Post-Migration Experiences, Cultural Practices and Homemaking

Post-Migration Experiences, Cultural Practices and Homemaking: An Ethnography of Dominican Migration to Europe

BY

SABRINA DINMOHAMED

*Center for Research of Caribbean Migration,
The Netherlands*

United Kingdom – North America – Japan – India – Malaysia – China

Emerald Publishing Limited
Howard House, Wagon Lane, Bingley BD16 1WA, UK

First edition 2023

Copyright © 2023 Sabrina Dinmohamed.
Published under exclusive licence by Emerald Publishing Limited.

Reprints and permissions service
Contact: www.copyright.com

No part of this book may be reproduced, stored in a retrieval system, transmitted in any form or by any means electronic, mechanical, photocopying, recording or otherwise without either the prior written permission of the publisher or a licence permitting restricted copying issued in the UK by The Copyright Licensing Agency and in the USA by The Copyright Clearance Center. Any opinions expressed in the chapters are those of the authors. Whilst Emerald makes every effort to ensure the quality and accuracy of its content, Emerald makes no representation implied or otherwise, as to the chapters' suitability and application and disclaims any warranties, express or implied, to their use.

British Library Cataloguing in Publication Data
A catalogue record for this book is available from the British Library

ISBN: 978-1-83753-205-6 (Print)
ISBN: 978-1-83753-204-9 (Online)
ISBN: 978-1-83753-206-3 (Epub)

INVESTOR IN PEOPLE

This book is dedicated to my mother, Chitra Ramnath, who always gave me the freedom to follow my own path. Her wisdom is beyond all books or degrees. This book is also dedicated to my father, Eugène Dinmohamed, who carries his Caribbeanness with so much pride that, without knowing, he inspired me to do research on Caribbean migration and culture.

Finally, this book is dedicated to my great-grandparents and grandparents, who migrated from India to Suriname and from Suriname to the Netherlands, and created a home in unfamiliar territories.

Contents

List of Figures and Tables	*ix*
Acknowledgements	*xi*

Chapter 1   Introduction: Dominican Immigrants, Cultural Practices and Homemaking   *1*

1.1	Dominicans' Homemaking Through Food Practices	*1*
1.2	Homemaking as an Alternative Lens for Exploring Immigrants' Settlement	*2*
1.3	Why Food Practices?	*8*
1.4	Researching Dominicans' Homemaking in the Netherlands	*10*
1.5	Aim of this Book	*15*
1.6	The Road Map of this Book	*16*

Chapter 2   Dominican Migration: Increasing Diversity in Destinations   *19*

2.1	Introduction	*19*
2.2	Emigration of Dominicans: Increasing Diversity in Destinations	*19*
2.3	Migration to the Kingdom of the Netherlands	*22*
2.4	Migration to the Netherlands	*30*
2.5	Conclusion: Diversification in Migration Destinations and Stepwise Trajectories	*38*

Chapter 3   Dominicans' Culture and Home After Migration to the Netherlands   *39*

3.1	Introduction	*39*
3.2	The Creation of Quisqueya in the Netherlands	*41*
3.3	The Encounters With Dutch Contextual Characteristics	*46*
3.4	Where is Home After Migration?	*57*
3.5	Conclusion: Attachments, Place of Home and Feelings of Home	*65*

viii *Contents*

**Chapter 4   The Differentiated Meaning of Dominican Food
After Migration**   *67*

4.1   Introduction   *67*
4.2   'Typical' Dominican Food: La Bandera, Sancocho or
       Something Else?   *68*
4.3   Dominican Food and Feelings of Home   *72*
4.4   Explaining Dominicans' Attitude Towards Dominican Food   *84*
4.5   Conclusion: Cultural Practices and Feelings of Home   *90*

**Chapter 5   *Habichuela Con Dulce* and *Noche Buena*: The Role of
Dominican Co-ethnics in Homemaking**   *93*

5.1   Introduction   *93*
5.2   Feelings of Home in the Dutch-Dominican Community   *94*
5.3   Food Practices, Business Opportunities and
       Dominican Sociability   *103*
5.4   Contested Homes in Communal Spaces   *107*
5.5   Conclusion: Co-Ethnics, Cultural Practices and
       Feelings of Home   *116*

**Chapter 6   Bread, Ugly Gravy and Boring Parties: Encounters With
Dutch Food Practices**   *119*

6.1   Introduction   *119*
6.2   Encounters with Dutch Food: Challenges and Opportunities   *121*
6.3   Finding Ingredients: The Importance of Other
       Caribbean Communities   *125*
6.4   Food Customs in the Netherlands: Adaptation and Rejection   *130*
6.5   Conclusion: Receiving Society Characteristics,
       Practices and Homemaking   *135*

Chapter 7   Conclusions   *137*

7.1   The Nature of Immigrant Homemaking   *137*
7.2   Immigrants' Cultural Practices and Post-Migration
       Experiences   *140*
7.3   Dominican Migration: An Agenda for Future Research   *141*

Appendix   List of Food Names   *145*

Bibliography   *149*

Index   *155*

List of Figures and Tables

Figures

Fig. 1.	Fefita La Grande, *Merengue Tipico* Perfomer, on Stage in The Hague.	13
Fig. 2.	Population of Dominican-born Persons in the Netherlands, 1996–2022.	34
Fig. 3.	*Habichuela con dulce* With a Dutch Biscuit.	83
Fig. 4.	Dominican Condiments and Seasoning.	108
Fig. 5.	Flyer for the Celebration of Dominican Independence Day.	108
Fig. 6.	The Carwash and the *Colmado*.	112
Fig. 7.	*Mangu Tres Golpes*.	115
Fig. 8.	Pedro's *Arroz Moro*.	132
Fig. 9.	Pasta Dominican Style With a Slice of Plantain on the Side.	133

Tables

Table 1.	Top 10 Destinations of Dominican Migrants Worldwide, 1990–2020.	22
Table 2.	Top 10 Destinations of Dominican Migrants in the Caribbean Region, 1990–2020.	23
Table 3.	Gender Distribution Among Dominican-born Persons in the Netherlands	34
Table 4.	Age Distribution of Dominicans in the Netherlands	35
Table 5.	Geographical Dispersal of Dominicans in the Netherlands.	36
Table 6.	Marital Status of Dominicans in the Netherlands.	37

Acknowledgements

Since I was a little girl, I have been fascinated by the lives of immigrants. At home in Amsterdam, my father would watch *Migrantentelevisie* ('migrant television') on the local television channels where immigrant groups in the Netherlands broadcast their own programmes. We watched to see programmes about Suriname and Surinamese people in the Netherlands, and I was always captivated by the immigrants' stories of their experiences in the Netherlands. Later in life, I was drawn by the Caribbean and Caribbean cultures. I always wondered why, despite being born and raised in the Netherlands, I could not feel at home there. When one would apply the widely accepted indicators of integration to me, my scores would be good and I would be declared a successful immigrant (in my case, second generation). How, then, to explain my lack of feeling at home? Are we, in our labelling of integration as 'successful', forgetting to take into account other factors and realities? It is with these questions in mind that I embarked on this research project. My aim, in addition to advancing the scientific debate, was to provide answers to a very personal question.

I thank several persons for inspiring, guiding and motivating me to do research. During my first year as a social sciences student at the Vrije Universiteit Amsterdam, courses in anthropology and about the Caribbean fascinated me. Anthropology lecturer Carel Roessingh was the first person to inspire me to become active in research. After getting my master's, during my years working as a researcher in Curaçao, the themes of migration and immigrants became really meaningful to me. Around then, I decided that I wanted to become an expert on the lives of immigrants. I am thankful to my then-boss at the Central Bureau of Statistics, Mike Jacobs, for when cleaning off his bookshelf, throwing a book at me saying, 'Look at this, it might interest you'. It was an anthropological study about the migration experiences of Dominican immigrants in Puerto Rico. That's when I knew: I wanted to study migrants from the Dominican Republic and their processes of finding a way in a new society.

A couple of years later, I crossed paths with Ruben Gowricharn. I thank him for introducing me to the concept of home as a perspective through which to examine immigrants' experiences. I thank Jan Rath for always reminding me that this is *my* research, thus instilling in me a sense of agency and strength. He also encouraged me to be myself in what, for me, was the uncomfortable world of academia, by being himself, including when 'the Afrikaanderwijk came out', as he expressed it.

xii *Acknowledgements*

My loved ones also played a part in my writing of this book. I thank everyone who supported me emotionally, financially and intellectually in Europe and the Caribbean (especially in Suriname, Curaçao and the Dominican Republic). *Dank je wel, dhan ye baad, gran tangi, masha danki* and *muchas gracias* to all of you who understood when I said I did not have time to meet up in those months of research and writing. You kindly responded, 'Just finish the thing, that is what's important now'. Another point: doing research without funding was a challenge. Wanting to finish the research in this life, but also having to earn an income posed serious challenges. However, these also proved an opportunity in disguise, as they showed me how many people were willing to offer support. The financial support of friends and family enabled me to concentrate on my research without having to worry about paying the rent or buying food.

While this book is a product of my own hard work, there is one person who always saw my intellectual capabilities and pushed me to explore them. That is my mother, Chitra. Without her, my path would not have been laid out, and I thank her for that. Then, there is the one person who encouraged me when doing the research became challenging. That is my sister Jane. She put me back in touch with my deep desire to do research on Dominican migration and brought back the sparkle that let me continue. Then, of course, without food you cannot function. Sometimes when trying to meet deadlines or being simply lost in my writings, my father, Eugène, would send me a message, *Heb je al gegeten?* ("Have you eaten?"). When I answered, 'I don't need food. I'll be at university until I die', he would soon be on his way to me with a meal. And Zorina, my little sister, thank you for inspiring me by being who you are, you strong warrior person.

Then there are my dear Dominican people. I thank Gladys Carrasco, who introduced me to so many Dominicans in different parts of the Netherlands and of different walks of life. And my respondents! I am indebted to all of you and all the other Dominicans I met on my journey in trying to understand Dominican migration and culture. Without your willingness to share your stories, I would not have been able to write this book. Without your love and warmth, doing the fieldwork would not have been as much fun. I also thank Françios Bérénos, Luz Teresa Mena Decena and Miguel Rodriguez Castro for always receiving me with so much love in San Pedro de Macoris and in their home. *Muchas gracias por su amor y calor.*

Through the stories presented in this book, I came closer to answering my own questions about home, and, as such, this research brought me home. Readers, I hope through this book you can smell the Dominican flavours and feel the Dominican *ambiente.*

Sabrina Dinmohamed

Chapter 1

Introduction: Dominican Immigrants, Cultural Practices and Homemaking

1.1 Dominicans' Homemaking Through Food Practices

At the Starbucks in Rotterdam Central Station, I spoke with 40-year-old *Bryan*, who had been living in the Netherlands for the last 20 years. He spoke of his childhood in the Dominican Republic, his mother's insistence that he come to the Netherlands, and the difficulties he had encountered in building a new life there. He told me about his accomplishments and where he considered to be home and shared thoughts on Dominican culture and its importance in his own life. In fact, he said, he cared little about Dominican cultural practices, which he considered narrow-minded. At the same time, he thought that if he had grown up differently and lived in better economic circumstances in the Dominican Republic, he might have different memories and miss the country and its culture. As it was, he equated the Dominican Republic with poverty, which he had no desire to recreate. Of his food memories, he said, 'You just had to eat whatever was put in front of you. Otherwise, you'd stay hungry. Some days, for example, my parents had no money to buy food. They gave you whatever they could'. Though *Bryan* loved Dominican food, he did not need food to create a sense of home in the Netherlands.

In Afrikaanderwijk, a neighbourhood in southern Rotterdam, 54-year-old *Sandra*, who had also lived in the Netherlands for 20 years, spoke lovingly of the Dominican Republic. She specifically mentioned how important Dominican food was to her. She consumed it every day and often went to Dominican restaurants. Even after so many years in the Netherlands, and having previously lived in Curaçao and Sint Maarten, she maintained Dominican food customs. For example, during *Semana Santa* (Holy Week), she made *habichuela con dulce*, a sweet bean dessert that in the Dominican Republic is prepared in every household and shared with family and friends. It is not a dish to eat alone, *Sandra* told me. You make it, she explained, 'and call everyone you know and say, "I have *habichuela con dulce*. Are you coming to pick it up, or shall I bring it or send it to you?" ' *Sandra* had continued this practice in the Netherlands and also fostered by the proximity of other Dominicans.

Post-Migration Experiences, Cultural Practices and Homemaking:
An Ethnography of Dominican Migration to Europe, 1–18
Copyright © 2023 by Sabrina Dinmohamed
Published under exclusive licence by Emerald Publishing Limited
doi:10.1108/978-1-83753-204-920231001

2 Post-Migration Experiences, Cultural Practices and Homemaking

At a restaurant in western Amsterdam, 36-year-old *Valentina* described her love of Dominican food. As a student living in what she described as the predominantly 'white' suburban Amstelveen, she would travel on the weekends to the Bijlmer, one of Amsterdam's more multicultural neighbourhoods, to buy cooking ingredients. On these trips, she took a grocery trolley to a specific area in the Ganzenhoef neighbourhood. The many Surinamese and Curaçaoan stores there made it easy to obtain yucca, plantains and specific condiments to prepare her favourite dishes. The unavailability of these products nearer to her own home thus did not prevent her from continuing to make Dominican food. After graduating, she said she left Amstelveen and chose her current residence for its proximity to products for Dominican dishes.

These stories, drawn from my research on Dominican migration to the Netherlands, reveal several aspects of immigrants' attachments to cultural practices from their country of origin and creation of home after migration. *Bryan*'s story demonstrates that cultural practices from the country of origin do not necessarily evoke feelings of home. Pre-migration circumstances – in his case, poverty – and personal preferences are also meaningful and influence the importance of Dominican practices after migration. Immigrants have different attachments to social and cultural practices from their country of origin. Some may feel no need to recreate these in their new context after migration. *Sandra*'s vignette suggests the importance of co-ethnics in maintaining traditions. Her work, social life and cultural activities kept her in contact with other Dominicans. Also, she lived in Rotterdam, which has a large concentration of Dominicans. Proximity to other Dominicans made it easy for her to keep up Dominican traditions. *Valentina*'s vignette demonstrates her determination to continue making Dominican dishes even though her 'white' neighbourhood's shops lacked the necessary ingredients. Receiving contexts undoubtedly affect the practices immigrants bring from their countries of origin, and immigrants have various ways of dealing with the differences they encounter.

These points illustrate the central argument of this book: there are different forms of creating home after migration, and immigrants' homemaking practices are influenced not only by their individual characteristics, choices and preferences but also by the characteristics of their context. This book is about Dominican immigrants, their relationship with cultural practices from the Dominican Republic and the role these cultural practices play in creating home post-migration. I explore immigrants' settlement processes, the way they position themselves in the new society and how they root and create home after migration. Thus, moving away from questions of integration, this book focuses instead on stories of immigrants' daily lives and practices on a micro-level.

1.2 Homemaking as an Alternative Lens for Exploring Immigrants' Settlement

Oh my children I will surely return, do not blame me if I have left you alone. I want to build many things for you that I have dreamed of in my life. I would like to go back, but I can't, I have goals to achieve (Translated by the author).

Introduction **3**

In this bachata song, singer Frank Reyes tells the story of a migrant who feels guilty for leaving his children behind in the Dominican Republic, but he wants them to know he has done this to secure them a better future. In the meantime, he struggles with daily life, missing his family and the town he was born in.

While doing my research on Dominican immigrants in the Netherlands, I stumbled on a newspaper article quoting Rotterdam's then-deputy mayor Bert Wijbenga who stated that the Dominican community was 'headed in the wrong direction'. He expressed 'concern about their socioeconomic position' (Liukku, 2020) and went on to suggest that research was needed on what he saw as a problematic community. I paused over the article, stunned. How could he be so unnuanced in his statements? The Frank Reyes song and the deputy mayor's words seemed to come from two different worlds. At that moment, I appreciated how very necessary my research was, particularly the specific approach I had adopted, seeking to understand the community from within by exploring its members' attachments and emotions. The question that weighed on me was, how can we better understand immigrants' settlement and incorporation processes?

1.2.1 Attention to Emotions and Micro-level Experiences

Studies of settlement processes have applied several concepts to understand and describe the positions of immigrants in the receiving society. The concepts of integration and assimilation, for example, are often used to explore and understand immigrants' participation in the economic, political, social and cultural spheres. They are also used to assess the 'success' of immigrants' settlement and participation. But what is successful migration, and who decides when and if it is achieved?

Some migration scholars have criticized previous work as too focused on how well immigrants participate in various spheres of the receiving society, while bypassing other aspects of immigrant experiences. To better understand immigrants' struggles, attitudes and attachments, they argue, three elements should be brought into the study arena: emotions, experiences on a micro-level and the meaning of daily practices (Boccagni, 2013; Hondagneu-Sotelo, 2017; Philipp & Ho, 2010). While I do not reject existing approaches to studying, describing and explaining immigrants' post-migration life, I agree that these are insufficient to grasp their settlement experiences. Hondagneu-Sotelo (2017) suggests that focusing on everyday practices, materiality and the meaning of place may shift our theoretical understanding of migration experiences away from simply integration, assimilation or transnationalism towards a perspective that acknowledges the right to make home. After all, as immigrants navigate their new environment, they not only deal with practicalities such as getting a job, finding housing and learning a new language but are also confronted with the absence of familiar places and social and cultural practices. Even if these were taken for granted before migration, they may become significant, if not essential, in the process of managing migration and putting down roots in a new place. I too have found that studying daily practices, like those surrounding food, places, materiality and emotions, is valuable for delving into how immigrants – and specifically, the Dominicans in my research – find their way in the receiving society.

4 *Post-Migration Experiences, Cultural Practices and Homemaking*

The concept of home seems appropriate for treating these underexposed aspects of the immigrant experience. According to Boccagni (2017), viewing migration through the lens of home is useful because it illuminates the bases of migrants' belonging and identification with place. The concept of home has been used to study immigrants' attachments and rootedness, especially their emotional attachments. Lam and Yeoh (2004) present the concept as offering an important clue to where the roots of migrants are anchored. Wiles (2008) argues that both home and the idea of home structure the experience of migration, and that discursive and material aspects of the country of origin form a framework for everyday life as migrants. These provide a way of establishing the self and the group, as well as a sense of belonging, and of demarcating who belongs and who is excluded. According to Phillip and Ho (2010), the concept of home, furthermore, enables exploration of attachments to the country of origin and receiving society. They state that 'migrants' subjective homemaking experiences are just as important as objective labour market performance indicators in providing an understanding of migrant settlement outcomes' (Phillip & Ho, 2010, p. 81).

What home exactly is cannot be unequivocally described, as it has different dimensions and exists on different scales. It has emotional and psychological components, for example, but is also linked to geographical place, a physical dwelling, social relations and materiality (e.g., objects, furniture). Various researchers provide definitions of home. Després (1991), for one, defines it as security and control, a reflection of one's ideas and values, a relationship with family and friends, a centre of activities as well as a refuge, shelter of privacy, indicator of personal status, material structure and place to own. More than a decade later, Mallett (2004, p. 62) raised the question of 'whether or not home is (a) place(s), (a) space(s), (a) feeling(s) and/or an active state of being in the world', suggesting that it all depends on the situation.

Scholars have also challenged the idea of home as a bounded, stable and closed place. According to Blunt and Varley (2004, p. 3), home must be understood not just as a fixed, delimited location, but as

> traversing scales from the domestic to the global in both material and symbolic ways and located on thresholds between memory and nostalgia for the past, everyday life in the present, and future dreams and fears.

While home is difficult to define, scholars have posited its main constituting elements as specific emotions related to places, persons and objects such as familiarity, security and a sense of community (Boccagni, 2017; Duyvendak, 2011; Hage, 1997).

1.2.2 Immigrant Homemaking and Differentiation in Post-migration Practices

The first argument advanced in this book is that immigrants have different relationships with practices from their country of origin and are not orientated only on the country of origin in making home. But what exactly is making home or

Introduction 5

homemaking? One definition is daily practices rooted in time and space with the aim of creating a domestic sphere (Bhatti & Church, 2000). Another is social practices in and around the house (Dayaratne & Kellet, 2008). Moreover, homemaking is considered a fundamental activity that anchors an individual in the world within the universe of the space, things, people and events in which they exist (Bachelard, 1964, cited in Dayaratne & Kellet, 2008). Homemaking, thus, has several dimensions including the material, social and personal. Examples of material practices are building a dwelling and furnishing or decorating its interior. Social practices involve relationships with other members of the household, while personal practices relate to individual self-expression within the home.

International migration causes detachment from familiar places and activities and, in the receiving context, a search for new attachments and new relationships with people and places (Al-Ali & Koser, 2002; Boccagni, 2013, 2017; Nowicka, 2007). Thus, while transforming a space or place into one that feels comfortable and safe is an activity that both non-migrants and immigrants engage in, it is different for immigrants. The uprooting that accompanies migration means that immigrants may, in a short period of time, lose familiar elements in their daily lives including attachments to people, places and things. The uprooting from everything that was once familiar and the settlement in a different geographical, social and/or cultural environment may compel immigrants to recreate what they left behind and lost. No doubt this also depends on whether what was left behind is something the immigrant *wants* to recreate. It is worth emphasizing that some may migrate because they do not feel at home. This has received less attention in the immigrant home literature but is elaborated on in the upcoming chapters.

Scholars have tried to understand what is at the core of homemaking for immigrants. According to Hondagneu-Sotelo (2017, p. 15), homemaking is about creating places of belonging, 'where people seek to transform the physical surroundings in ways that they find agreeable and that will support their utilitarian purposes of social reproduction and restoration'. Hoffman (1989) calls immigrant homemaking 're-creating soils of significance', in which the affective qualities of home cannot be separated from the concrete materiality of rooms, objects and rituals. This is a useful conceptualization, as it connects emotions and practices. Petridou (2001, p. 87) underscores the importance of meaning stating that immigrant homemaking is about 'the dynamic way in which everyday practice makes the home meaningful to those who inhabit it'. Boccagni (2017) refers to the ordinary interactions through which individuals try to appropriate and make a place meaningful, personal and secure:

> What I propose to frame as homing ... is a range of *spatialized social practices through which migrants* – as exemplary of people who went through extended detachment from their earlier homes – *try to reproduce, reconstruct and possibly rebuild meaningful home-like settings, feelings and relationships.* (Boccagni, 2017, p. 26, italics original)

6 *Post-Migration Experiences, Cultural Practices and Homemaking*

Boccagni (2017) calls attention to home as a process, naming it 'homing'. This refers to people's potential to attach a sense of home to their life circumstances in light of their assets and the external structure of opportunities. This book elaborates on these assets and opportunities, as well as the interplay between them, to provide a comprehensive picture of immigrant homemaking. In my research, homemaking encompasses social and cultural practices inside the home and outside (in communal and public spaces). These practices may evoke feelings identified in the home literature as elements of home. Maintenance of practices from the home country is not an absolute, but can change as immigrants' relationship with the country of origin and the receiving society evolve.

One limitation of existing studies on immigrant homemaking that stands in the way of a nuanced yet comprehensive understanding of homemaking processes is the tendency to focus on how practices from the country of origin are recreated (Dinmohamed, 2023). This in itself is not surprising, as Duyvendak (2011, p. 31) observes:

> [Immigrants] are not acquainted with the particularities of the places they have come to live in, and not necessarily interested in them for they do not help them feel at home. When they establish home away from home, immigrants often recreate places that look and smell, at least to a certain extent, like the places they left behind.

However, whether immigrants always strive to recreate what they left behind is an open question. Do they have a homogenous wish to recreate familiar practices from the country of origin? If so, how can we make sense of *Bryan*'s food practices, which are not orientated to the Dominican Republic? Brubaker (2002) has criticized the idea of an ethnic group being internally homogenous, externally bounded and perceived as a collective of totally similar actors with common purposes. Rather, he argues for a more nuanced understanding, moving beyond groupist assumptions and towards empirical investigations of the circumstances under which people do (or do not) feel and act as members of specific ethnic/racial/national categories. Pursuing this line of inquiry, I wondered how this might be reflected in practices after migration. Moreover, immigrant homemaking studies do not always clarify what feelings are evoked by practices and whether they are indeed feelings of home. Duyvendak (2011, p. 42) suggests that while home studies have examined the 'harder' context of place, the emotional side has been neglected:

> [T]he emotion of feeling at home attracted less interest than the object of the feeling, the place qua place. This neglect of emotion-as-emotion appeared to suggest that 'feeling at home' meant and was experienced by everybody as the same thing.

Before considering all practices from the country of origin as homemaking practices, more must be understood about the relationship between practices and the feelings they evoke.

Introduction 7

The Dominican community in the Netherlands is an ideal subject to explore differentiation in homemaking practices. Indeed, in my dealings with some Dominican immigrants, I noticed a negative attitude towards other Dominicans. They avoided socializing with co-ethnics who, they said, acted 'too Dominican', referring to practices such as consuming only Dominican food, talking loudly and seeming unmotivated to progress in life. These opinions of Dominicans about other Dominicans in the Netherlands clued me into differentiation in practices. I learned that there were Dominican immigrants whose practices were indeed orientated towards the Dominican Republic, but also others who, while they felt Dominican, had no urge to perform 'typical' Dominican practices, to return to their country of origin or to socialize exclusively with other Dominicans.

1.2.3 Contextual Embeddedness of Immigrant Homemaking

The second argument put forward in this book is that immigrants' homemaking practices are influenced not only by their own individual characteristics, choices and preferences but also by characteristics of their context. Context is important to consider because immigrants bring practices from place to place, with each place having its own unique characteristics. A few scholars, mostly from the field of housing studies and architecture and design, note that factors such as spatiality, regulations, construction norms and availability of products for purchase in the receiving society may affect or suppress immigrants' attempts to transform the spaces they live in into meaningful places to which they can relate (Gram-Hanssen & Bech-Danielsen, 2011; Hadjiyanni, 2009). As such, Gram-Hanssen and Bech-Danielsen (2012) explored the extent that immigrants could identify with Danish housing, and whether Danish housing allowed immigrants to arrange their houses (and thus their homes) according to their own wishes. They found that preferences regarding housing and interiors depended on the residents' country of origin and what they were accustomed to, leading them to conclude that Danish housing codes limited immigrants in arranging their homes to their satisfaction. Beyond material restrictions, homemaking is affected by social and cultural conditions. According to Meijering and Lager (2014), language and social structures (e.g. people's coldness or warmth) affect Antillean migrants' sense of home in the Netherlands. For these migrants, the individualist nature of the Dutch people and society is an impediment to their feeling at home. How material and socio-cultural conditions lead to negotiations in practices and feelings of home as well as how these negotiations affect feelings of home, warrants greater attention. In the case of *Valentina*, this would mean asking what challenges, besides the limited availability of products for making Dominican food, stand in the way of her preferred food practices. How does she deal with those conditions and do they affect her feelings of home? The small size of the Dominican population, and its limited social and cultural infrastructure in Dutch society, present an interesting context in which homemaking takes place. How does such a relatively small community – with no visible cultural infrastructure, at least not seen by the untrained eye – create or recreate food practices and stay connected to their customs in a society that differs so markedly from their

8 Post-Migration Experiences, Cultural Practices and Homemaking

country of origin. The situation in the Netherlands is a sharp contrast to that in Puerto Rico, Spain and neighbourhoods of New York City, all of which have well-developed Dominican infrastructures.

The existence of a co-ethnic community in the receiving context is considered to play a role in making home. Some studies point to the role of co-ethnics, as part of the receiving context, in providing amenities, such as restaurants, grocery stores, bakeries and cafés (Philipp & Ho, 2010; Wiles, 2008). Co-ethnics also enable recreating ways of socializing. This socializing occurs within the domestic space, but also outside it, in communal spaces. Boccagni (2013, p. 283) found that immigrants' 'homemaking symbols and practices were not necessarily circumscribed to their dwelling places'. Homemaking outside the house, according to this author (2013, p. 283), involves 'ways of staying together and consuming leisure time in the public space: football matches, picnics, religious or cultural events, or the simple "hanging out" together'. Being with co-ethnics makes it possible to inhabit space and time in a familiar way (Boccagni, 2013) or to recreate social activities, the homeland or forms of recreation that immigrants were used to in their country of origin (Hondagneu-Sotelo, 2017; Meijering & Lager, 2014). While the role of co-ethnics in homemaking has been touched upon, it remains unclear how and whether the opportunities provided by co-ethnics evoke feelings of home. For example, in the case of *Sandra*, what food-related opportunities did other Dominicans provide? And did such opportunities evoke feelings of home? Delving into the lifestyles of Dominican immigrants allowed me to explore how homemaking may unfold beyond the home. In this community, like many non-western European communities, there is no sharp public–private divide; that is, where the home starts and ends is fluid. Home in the Dominican Republic is not only inside the house but also outside, with others. Considering this community, I could explore how certain activities normally associated with the home might unfold in communal or public places, presenting these sites as shared open-air homes (Hondagneu-Sotelo, 2017).

In sum, a singular focus on immigrants' recreation of the country of origin in homemaking and lack of regard for the context in which this takes place leads to a simplistic picture: that people migrate and transplant their practices in post-migration life without challenges and negotiations. I argue that there are many different forms of creating home after migration, some of which do not involve recreation of practices from the country of origin. The ways immigrants create home after migration are influenced by a variety of factors. On an individual level, they are influenced by pre-migration and post-migration factors, as well as personal changes not necessarily related to migration. In addition to individual characteristics, choices and preferences, immigrants' homemaking practices are influenced by characteristics of their context, including the co-ethnic community, if such exists, and the wider receiving society. These components of the context both facilitate and obstruct practices and feelings of home.

1.3 Why Food Practices?

Food is one of many practices that immigrants bring from their country of origin. Previous research has examined the food practices of immigrants in relation

Introduction 9

to their adjustment, ethnobiology, housing, geography, consumption and nutrition. These studies encompass aspects including food consumption, preparation, celebrations, customs and grocery-shopping (Longhurst, Johnston, & Ho, 2009; Rabikowska, 2010; Weller & Turkon, 2015). There are also studies that focus specifically on food as a homemaking practice and explore how practices such as consuming food from the country of origin evokes feelings of familiarity and community (Petridou, 2001; Sandu, 2013). A practice such as grocery-shopping, for example, can 'bring back' an immigrant to the country of origin (Philipp & Ho, 2010; Sandu, 2013). Some studies demonstrate that social practices surrounding food, such as eating with co-ethnics, can feel like being in the country of origin and foster social bonds (Petridou, 2001; Philipp & Ho, 2010; Sandu, 2013). Food thus seems to play a prominent role in post-migration life and even evoke what home studies have identified as 'feelings of home'.

Why choose to examine immigrants' food practices rather than practices related to housing, material objects or religion to show differentiated orientations in immigrant homemaking and its embeddedness in context? Firstly, people's experiences with food tell us about their emotional and affective relations with place. For some immigrants, food is a symbolic anchor to the country of origin that helps them feel at home and fight homesickness while serving as a bridge to a new home. For others, however, food does not always evoke good memories. Mankekar (2002) observed that food practices could elicit nostalgia and reproduce Indian culture in California, but it did not evoke nostalgia among all members of the community. Diner (2001) found that Irish migrants associated food with famine and hunger in their country of origin. As a consequence, food did not play a part in the construction of Irish identity or recreation of traditions. These findings underscore the need for a further exploration of familiarity as a driver in homemaking.

Second, food practices may differ markedly from one country to another. Furthermore, they are not always transplantable to a different context, or at least, not without challenges. Immigrants' food practices may be influenced by the new situation in the receiving country including laws, regulations, institutions and social and cultural customs. Food practices are subject to trade agreements concerning the import of ingredients or foods considered rare or even dangerous by members of the host society (Kershen, 2002; Komarnisky, 2009). Studies also demonstrate that practices can change or hybridize due to the encounter with contextual characteristics and immigrants' negotiations of these. According to Parasecoli (2014, p. 420), '[food] undergoes various degrees of transformation due to availability of ingredients, people's exposure to different flavours and techniques and the need to adapt to a dissimilar rhythm of life'. Research on the process of ingredient finding, for example, may reveal how unavailability in the receiving society affects dishes. Examination of preparation and consumption processes may uncover ways in which changes in social organization influence preparation or consumption of food from the country of origin. For example, if post-migration women must work outside the home, they cannot cook time-consuming meals (Srinivas, 2006). Focusing on food practices, therefore, provides a window to explore how receiving society characteristics interfere with homemaking and how immigrants negotiate these.

10   Post-Migration Experiences, Cultural Practices and Homemaking

Third, the segment of the receiving society comprising a co-ethnic community can foster certain practices. Co-ethnics facilitate the maintenance and continuation of food practices from the country of origin through shared preparation and consumption forms (Diner, 2001), celebrations and amenities (Mankekar, 2002; Philipp & Ho, 2010; Sandu, 2013). Food practices in a co-ethnic community context may reveal homemaking as an immensely social event, occurring in a social context and in social interaction. Studies demonstrate, for example, that food connects co-ethnics: food is a 'symbol of common descent' and 'reinforcer of social bonds' (Van den Berghe, 1984, p. 393).

Food practices permit an exploration of how home is made not only with co-ethnics, but also in communal spaces. Food practices travel outside the home, meaning that homemaking practices can take place on a community level, publicly and transnationally. Grocery stores, for example, are important places enabling construction of the country of origin and identity (Mankekar, 2002; Philipp & Ho, 2010; Sandu, 2013). They are a 'crucial node in the transnational circulation … of commodities' (Mankekar, 2002, p. 76). Restaurants and takeaway venues can also be important places where home is recreated outside the house. Celebrations reveal immigrants' social relationships within the community and beyond as well as food's bridging function. In the words of Hirschman (1996), commensality, that is, sharing food 'melds the public and private spheres'.

1.4 Researching Dominicans' Homemaking in the Netherlands

This book is based on fieldwork that I conducted from 2016 to 2020 and from 2022 to 2023. Employing an ethnographic approach, I sought to gain insight into Dominicans' post-migration experiences in the Netherlands. That strategy, I believed, would provide a nuanced understanding of the lived experiences of Dominican immigrants and their practices. Being immersed in their community, insofar as we can speak of 'one' community, enabled me to gain a detailed and multiperspective understanding of their practices, the meanings of these and the context in which they occurred.

1.4.1 Doing Ethnographic Fieldwork: 'Tu eres mas dominicana que un plátano'

My first data collection method was semi-structured interviews. These allowed me to maintain focus while leaving room for creativity and enabling complementary issues to emerge. Interview topics included pre-migration life, migration motives, the place of home, connections with the Dominican Republic, contacts with the Dominican community in the Netherlands, Dominican cultural practices in daily life, food practices and future plans. As my aim was to get an impression of the respondents' lives before and after migration, I asked questions in chronological order from childhood in the Dominican Republic to respondents' current lives in the Netherlands. In this, my ability to speak Spanish, my knowledge of Dominican Spanish and my familiarity with the Dominican Republic, its culture

Introduction   11

and its social practices were an advantage, enabling me to reach a wider group of respondents and to better understand nuances.

The respondent population consisted of first-generation Dominican immigrants, thus people born in the Dominican Republic, who had experienced leaving one place behind and creating a new life elsewhere with the intention to stay in the Netherlands. Ultimately, this selection led to 48 interviews, with 31 women and 17 men, ages 27–65. Their educational levels varied from high school to PhD. Respondents originated from different parts of the Dominican Republic, with some from cities and others from rural areas. Length of residence in the Netherlands ranged from 34 years to nine months at the time of our interview. There was also variation in migration trajectories. Some came directly from the Dominican Republic, while others arrived in the Netherlands via the Dutch Caribbean islands or via other European countries. Migration motives differed too, examples being marriage to a Dutch spouse, schooling and family reunification. Finally, settlement areas in the Netherlands varied, with some respondents living in large cities, while others resided in smaller cities, towns and suburban areas. All respondents were offered anonymity to make it easier to answer the questions freely. Not everyone found anonymity important, but I chose to anonymize all names for the sake of consistency.

One concern I had at the start of the fieldwork was that respondents would be unwilling to participate. While I knew Dominican immigrants from places where I socialized, such as restaurants and bars, asking them to tell me their migration stories in a research context seemed an entirely different matter. Why would they take the time to share their experiences with me? What was in it for them? However, this proved much easier than I could have imagined. Moreover, respondents were quite positive about the idea of someone, especially someone not of Dominican descent, doing research on Dominican immigrants and their culture in the Netherlands. Another factor that facilitated my access was my knowledge of Dominican culture and respondents' appreciation of that. Nonetheless, this familiarity was a source of worry as well. For example, I recruited some respondents at a bar I frequented to dance bachata. At first, I was afraid that would affect me being taken seriously as a researcher, if respondents saw dancing at a club as somehow inconsistent with my role as a serious researcher. Fortunately that proved not to be the case. Respondents seemed to respect me because I knew about their culture, in which dance and music are important aspects, and they were happy to help me with my research. At an event to celebrate the anniversary of a Dominican cultural foundation, one of my respondents, who was also present, said to me, *tu eres mas dominicana que un platano*, which can be translated as, 'you are more Dominican than a plantain', meaning you are really, really Dominican. The reason for saying this was my skill in dancing (as dancing is major part of Dominican celebrations), the fact that I spoke Spanish and understood Dominican Spanish, and the way I fit into the Dominican ambiance. It was an expression of praise, but also an indication of my acceptance in their community, being officially part of them. Thus, the dancing which had initially been a cause of worry actually helped afford me a place in this community.

12 Post-Migration Experiences, Cultural Practices and Homemaking

While I had participated in Dominican social and cultural events for years, and some people I met considered me part of the community, I was not an insider for every Dominican or always. I was perceived differently depending on whom I was with and the situation (Bucerius, 2013; Ryan, 2015). Many Dominicans who had lived in the Netherlands for a long time recognized me as being of Surinamese descent. When talking about procuring ingredients at Hindustani shops, for example, they would say, 'You use the same products we do'. Or when they spoke of their experiences as immigrants in the Netherlands, they would include me as one of them. When talking about the variety of foods they came to know in the Netherlands, some would say, 'I really like "your" food', often referring to the typical Hindustani-Surinamese *roti* (a large flat pancake type bread served with meat, potatoes and vegetables). When I asked one respondent whether it was easy to find Dominican products in the Netherlands, she answered:

> Yes, of course, at the Surinamese. In the Surinamese supermarkets, they also sell Dominican products, because your food is similar to ours. It is different seasoning, but almost the same. So, even if the products come from Surinam or another country, it is also Dominican.

It was interesting to note that she considered me to be of Surinamese descent, without ever having asked me about it. I believe that this perception of me as part of an immigrant community – as opposed to native Dutch – worked in my advantage in the sense that my respondents felt more comfortable talking to me (Ryan, 2015).

However, the Surinamese are considered very different from Dominicans by Dominicans themselves because of the language difference as well as cultural and religious dissimilarities. However, my speaking Spanish and knowing about the Dominican Republic and its culture meant that respondents saw me as a different type of Surinamese ('Surinamese don't speak Spanish, how wonderful that you do'). This unexpected proximity to them gave me added credibility and led them to be more open to me as a researcher and as a person. My knowing about cultural elements and sensitivity for social codes made me a trusted outsider (Bucerius, 2013).

The second data collection method was participant observation. I immersed myself in the Dominican community visiting cafés, hair salons, radio broadcasting stations and cultural events. These provided me a view on Dominican activities in the Netherlands, interactions between Dominican immigrants and the role of food at events. Then there were specific food-related places I visited in cities across the Netherlands such as grocery stores and restaurants. At these places, I looked at menus and observed visitors and their interactions with their surroundings. Lastly, I was closely involved in the lives of six respondents, with whom I had regular contact. I was a guest at birthday parties, where I got the chance to observe the food served, forms of joint food consumption and the general atmosphere. I also attended several cooking sessions, which enabled me to observe preparation and use of ingredients while hearing food-related stories, such as the art of peeling a plantain and the importance of good Dominican salami.

1.4.2 Longstanding Interest in Dominican Migration and Culture

My interest in Dominican immigrants, their cultural practices and stories about migration began prior to this research. Between 2003 and 2010, I was living and working in Curaçao (one of the Dutch Caribbean islands). In that period I came into contact with Dominican immigrants and their cultural practices related to food, music and dance. I also came into contact with Dominicans' stories of migration and, in particular, their migration experiences in Curaçao. At that time, I began to see how migration to Curaçao was sometimes a step towards an eventual migration to the Netherlands. In the Netherlands, from 2010 onwards, in an attempt to deal with my homesickness for Curaçao and the specific Dominican atmosphere, which I missed, I started to visit places where I could listen to and dance to bachata music. From there, I got to know Dominican immigrants in Amsterdam, Rotterdam and The Hague. I attended several types of gatherings including social gatherings (e.g. bingo on Sundays and birthday parties), festivals such as national holidays of the Netherlands (e.g. Queen's Day) and the Dominican Republic (e.g. Independence Day and Dominican Mother's Day) and many concerts of bachata and merengue artists performing on stages in the Netherlands (Fig. 1).

Fig. 1.   Fefita La Grande, *Merengue Tipico* Perfomer, on Stage in The Hague.

14 Post-Migration Experiences, Cultural Practices and Homemaking

Being immersed in the Dominican community raised in me questions that have also come up in other types of research wherein the researcher is already familiar with the research subject. Particularly, I worried about my ability to look at familiar situations with 'objective' eyes. In this same vein, Van Ginkel (1994, p. 11) asked, 'How is it possible to prevent overlooking important matters and patterns that one sees, hears and smells every day?' This author's answer, like others (Narayan, 1993), was that we should not confuse distance with objectivity and/or familiarity with bias. While being aware of this, I still felt the need to defamiliarize because knowing so much about the cultural and social codes did cause me to be less probing and critical during some of my first interviews. A degree of reflexivity is needed to stay cognizant of one how is located within the field and how that positioning may influence methods, interpretation and knowledge production (Kempny, 2012; Ryan, 2015). I became aware of my biases and assumptions during my observations where I was confronted with certain assumptions that I held about 'Dominican culture'. One was at a birthday party where I saw all kinds of what I considered to be European snacks on the table like cheese and olives. I was stunned: is this Dominican birthday celebration food? I realized then that there are many subcultures and subgroups within 'the community' and that the food traditions I had come to know in my encounters up until then, and considered 'typical Dominican', might not be the traditions of all Dominicans. In short, the Dominican community in the Netherlands was much more heterogeneous than I expected.

I also did volunteer work from August 2017 to August 2018 at Casa Migrante, a social welfare organization for Spanish-speaking immigrants in Amsterdam. I learned about the organization through a Dominican respondent who volunteered there and said that lots of Dominicans went there for assistance with the many things they did not understand about the Netherlands. I thought this would be a good way to learn about challenges Dominicans face when settling in the Netherlands to get a broader sense of their experiences beyond questions concerning home and food practices. One client at Casa Migrante, for example, needed help resolving three issues, concerning taxes, a health care bill and a letter from the government agency dealing with student grants (for her daughter). I learned that she had left the Dominican Republic 14 years ago for Spain. She liked life in Spain, but the economic crisis there compelled her to come to the Netherlands so her daughter could have better educational opportunities. She prepared her daughter well for migration and sent her to English classes in Spain. At the time of our interview, the daughter was studying at the University of Maastricht, and the client said that when she graduated, she herself would return to the Dominican Republic, where she had already built a house. She was living in Amstelveen and searching for an apartment in Amsterdam, which was difficult. She said she would not live in 'Bijlmer' (a multicultural neighbourhood in Amsterdam) because 'all those Dominicans in one place' was too much for her. She liked quiet and tranquillity. This client's story reflected a stepwise migration process, which many Dominicans in the Netherlands underwent. It also showed that being in Europe was temporary, served a certain purpose and that she was well prepared for a return to the Dominican Republic. It additionally revealed her perception of Dominican co-ethnics in the Netherlands.

Introduction **15**

While I had vacationed in the Dominican Republic a number of times before the start of my research, during the formal research period I visited the country twice in 2019 and 2022. These two visits provided me opportunities to pay closer attention to the food practices of Dominicans in the Dominican Republic, as well as regional variation, Dominican migration and Dominican culture. While my trips took me to different parts of the country, I always stayed for a couple of days with a Dominican family in San Pedro de Macoris. Talking to this host family, I realized that a 'Dominican culture' *per se* does not exist. Rather, there are many Dominican cultures and social contexts, mirroring my findings from my fieldwork in the Netherlands. In the Dominican Republic, I also came to understand more about Dominican migration including the fact that some Dominicans do not want to migrate and what return migrants found difficult about living in Europe. In light of my interactions within the country, I could better understand why a number of Dominicans in my research said they found the silence in the Netherlands deafening; after all, they came from a country where there was always music, talking on the streets and the sound of *motoconchos* (small motorcycles, also used as cheap taxis). I understood more about the transition from a country where people stop by your house at any time of day without calling ahead. I also understood more about missing human warmth in the Netherlands, as my respondents came from a country where a standard question was, *Cómo está la familia?* ('How is your family?').

1.5 Aim of this Book

The first aim of this book is to bring migrant settlement into focus by exploring how immigrants position themselves in a new society, how they root and how they create a home after migration. The research, thus, moves away from questions of integration to examine stories of immigrants' daily lives and practices on a micro-level, echoing Sørensen (1994, p. 108):

> When one rejects traditional approaches to migration and focuses instead on the lived experience of migration, cultural meeting places and the generation of transnational lives, meanings and identities, then one must also reject the various models put forward earlier about forms of cultural integration. Neither the 'melting pot' model of cultural assimilation (presented in cultural theories of the world as existing of different distinct cultures) nor the 'salad bowl' model of cultural pluralism (also called the cultural mosaic) can be accepted as appropriate tools any longer. Ideas of assimilation, integration, fusion or pluralism and the related metaphors of either melting pots or pressure cookers, mosaics or powder kegs, cannot grasp the cultural complexity of migration processes (though these metaphors may disclose important global power structures and specific local gender relations).

Neither Sørensen (1994) nor I reject existing approaches to studying, describing and explaining immigrants' post-migration positions, but we consider them

16   Post-Migration Experiences, Cultural Practices and Homemaking

insufficient to grasp immigrants' settlement and incorporation experiences. By studying immigrants' attachments to practices from the country of origin and the emotions related to them, I sought to capture immigrants' daily realities, micro-level experiences and the material side of incorporation. These aspects offer a window onto the complexities and struggles that migration processes entail as well as immigrants' attitudes and expectations towards both the country of origin and the receiving society (Boccagni, 2013; Hadjiyanni, 2009; Villar-Rosales, 2010).

A second aim is to complement immigrant homemaking studies. There are many wonderful studies about immigrant practices and how immigrants create home after migration. This book adds to these by providing a comprehensive picture of processes and determinants. In particular, I follow Boccagni (2017), who calls attention to home as a process wherein people attach a sense of home to their life circumstances depending on their assets and the external structure of opportunities. I pursued this in several ways in my research. Firstly, I connected practices to feelings to shed light on how practices contribute to specific feelings of home. Secondly, I developed a picture of processes: the migration, social interactions and changes. Thirdly, I delineated determinants of homemaking on both individual and contextual levels. Fourthly, I included spaces outside the house as spaces where home can be made.

The third aim of this book is to expand the literature on contemporary migration flows from the Caribbean to Europe. Most research on Caribbean immigrants in the Netherlands focuses on those from the former colony of Suriname or the Caribbean parts of the Kingdom of the Netherlands. However, immigrant communities from other Caribbean countries are growing including Dominicans, Guyanese and Jamaicans. This book advances knowledge about the Dominican diaspora. While Dominicans' migration to the United States and Spain, their settlement processes and even development of the second generation have received much attention in scholarly research, their migration the Netherlands has not. Moreover, by studying Dominicans through a lens of attachments and emotions, I hope to bring a different perspective on immigrants' settlement and incorporation processes, responding to Duany (2008, p. 60):

> Although researchers have drawn clearly the socioeconomic contours of Dominican migration, the everyday life of Dominicans in New York City remains outside the fringes of academic discourse …. By focusing on the socioeconomic components of the migratory process, most scholars have overlooked the cultural dimensions of Dominican exodus.

1.6 The Road Map of this Book

Following this introduction, Chapter 2 discusses the migration of Dominicans to the Netherlands and their settlement patterns. The chapter describes characteristics of the Dominican population in the Netherlands, presented mainly via

Introduction **17**

a statistical overview using data from the Dutch statistical office. In particular, I compare the years 1996, 2000, 2005, 2010, 2015, 2020 and 2022 to trace developments in population size, gender distribution, age distribution and geographic dispersal.

Chapter 3 assesses what home is for Dominicans in the Netherlands. Divided into three sections, it first describes the emergence of what can be called a Dominican community and cultural infrastructure in the Netherlands, dealing with how the first flows of Dominican immigrants recreated practices, spaces and places from the Dominican Republic in the Netherlands and their efforts to recreate some familiarity. Second, it describes their experiences of, and opinions about, unfamiliar characteristics of life in the Netherlands, which exposes challenges they faced *vis-á-vis* feeling at home. Thirdly, the Dominicans' sense of home is described, bringing to the fore that the place of home is not fixed and depends on various factors including appreciation for specific characteristics of each country and personal changes.

Chapters 4–6 zoom in on food practices, which form the core focus of this book's analysis. Chapter 4 examines what Dominicans consider Dominican food. It then describes consumption habits of Dominican immigrants after migration to the Netherlands and the meaning of these practices with regard to feelings of home. This leads to a categorization of different types of homemakers. Overall, the chapter explores whether Dominican food is a homemaking practice. The last section details which migration-related and individual characteristics lead to differentiation in practices.

Chapter 5 deals with how co-ethnics and the opportunities they provide affect food practices and feelings of home. Looking into the role of co-ethnics reveals homemaking as a social matter which also occurs in spaces other than only the domestic (the house). The first section describes the Dominican community in the Netherlands, in which the co-ethnic community is found to evoke feelings of home but also be divided. As such, it provides an entry point to understand the different attachments to and functions of the community. The second section explores the opportunities co-ethnics provide to keep familiar Dominican food practices alive and, in so doing, the role co-ethnics may play in making home. The third section focuses on food institutions; thus, opportunities outside the domestic space function as communal space such as restaurants and grocery stores.

Chapter 6 explores how homemaking is embedded in, and influenced by, the receiving context. In this case, the context is the Netherlands, a country with very different cultural and social characteristics. The first section describes the encounter with what I call 'material' characteristics, and thus 'traditional' Dutch food, products and ways of preparing food, and how Dominicans experience these. The second section discusses, as another part of the material characteristics, how other immigrant communities help in homemaking through food. As no extensive Dominican food infrastructure exists in the Netherlands, Dominicans rely on other Caribbean communities with similar product needs and established grocery stores. The third section focuses on the social characteristics of the receiving context, particularly unfamiliar food customs that Dominicans encounter related to Dutch social organization and celebrations. I link these material and social

18   *Post-Migration Experiences, Cultural Practices and Homemaking*

encounters to Burke's (2009) categorization of acceptance, resistance, segregation and adaptation to show how Dominicans deal with the encounters in the Netherlands.

The closing chapter discusses the significance of this study's findings for the homemaking concept and for the study of immigrant settlement. In addition, new points of departure are provided for future research on homemaking and Caribbean migration to Europe.

Chapter 2

Dominican Migration: Increasing Diversity in Destinations

2.1 Introduction

Seeking a visa of cement and limestone
And in the concrete jungle, who will I meet?
Seeking a visa; a reason to be,
Seeking a visa; never to return.
Necessity, how it enrages me!
A powerful blow, what else can I do?
To be shipwrecked, food for the sea
A reason to be; never to return.

(Translated by the author)

This song, 'Visa para un sueño', by Juan Luis Guerra, provides a social commentary on the challenges of obtaining a visa to travel to the United States to work, improve life conditions and escape poverty. There are many such songs about migration in merengue and bachata music, reflecting how ingrained the migrant experience has become in Dominicans' lives, among those who migrate and those who do not (Gill, 2012). In my research, Dominicans expressed great love for their country and pride to be Dominican. Why then do so many choose to build a life elsewhere?

This chapter discusses the emigration of Dominicans. In particular, it examines their main migration destinations, migration flows to the Dutch Caribbean islands and their settlement patterns in the Netherlands in Europe.

2.2 Emigration of Dominicans: Increasing Diversity in Destinations

Several events have given rise to large-scale emigration from the Dominican Republic. The first wave of Dominican emigration followed the assassination of President Rafael Leonidas Trujillo. For more than 30 years, from 1930 to 1961, Dominican

---

Post-Migration Experiences, Cultural Practices and Homemaking:
An Ethnography of Dominican Migration to Europe, 19–38
Copyright © 2023 by Sabrina Dinmohamed
Published under exclusive licence by Emerald Publishing Limited
doi:10.1108/978-1-83753-204-920231002

20   *Post-Migration Experiences, Cultural Practices and Homemaking*

citizens lived under the Trujillo dictatorship. Emigration at that time was restricted because Trujillo believed the country needed all potential workers to build the economy, but he also feared that his opponents would organize against him from abroad (Grasmuck & Pessar, 1991; Hernández, 2002; Levitt, 2001). Migration barriers were lifted after Trujillo's 1961 assassination, signalling the start of a migration exodus, primarily to the United States. The first to leave the country were political migrants, thus persons related to the Trujillo dictatorship: conservative political leaders, government employees and persons from the ruling class.

At the end of the 1960s, a second wave of emigration began due to the economic difficulties in the country at the time. In this period, it was mainly those with relatively high levels of formal education and good jobs who went abroad looking for a better job or higher salary. '[T]he migrants were workers who, precisely because of their relatively advantageous position, were able to finance the expensive move to the United States' (Grasmuck & Pessar, 1991, p. 95). Dominican migration to the United States was encouraged by the growing demand for cheap labour there, alongside the abolition of immigration quotas by national origin in 1965 and the passing of the Immigration and Naturalization Act of 1965 with its emphasis on family reunification.

During the 1970s, the economy of the Dominican Republic was transformed from a rural agricultural model to one that was urban-based, causing thousands of Dominicans to migrate to the cities in search of employment. However, the economy did not provide sufficient job opportunities, leading to high levels of unemployment and a burgeoning informal sector. While the outflow of highly skilled people with good jobs continued, the poor could not leave because of the high costs associated with migration.

From the 1980s, the group of migrants diversified. Throughout the 1980s, unemployment, inflation and weak public services propelled emigration among all social classes. Migration became a survival strategy for the lower and middle classes. Those who could not obtain a visa for mainland United States chose other destinations. Given the increasing restrictions on visas for the US mainland, many chose to travel illegally in so-called *yolas* (small wooden boats) through the Mona Passage to Puerto Rico. According to Duany (2005), Dominican migration to Puerto Rico was different from that to the US mainland: those who went to Puerto Rico generally had lower levels of formal education and originated from non-urban contexts.

Though the Dominican Republic has registered economic growth since 2010, this has not stemmed emigration. Wealth distribution in the country has remained unequal, the informal sector is large, and the quality of work and living conditions are precarious for much of the economically active population (International Organization for Migration, 2017). The lack of opportunities in the country keeps its population in a continuous pursuit of emigration, seeking betterment elsewhere. A recent study carried out by the Pontificia Universidad Católica Madre y Maestra (Santo Domingo), focused on Dominicans between the ages of 17 and 24, showed that their main motivations for leaving the country were the search for opportunities regarding work and study and basic human rights (Guilamo, Flores, Reyes, & Perez, 2023).

Dominican Migration **21**

The mainland of the United States has been the most popular destination for Dominicans, followed by Puerto Rico and Venezuela (OECD, 2017). Puerto Rico's importance as a destination is especially, for some, as a hub for emigration to the US mainland. Venezuela was particularly important as a destination for Dominicans during the 1970s and early 1980s in the context of the oil boom there. Since then, destinations have become more diverse and now include Spain, Switzerland, Germany, Canada, Panama and the Netherlands. The share of Dominicans choosing European destinations has increased over time from 7% of the total emigrant stock in 1990 to 17% in 2015 (OECD, 2017). Table 1 presents the top 10 destinations for Dominican emigrants from 1990 to 2020. Principal European destinations are Spain, Italy, Switzerland, the Netherlands and Germany. (While the United Nations Department of Economic and Social Affairs uses country of origin to indicate who is Dominican and I use country of birth, these UN data still give good indications of who is a first-generation Dominican.)

Spain has the largest community of Dominican immigrants in Europe. However, the country's largest immigrant populations are from Morocco, Romania and Colombia. According to data from the Spanish statistical office, immigrants from the Dominican Republic are in the 11th place. While the Dominican community is not one of the largest in Spain, it is growing, having tripled in size from 2000 to 2020. In 2021, Spain counted 186,395 Dominican-born persons. Their migration to Spain started in the mid-1980s, dominated by women who came to Spain for domestic services jobs (Lilón & Lantigua, 2004; Romero Valiente, 1997). At first, Dominican migration to Spain was spurred by an intensification of relations between the two countries as well as economic development in Spain which generated a labour demand that the local population could not satisfy. Most Dominicans emigrating to Spain were born in the south-western region and left due to poverty. By comparison, Romero Valiente (1997) found low participation of Dominicans from the south-west region in emigration to the US mainland, Puerto Rico and Venezuela. Without such initial flows, there is reduced chance of people from this region generating migratory chains to these destinations, where natives of the regions of Cibao and Este are prominent (respectively, on the US mainland and Puerto Rico). Within Spain, Dominicans have settled primarily in Barcelona and Madrid.

Italy holds the second place, after Spain, among the European destinations of Dominicans. Italy's three largest immigrant communities are Romanians, Albanians and Moroccans. Compared to these, the Dominican community is small. However, it is increasing in size and numbered 48,083 Dominican-born people in 2020. Like in Spain, Dominican migration to Italy has been dominated by women. Data from the Italian statistical office show that they have settled primarily in the regions of Lombardy, Liguria, Veneto and Tuscany.

In Switzerland, the Dominican population is substantially smaller than that country's largest immigrant groups, which are from Germany, Italy, Portugal, France and Turkey. In 2020, Switzerland counted 12,377 Dominicans, representing a doubling over the previous 20 years. Petree and Vargas (2005) identify Dominican migration to Switzerland as part of a larger wave of migration to Europe that began in the 1980s. Several initial pull factors helped spur Dominican migration to Switzerland: the emergence of an international tourism industry in the Dominican

22   *Post-Migration Experiences, Cultural Practices and Homemaking*

Republic, temporary labour migration opportunities for work in Switzerland's cabaret bars, and growing transnational social networks facilitating migration for marriage and family reunification (Petree & Vargas, 2005). In terms of geographic concentration, most Dominicans have settled in urban areas in Switzerland including both larger and smaller cities such as Zurich, Basel, Geneva, Bern, Lausanne, Lucerne, Aargau and the canton of Ticino. On the sending side, most Dominican immigrants to Switzerland come from urban and semi-urban contexts. Most are from poor families and have low levels of formal education.

Information regarding the settlement experiences of Dominicans in Germany is limited. In 2020, Germany counted 12,304 Dominicans. Like elsewhere, however, the community is increasing in size and registered a 37.8% increase from 2010 to 2020 (see Table 1). According to 2021 data from the German Federal Statistical Office, Dominicans have settled primarily in the districts of Berlin, Hamburg, Frankfurt am Main, München and Hannover.

Table 1.   Top 10 Destinations of Dominican Migrants Worldwide, 1990–2020.

	1990	1995	2000	2005	2010	2015	2020
United States mainland	347,858	524,698	705,139	761,989	843,720	1,086,819	1,167,738
Spain	15,160	21,654	36,953	73,049	136,976	156,905	184,832
Puerto Rico	37,207	49,325	61,563	66,983	63,981	57,891	46,905
Venezuela	18,280	16,240	14,293	14,286	14,423	14,743	13,899
Italy	9,060	13,427	17,793	30,028	40,445	41,853	48,083
Switzerland	4,751	5,976	7,223	8,107	9,532	10,960	12,377
Canada	2,668	3,841	5,106	6,737	8,450	10,535	11,414
The Netherlands	2,403	3,933	5,593	6,995	7,751	8,585	9,541
Panama	1,474	3,554	5,859	5,798	6,914	8,095	9,711
Germany	1,012	2,828	4,643	7,013	8,932	9,168	12,304

Source: United Nations Department of Economic and Social Affairs, Population Division (2020). International Migrant Stock 2020.

2.3 Migration to the Kingdom of the Netherlands

Migration, particularly intra-regional migration, can be seen as a tradition and inherent aspect of Caribbean cultures (Pizarro & Villa, 2005; Thomas-Hope, 1992).Thus, while migration of Dominicans to the Netherlands in Europe is a relatively new phenomenon, migration to the Dutch Caribbean islands is not. (The Dutch Caribbean islands comprise the constituent countries of Aruba, Curaçao and Sint Maarten as well as the 'special municipalities' of Bonaire, Sint Eustatius and Saba.) Migratory flows between the Dominican Republic and these Caribbean destinations have existed for centuries.

Dominican Migration **23**

2.3.1 Migration to the Dutch Caribbean Islands

The Dutch Caribbean islands are among the top five destination countries of Dominican migrants within the Caribbean region (Table 2).

Nowadays, the main migration flows between the Dominican Republic and the Dutch Caribbean islands, in terms of size, are towards Curaçao, Sint Maarten and Aruba. However, prior to 1900, migration between the Dominican Republic and the islands was in the reverse direction: from the Dutch Caribbean islands towards the Dominican Republic. The first flow started in 1516 (see Abaunza, 2017; De Boer, 2016 for more detail). Following Columbus' arrival on the island, which was then named Santo Domingo, or Hispaniola (the present territory of the Dominican Republic and Haiti), it became the first European settlement in the Americas. Soon, however, there was a drop in the number of indigenous inhabitants due to diseases the Spaniards brought with them. To remedy the labour shortage on Hispaniola, almost the entire indigenous population of Curaçao, Aruba and Bonaire, estimated at 2,000 people, was forcibly brought to Hispaniola to work in the sugar industry and copper mines (Moya Pons, 2008). This population displacement can be considered the first direct contact between Hispaniola and these three islands in the colonial era. Subsequent migration flows to the Dominican Republic included the labour migration of Sephardic Jews from Curaçao to the

Table 2. Top 10 Destinations of Dominican Migrants in the Caribbean Region, 1990–2020.

	1990	1995	2000	2005	2010	2015	2020
Puerto Rico	37,207	49,325	61,563	66,983	63,981	57,891	46,905
Curaçao					5,260	5,715	6,665
Aruba	2,042	2,829	3,615	3,903	4,114	4,327	4,839
United States Virgin Islands	533	1,861	3,194	3,915	4,638	4,641	4,642
Haiti	2,406	2,285	2,170	2,061	2,164	2,272	2,377
Sint Maarten (Dutch part)				1,701	3,403	3,546	3,762
Turks and Caicos Islands	349	520	692	722	1,354	1,756	1,989
British Virgin Islands	748	879	1,010	1,157	1,526	1,745	1,979
Antigua and Barbuda	621	1,044	1,466	1,572	1,678	1,784	1,865
Guadeloupe	3,440	2,517	1,593	1,253	913	874	864
Bahamas	44	64	84	177	269	291	310

Source: United Nations Department of Economic and Social Affairs, Population Division (2020). International Migrant Stock 2020.

24   Post-Migration Experiences, Cultural Practices and Homemaking

Dominican Republic (between 1800 and 1900) and the labour migration of formerly enslaved Africans. After the abolition of slavery in 1863, many Curaçaoans worked as seasonal agricultural workers on other islands, including the Dominican Republic, supplying labour for the region's post-plantation economies (Allen, 2006).

From the 1900s, the direction of the migration flow changed and became orientated away from the Dominican Republic towards the Dutch Caribbean islands. Currently, the largest flows occur between the Dominican Republic and Curaçao, Sint Maarten and, to a lesser extent, Aruba (De Boer, 2016; Dinmohamed, 2007, 2008, 2017, 2021).

2.3.1.1 Curaçao.   Studies on Caribbean migration characterize Curaçao as both a sending and a receiving society of labour migrants. The establishment of the Royal Dutch Oil Company in 1918 changed the socio-economic conditions of Curaçaoan society. Curaçao was thus transformed from a commerce-focused and agricultural society into a more complex, modern and industrial society (Allen, 2003). The island became a major international hub as well. In this period, 'economic prospects changed population movement on the island so that it became a receiving, rather than a sending, society' (Allen, 2006, p. 83). Due to insufficient labour availability, Curaçao attracted migrants from different parts of the world. Thousands of persons migrated to the island from within the Caribbean, but also from Europe, the Middle East and Asia, to work at the refinery. A second wave of immigrants arrived in the 1990s. At this time, the tourism industry in Curaçao was growing, and due to a lack of local workers, migrants from the Caribbean and South America were attracted to the island. Due to emigration of Curaçaoans to the Netherlands, gaps in the labour market arose that were filled by these immigrants from abroad. Unlike those in the previous period, the migrants who came at this time were predominantly regional and are nowadays referred to as 'new migrants' (Dinmohamed, 2017). Immigrants in this group originate mainly from the Dominican Republic, Colombia, Venezuela, Haiti, Jamaica and Surinam. (See the work of Rose Mary Allen who has published extensively on intra-regional migration to Curaçao.)

Research on Dominicans' migration experiences in the Dutch Caribbean islands is limited, and knowledge about migration motives is scarce. Several studies mention migration as a livelihood strategy for Dominicans, a way out of poverty and a way of providing for the family (Gutierrez, 2006). In my research on Dominicans in the Netherlands, I learned more about Dominicans' choices for the islands. Migration to the Dutch Caribbean islands is in most cases considered an opportunity to better one's conditions. Some target these islands specifically to obtain a Dutch passport (*para hacer papeles*), which was easy in the 1980s, according to *Analisa*, originally from San Juan de la Maguana. Her story illustrates the importance of social networks in migration decision-making processes and post-migration settlement. Her sister, who had gotten married in Curaçao, arranged for her to come. She stayed for one and a half years and then returned to the Dominican Republic, after which she departed for the Netherlands. About her reasons for migration she said:

To search for a better life (*buscar una mejor vida*). You already know that in our country, you work and work, and it is only enough to [afford to] eat. But when you arrive in another country, you have the opportunities to progress more.

In other cases, women sought business opportunities in Curaçao. Often they met Curaçaoan men on their travels. *Francisco* told me about his mother, who had gone to Curaçao 'in search of a better life', as he put it. At that time, Curaçao was one of the countries in the region where no visa was needed for travel. Faced with difficult economic circumstances at home, *Francisco*'s mother decided to go to Curaçao to buy clothes in the Free Zone and sell them in Santo Domingo. When he was 10 his mother brought him to live with her in Curaçao:

> Curaçao at that time was one of the few countries where you could travel without a visa. Things in Santo Domingo were a bit tight. My mom went to Curaçao to do the job of selling clothes, the business of the Free Zone. She bought five or six suitcases of clothes and sold them. And she also met a man from there, my stepfather. My mom got to know him, she kept on travelling and in the end she got married. She became a resident in Curaçao and she went to live in Curaçao. I suffered from asthma and in Santo Domingo there was no cure for asthma, so my mom took me to Curaçao in 1978. When I went to Curaçao [I was confronted with] a different language, different people, different ways. I felt like a Martian on earth. Like ET.

Another story, that of *Victor*, confirms the important role of migration among Dominican women as a livelihood strategy and means of ensuring the well-being of their children (Gutierrez, 2006). According to *Victor*, poverty and lack of prospects in the Dominican Republic made his mother decide to go to Curaçao:

> He was on a holiday there. They [Curaçaoan men] usually vacation there for the music, but also, they know that there are beautiful women there. That's just life. And they get to know each other and he says, 'I want to take you to Curaçao'. She thinks, 'I have to leave my environment, but my son has no future, so I will'. She knows that her son goes to school, but whether he gets a job depends on connections and we don't have those. So that won't work at all. She goes there with him, she arrives in Curaçao. Then she has to deal with the viciousness of Curaçaoan women, because a Curaçaoan man is married to a Dominican woman. [Those women say,] 'they are all whores and take our men away'. Those were the ideas at that time.

Dominicans form Curaçao's second largest immigrant group (after immigrants born in the Netherlands) and the largest group of regional immigrants. The first Dominican migrants arrived in Curaçao between 1920 and 1929. A significant

26 *Post-Migration Experiences, Cultural Practices and Homemaking*

increase of Dominicans in Curaçao occurred between 1970 and 1979, with exponential growth between 1990 and 2000. After 2000, the number of Dominicans moving to Curaçao diminished, but the community has continued to grow. Based on census data, the number of Dominican immigrants registered on the island increased from 1,485 in 1981 to 3,474 in 1992, 4,191 in 2001 and 5,405 in 2011 (Dinmohamed, 2017). In 2020, there were 6,665 persons from the Dominican Republic in Curaçao (Table 2).

2.3.1.2 Sint Maarten. In 2020, Sint Maarten counted 3,762 Dominicans, making them the country's largest immigrant community (Table 2). Even so, the actual size of the Dominican population is likely larger, as many Dominicans on the island are undocumented (Restler, 2006). Other large immigrant communities on Sint Maarten are from Haiti, Guadeloupe, Jamaica and Dominica. While movement from the Dominican Republic to Sint Maarten is relatively new, movement in the reverse direction, from Sint Maarten to the Dominican Republic, is not. *Luis*, for example, was born in Santo Domingo, but grew up in Sint Maarten, where his family had roots. His parents were living in Sint Maarten when his mother got pregnant, but she wanted to give birth to the child in the Dominican Republic. Thus, he was born in Santo Domingo and returned to Sint Maarten with his mother when he was three months old. He told me about his paternal great-grandfather, who was originally from Sint Maarten and migrated to the Dominican Republic:

> My great-grandfather, that is, my grandmother's father, lived in the Dominican Republic …. There he met my great-grandmother. They got together, had ten children and lived there for many years. He lived there practically all his life, he felt Dominican, but from Sint Maarten. After my great-grandmother died, my grandmother decided to migrate to Sint Maarten, because she and her siblings began to realize, 'if my father is from Sint Maarten, I have French nationality'. So from there my grandmother travelled to Sint Maarten, worked and built a life there. And she began to bring her brothers and sisters over from the Dominican Republic.

2.3.1.3 Aruba. Migration has played a crucial role in Aruba's demographic development (CBS Aruba, 2004). During the late 1920s, the Aruban economy experienced an economic boom when two oil refineries were established on the island: Eagle Petroleum Company Incorporated (a subsidiary of Royal Shell) and Lago Oil and Transport Company. Like in Curaçao, the oil industry attracted labourers from throughout the region. In 1948, the majority of immigrants originated from the islands of the British West Indies. Another large group of immigrants at the time were from Venezuela and Colombia. Historically, close ties exist between Aruba and Venezuela, and Aruba has traditionally been an important destination for Venezuelan business people. Substantial intermarriage occurred between people from the island and Venezuelans. This was also the case, though to a lesser extent, among Colombians.

Dominican Migration 27

In 1985 the Lago refinery was forced to close its doors, prompting many citizens, both Aruban and foreign-born, to leave the island (CBS Aruba, 2004). Aruba thus lost its attraction as a migration destination, and immigration dropped. In an effort to counter the devastating effects of the refinery's closure, the government sought to develop Aruba as a prime tourist destination. Consequently, the construction sector on the island experienced an enormous boom. The 1991 census registered the largest group of foreign workers as originating from the Dominican Republic (CBS Aruba, 2004). Dominican women went to Aruba to work as domestic servants, filling a gap caused by the higher participation of Aruban women in the labour market. *Irvin* told me about his mother, who while working at a hotel in Punta Cana was offered a job in Aruba. She went in the 1970s to work as a dishwasher at the Holiday Inn hotel:

> In 1976 my mother migrated to Aruba for work. She was then 23-years-old with four children. I was 3-years-old. My father stayed behind with us. In the end, my mother decided not to go back to Dominican Republic. She offered for our father to come to Aruba, but he didn't want to. He said, 'I am fine here'. Then she had to decide what to do with us. In the end, my father decided we were better off in Aruba than the Dominican Republic. So, we went and he stayed.

In 2020, immigrants from the Dominican Republic formed the fourth largest community in Aruba, after the Venezuelans, Colombians and Dutch. The number of Dominican immigrants registered on the island increased from 2,042 in 1990 to 3,615 in 2000, 4,114 in 2010 and 4,839 in 2020 (Table 2).

2.3.1.4 Bonaire, Sint Eustatius and Saba. Migration to Bonaire, Sint Eustatius and Saba is relatively small, and research on the Dominican community on these islands is limited. Data from the Dutch statistical office (CBS) shows that in 2020, Bonaire counted 1,311 Dominican-born persons, Saint Eustatius 291 and Saba 99.

Sullivan (2006) studied the Dominican community in Saba and describes a general influx of migrants starting in the 1960s. Establishment of the Saba University School of Medicine, in particular, brought a rise in the number of Americans and Canadians living on the island. Labour migrants from the Dominican Republic, Dominica, Haiti, St Vincent, Colombia and other Caribbean islands came to work in the tourism industry. The Dominican presence in Saban social life is notable, and Sullivan (2006, pp. 462–463) observes, 'the general influence of these Spanish-speaking groups can be seen in the grocery stores that now sell foods like empanadas, the clubs that regularly have Spanish nights, and the schools that now struggle with increasing demands for bilingual education for adults and children'. A main characteristic of this migration flow from the Dominican Republic is that the majority is female.

2.3.3 From the Dutch Caribbean Islands to the Netherlands

The Dutch Caribbean islands have often been presented as a springboard for migration to Europe, particularly the Netherlands (Gutierrez, 2006; UN-INSTRAW,

28   Post-Migration Experiences, Cultural Practices and Homemaking

2006). But the question arises as to whether Dominicans, when making the decision to leave the Dominican Republic, already see the Dutch Caribbean islands as a gateway to a better life in Europe. Do they migrate from the Dominican Republic to these islands with the whole process already in mind? Or does the idea emerge while on the islands? The stories I have heard indicate that many, when they left the Dominican Republic, did not consider the islands a springboard to the Netherlands. More common was the idea of going to earn money on the Dutch Caribbean islands and eventually return to the Dominican Republic. Paul and Yeoh (2021, p. 12) mention that

> few migrants fully grasp the range of destination options available to them before they leave their country of origin. It is only after they embark on their journeys and once they are overseas that their mental maps of the world open up and shift in significant ways, directly impacting on their subsequent migrations.

Graziano (2006), in the case of Dominican migration to Puerto, elaborates on two scenarios. The first is travel by Yola to Puerto Rico and continue by air to the mainland. The second is choosing Puerto Rico as the final destination from the start because of family reunification, a desire to be closer to the Dominican Republic, a preference for an atmosphere that is culturally and linguistically more similar and avoiding the risks of moving to the unfamiliar mainland. Much more research is needed regarding Dominican immigrants' migration motives and decision-making processes to understand their choice for the Dutch Caribbean islands.

Nonetheless, the Dominicans in my research often mentioned the islands in their migration stories, offering some clues regarding their motivation to migrate a second time to the Netherlands. Many had economic reasons. *Analisa* decided to go to the Netherlands after having lived for a while in Curaçao. One sister and one aunt were already in the Netherlands, which encouraged her and another sister to take the step to Europe. Staying in Curaçao was not an option, and *Analisa*'s story illustrates again the importance of social networks in migration decision-making processes:

> Curaçao is almost the same as Santo Domingo. The only thing different is that it has the guilder, but it's almost the same. I got to know Holland through my sisters. I have a sister and she was here [the Netherlands] for a while. She got married, then arranged for my oldest sister to come, then me. Let's say we helped each other: one helps one and the other helps the other, like that. I came here with my older sister and a younger one. We have an aunt here, and she put herself in charge of us.

Luis' story, too, points to the role of social networks in facilitating migration to the Netherlands. He said that when he lived in Sint Maarten he had never heard of the Netherlands, but while exploring his options for further

Dominican Migration   **29**

studies he came across it. His plan had been to go to France, but because his family had acquaintances in the Netherlands, his parents preferred for him to go there. The family acquaintances received him, and he stayed with them his first two years.

Some Dominican women arrive in the Netherlands' sex industry through ties with sex work in Curaçao. In 1949, Campo Alegre, a state-owned brothel, was founded in Curaçao at the initiative of the Dutch government, the Catholic Church, the US Army and various business representatives (Janssen, 2007). Campo Alegre was the only spot on the island where prostitution was tolerated. Women were drawn to work there from throughout the region, with most initially coming from Venezuela, the Dominican Republic and Cuba. Some entered the country as tourists, and some received work permits for employment at hotels or night clubs. During the economic crisis in the 1980s, in particular, large groups of Dominican women came to work at Campo Alegre. Yet, up until its closure in 2020, women were allowed to work at the club for just three months in order to prevent relationships from forming with customers. Due to the international oil crisis and the closing of Shell in Curaçao, the economic situation in Curaçao deteriorated, causing not only Curaçaoans but also these Dominican women to migrate to the Netherlands.

Some Dominican women chose migration to the Netherlands because of their children. *Carolina* came to the Netherlands after living in Curaçao for more than 20 years. Her motivation was to provide a better future for her two handicapped children:

> I lived in Curaçao for twenty-some years. I went to school there and my children were born there. My mom came here [the Netherlands] first. Then I followed. I had two sick children. One of my eldest sons has epilepsy. After that he became diabetic. My daughter is mentally retarded and she also had epilepsy at the time, and now is also diabetic. So, look, it was quite turbulent. I was a single mother and I had to do everything. And at that time there were no possibilities in Curaçao, for example, special schools or treatments for that type of children. I do not know now, but at that time there was nothing. So when I came I said I am going to give my children a chance here. My oldest son was already with my mother, and afterwards I came with my daughter and my other son. And I left two others there, because I could not afford to bring them all at once. When I came, I had to start from scratch. A single mother with children.

Sandra's story is different. She loved living in Sint Maarten, but she decided to leave the island due to the frequency of hurricanes and the desire to ensure her daughter a safe future. Her migration story began when she migrated to Curaçao at age 11. She lived in Curaçao until she was 23. Then she went to the Netherlands, after which she migrated back to the Caribbean (Sint Maarten), where she lived for eight years. She told me about her decision to leave the island:

30 Post-Migration Experiences, Cultural Practices and Homemaking

I felt at home, I felt like I was in the Dominican Republic. I always thought, 'I feel very good here, I like this place a lot, I have my job, I have my life, I am not going anywhere'. And I stayed there until 1998. I got married, I had a little girl. But then in 1995, 1996, 1997, almost every year, a hurricane came, and ruined everything you had. So packing, unpacking. I said, 'I'm not going to do this anymore'. My girl was one year old. And I saw what was happening with my nephews and nieces, nervous whenever it started to rain. And I said, 'I don't want this for my daughter'.

2.4 Migration to the Netherlands

'What an interesting choice, I have never heard of Dominicans in the Netherlands'. This was a recurring comment when I told colleagues about my research. While I could not imagine the Netherlands without the Dominican cultural and social scene, as it had given me so much warmth and joy, this immigrant community was invisible to the majority of people in the Netherlands. Compared to the Netherlands' larger and more prominent immigrant communities, the Dominican community is small, though increasing, in size. This section introduces the Dominican population in the Netherlands by way of an overview using data from the Dutch statistical office. I compare the years 1996, 2000, 2005, 2010, 2015, 2020 and 2022, tracing developments in population size, gender distribution, age distribution and geographic dispersal. But first, why do Dominicans come to the Netherlands?

2.4.1 Migration Motives: Not Only Dominicans From Poor Contexts

The Frank Reyes song in the previous chapter exemplified the struggles of a Dominican in post-migration life. It also provides a key reason for leaving the Dominican Republic, namely, to provide a better future for children. While migration of Dominicans has been considered a livelihood strategy, a way to survive, my research underscores that the reality with regard to the choice of migration is more diverse.

Dominicans' migration motives in my research can be classified into several categories, somewhat correlated to the period in which the immigrant arrived in the Netherlands. Almost all who came in the 1980s and 1990s came for economic reasons in search of a better life (*para buscar una mejor vida*). Children also play a role in the decision-making process. Several studies have found that Dominican women's migration to Europe and the Netherlands is often motivated by the desire to provide a better future for their children (Brennan, 2004; Gutierrez, 2009). Yet, when migrating, these women must typically leave their children behind in the Dominican Republic, to be cared for by a female relative, usually the migrant's sister or mother. Many of the Dominican women who participated in my research had met Dutch men in the Dominican Republic and chosen to join them in the Netherlands, while their children from prior relationships stayed with grandparents or other family members until they could follow. For women from poor contexts, marriage to citizens of other countries may be an avenue to legal

Dominican Migration **31**

migration off the island (Brennan, 2004). *Victor* and *Oscar* told me how their mothers made the decision to come to the Netherlands:

> My mother's cousin had gone to Holland, also via a Curaçaoan man. She said, 'Come to the Netherlands, because if you come here, you will get everything. You get a house, and this and that'. Then you have to imagine someone who has nothing at all, who hears that you'll get a house, your children will go to school, everything. You think, 'Wow, could this be true?' Back then you didn't have the internet, Facebook, things like that. You have to realize that. And she says, 'I have nothing to lose, I have nothing left. So I have this passport, let me have a look'. She comes here [to the Netherlands] and she leaves us with grandma. (Victor)

> That Italian man [his mother's husband] lived here in the Netherlands at the time, but often went to the Dominican Republic. So at the time my mother had made a choice for a better life. It was actually more a choice of, 'I just want to go to the Netherlands and then have my children come'. What happened next was one of the toughest moments of my life. My mother went away without telling us. We didn't really know anything, although I already had a premonition. (Oscar)

Between 2000 and 2010, migration motives were much more varied. Some Dominicans had never intended to leave the Dominican Republic, but came to the Netherlands to be with a spouse. According to Lilón and Lantigua (2004), in addition to the regional economic crisis of the 1980s and the increasing difficulty of migrating to the US mainland, Puerto Rico and Venezuela, there was another factor that affected Dominican migration to Europe: the rapid development of the tourism industry in the Dominican Republic during the 1980s and 1990s. Tourism, which mainly targeted middle-class Europeans, brought an inflow of Spanish, German, Swiss and French vacationers and 'led to a large number of marriages between (mainly female) Dominicans and Europeans' (Lilón & Lantigua, 2004, p. 134). *Aurelia* said she had never thought of migration. Born and raised in Esperanza, she had a good childhood surrounded by family. When she was 29 years old, she came to the Netherlands after meeting a Dutch man who was on holiday in the Dominican Republic. She described the process of getting to know each other and organizing the paperwork to enable her move to the Netherlands:

> Well, I had no plans to leave my country. I am very Dominican. But in 2001 my best friend met the man who is now my husband on a bus. He had gone to the Dominican Republic because a Dominican told him if he wanted to meet a woman he should go to the Dominican Republic, that there were many good, professional girls with a good heart. So he went with his dad. She started talking to me about him, that she had met... a blond Dutchman with blue eyes and bottle-bottom glasses. Then she introduced him to me over the phone. We exchanged e-mail addresses. I'm talking about 2001.

32 *Post-Migration Experiences, Cultural Practices and Homemaking*

MSN was beginning to grow but we never saw each other on camera, we always sent e-mails. At a given moment he returned to the Dominican Republic in 2002. I met him and he tells me that he fell in love in that moment. I put him to work there for a year and a half; I did not accept him as a boyfriend, because I had that fear of another country, I didn't know about the culture. I came first for two weeks to see how everything was. In the year and a half [I had known him] they could have told me many stories that were not true. We talked, I met everyone here [in the Netherlands], his family. He took me to his mom's grave. Well, that was in October 2003. In February 2004 we got married. On 23 January 2005 I came to live here. [Completing] all the procedures [was] very intense. But here I am.

A smaller group of Dominicans in my research had been sent to the Netherlands by the Dominican government or came to broaden their horizons to explore the world. Those in this group tended to have higher educational levels and professional jobs. *Mercedes* lived in Santo Domingo until age 22. She was always attracted to foreign languages and getting to know different countries. Her job with the Dominican government had taken her to live in London, Brussels and Denmark. Finally, she ended up in the Netherlands, where she had resided for five years at the time of our interview. She told me that she always found excuses to leave the Dominican Republic, where she 'had a great job, a nice car and a wonderful social life'. For her, migration was about independence and exploring the world.

From 2010 onwards, most Dominicans coming to the Netherlands with economic motives were those who had lived in Spain. When the 2008 financial crisis hit, many decided to leave Spain and seek work in the Netherlands. *Roberto* was 30 when he came to the Netherlands. When he was six, his mother had moved to Spain for work, and he had joined her there when he was 13. After the economic crisis hit the country, *Roberto* decided to look for work in the Netherlands, where his brother had already found a job.

2.4.2 Characteristics of the Dutch-Dominican Population

While Dominican immigrants have not been the subject of in-depth research in the Netherlands, the Dutch statistical office (CBS) has maintained basic data on Dominican immigrants from 1996 onwards. Before tapping into this data, however, it is worthwhile to specify who the institute categorizes as 'Dominican'. CBS has two main ways of categorizing a person as an immigrant. One is by country of birth; another is by so-called 'migration background', which includes both first-generation and second-generation migrants (CBS, 2016). As this book is interested in the experiences of persons who left one country and sought to make a home in another, I chose country of birth as an indicator of who is Dominican, thus leaving children of Dominican immigrants in the Netherlands out of the analysis.

2.4.2.1 Region of Origin. No quantitative data are available on the regions or cities/towns from which Dominicans in the Netherlands originate. However, data from Curaçao and Spain are available and give some indications, as a portion of the Dominicans in the Netherlands had previously lived in those countries. The

Dominican Migration **33**

majority of Dominicans in Spain are from the southern regions of the Dominican Republic. According to Lilón and Lantigua (2004, p. 143), most come from

> rural areas, with very low educational level from south-western regions, from Vicente Noble and Barahona, followed by those from the east, the outlying zones of Santo Domingo and in fewer cases from the Cibao region.

In Curaçao, the majority of Dominican immigrants originates from small cities or rural areas, and 31% come from the capital, Santo Domingo (Ministerie van Sociale Ontwikkeling, Arbeid en Welzijn [SOAW], 2014).

The stories told by the Dominicans in my research provide indications as well. The majority of the Dominicans I spoke with came from Santo Domingo and cities and towns in the southern region (Bani, Higuey, Barahona, San Juan). Others came from the south-east (La Romana, San Pedro de Macoris, Higuey), and a minority was from the northern region (Santiago, Salcedo, La Vega, Mao). My respondents confirmed that a minority of Dominicans in the Netherlands was from the north, with most being from the south, the capital or the east of the Dominican Republic. Most of those from the north came here through marriages with Dutch tourists. On contacts between Dominicans and European tourists, and specifically in the northern coastal town of Sosúa, Brennan (2004) writes:

> International tourism began slowly, with the docking of cruise ships off Sosúa's shore and the construction of an international airport between Sosúa and Puerto Plata in the early 1980s. Up to this point, visitors to Sosúa had been wealthy Dominicans who built magnificent vacation houses in the hills overlooking the beach along with upper middle-class Dominicans who owned modest apartments for weekend getaways from Santiago, a city two hours away …. Canadians comprised the first foreign tourists … They dominated as tourists, foreign investors and business owners until the late 1980s, when new trans-atlantic flights opened the Caribbean to more arrivals from Europe.

Several of my respondents spoke of the diversity of the Dominican people, describing them as having very different ways of being even before migration, often associated with their different regions of origin. I, too, noticed that they all had their own ways and customs and were proud of their origins. Even respondents born in Santo Domingo would always mention where they were 'originally' from.

2.4.2.2 More Dominican Immigrants in the Netherlands. The first Dominican immigrant to the Netherlands, a woman, arrived in 1964. For more than a decade thereafter, Dominican arrivals were sporadic, but from 1976, the numbers increased annually. Population size data on Dominican-born people in the Netherlands reveals growth from 4,258 in 1996 to 10,250 in 2022 (Fig. 2). Dominican migration to the Netherlands has always been dominated by women (Table 3). However, numbers of men have increased over time. In 2022, the population was 33.2% male and 66.8% female. The second generation has increased gradually from 1,146 persons in 1996 to 6,670 in 2022.

Fig. 2. Population of Dominican-born Persons in the Netherlands, 1996–2022. *Source*: CBS, Statline (2022).

Table 3. Gender Distribution Among Dominican-born Persons in the Netherlands.

	Male		Female		Total
	Absolute	%	Absolute	%	
1996	1,220	28.7	3,038	71.3	4,258
2000	1,572	27.9	4,067	72.1	5,639
2005	2,044	29.0	5,000	71.0	7,044
2010	2,329	30.2	5,443	70.5	7,722
2015	2,721	31.4	5,951	68.6	8,672
2020	3,136	32.5	6,517	67.5	9,653
2022	3,408	33.2	6,842	66.8	10,250

Source: CBS, Statline (2022).

2.4.2.3 Dominicans in the Netherlands Ageing. Over the years, the age composition of first-generation Dominicans has changed. Comparing 1996 to 2022, the 0–15 category declined from 18% to 3.8%. The 15–30 category also declined, while the 30–45 and 45–65 categories both grew. The population is thus ageing. In 2022, 34.9% were in the 30–45 category and 37.6% in the 45–65 category (Table 4).

2.4.2.4 Changing Geographic Dispersal. The Netherlands comprises 12 provinces, and Dominicans have settled primarily in those of North Holland and South Holland. These represent the highly urbanized western part of the country, in which concentrations of Dominicans are traditionally found in the major cities of Amsterdam, Rotterdam and The Hague. Nonetheless, a comparison over the years reveals changes (Table 5). Firstly, the largest population is no longer in Amsterdam, as it once was, but rather in Rotterdam. Secondly, while in 1996, 54.1% of Dominicans lived in the three aforementioned cities, and this figure had decreased to 46.1% as of 2022. Dominicans have spread across the country to cities such as Almere, Groningen, Arnhem, Utrecht, Eindhoven, Tilburg and Dordrecht.

Table 4. Age Distribution of Dominicans in the Netherlands.

	1996		2000		2005		2010		2015		2020		2022	
	Absolute	%	Absolute	%	Absolute	%	Absolute	%	Absolute	%	Absolute	%	Absolute	%
0-15	766	18.0	737	13.1	509	7.2	424	5.5	408	4.7	420	4.4	391	3.8
15-30	1,690	39.7	2,018	35.8	2,363	33.5	2,190	28.2	1,943	22.4	1,547	16.0	1,472	14.4
30-45	1,276	30.0	2,036	36.1	2,606	37.0	2,950	38.0	3,075	35.5	3,356	34.8	3,582	34.9
45-65	468	11.0	783	13.9	1,388	19.7	2,003	25.8	2,833	32.7	3,569	37.0	3,857	37.6
65 and Older	58	1.4	65	1.2	118	1.7	205	2.6	413	4.8	761	7.9	948	9.2
Total	4,258	100	5,639	100	7,044	99	7,772	100	8,672	100	9,653	100	10,250	100

Source: CBS, Statline (2022).

Table 5. Geographical Dispersal of Dominicans in the Netherlands.

	1996		2000		2005		2010		2015		2020		2022	
	Absolute	%	Absolute	%	Absolute	%	Absolute	%	Absolute	%	Absolute	%	Absolute	%
Amsterdam	1,170	27.5	1,311	23.2	1,414	20.1	1,523	19.6	1,592	18.4	1,604	16.6	1,690	16.5
Rotterdam	709	16.7	1,002	17.8	1,334	18.9	1,370	17.6	1,549	17.9	1,714	17.8	1,780	17.4
The Hague	426	10.0	553	9.8	808	11.5	848	10.9	1,052	12.1	1,213	12.6	1,256	12.3
Total	4,258	54.1	5,639	50.8	7,044	50.5	7,772	48.1	8,672	48.4	9,653	46.9	10,250	46.1

Source: CBS, Statline (2022).

Table 6. Marital Status of Dominicans in the Netherlands.

	1996		2000		2005		2010		2015		2020		2022	
	Absolute	%	Absolute	%	Absolute	%	Absolute	%	Absolute	%	Absolute	%	Absolute	%
Single	2,102	50.3	3,044	54.8	3,919	56.3	4,197	54.6	4,547	53.0	4,967	52.0	5,331	52.5
Married	1,389	33.3	1,474	26.5	1,624	23.3	1,806	23.5	2,155	25.1	2,387	25.0	2,475	24.4
Widowed	80	1.9	93	1.7	134	1.9	168	2.2	212	2.5	243	2.5	284	2.8
Divorced	604	14.5	946	17.0	1,283	18.4	1,509	19.6	1,665	19.4	1,961	20.5	2,060	20.3
Total	4,175	100	5,557	100	6,960	100	7,680	100	8,579	100	9,558	100	10,150	100

Source: CBS, Statline (2022).

38 Post-Migration Experiences, Cultural Practices and Homemaking

2.4.2.5 Marital Status. Marital status of Dominicans in the Netherlands has been fairly stable. However, fewer Dominicans were married in 2022 than in 1996, and more were divorced (Table 6). There was a slight increase in the share of those who were widowed. Note that on this characteristic, the 'migration background' categorization had to be used as data based on country of birth was not available.

2.5 Conclusion: Diversification in Migration Destinations and Stepwise Trajectories

This chapter has offered clarification on why so many Dominicans choose to build a life elsewhere despite their deep love for the Dominican Republic. It explored factors that spurred emigration, the principal destinations and migration motives.

In short, emigration from the Dominican Republic started with the political migrants of the 1960s. From the 1970s onwards, economic turbulence and lack of jobs led to diversification of the group choosing to emigrate, in search of opportunities outside the Dominican Republic. Principal destinations were initially the mainland of the United States, Puerto Rico and Venezuela. Starting in the 1980s, destinations became more varied including other Caribbean countries as well as countries in Europe. The share of Dominicans choosing European destinations has increased over time with principal European destinations being Spain, Italy, Switzerland, the Netherlands and Germany.

In exploring Dominican migration to the Netherlands, a key role is reserved for the connection between the Dominican Republic and the Caribbean part of the Kingdom of the Netherlands. Population movements between the Dominican Republic and the Dutch Caribbean islands began some 500 years ago. Nowadays, the main migration flows between the Dominican Republic and the Dutch Caribbean islands, in terms of size, are towards Curaçao, Sint Maarten and Aruba. However, prior to 1900, most migration was in the reverse direction: from the Dutch Caribbean islands towards the Dominican Republic. Many Dominicans today choose to migrate onwards to the Netherlands after living in Aruba, Curaçao or Sint Maarten.

Dominicans' reasons for choosing the Netherlands are diverse and include economic circumstances, the desire to broaden horizons and marriage to a Dutch spouse. Statistical data show a gradual increase of first-generation Dominicans in the Netherlands, and confirm that Dominican migration to the Netherlands has always been dominated by women.

Chapter 3

Dominicans' Culture and Home After Migration to the Netherlands

3.1 Introduction

> People change there, I changed a lot, Europe has changed me. I now enjoy doing more things on my own. Before I used to always do everything with a friend. Now I am not used to that anymore; I am even more independent than before …. It will always be my home country, it will always be where my heart is, but my mind is not there anymore. I know what I want now. Now I am 40 and when I was 20 maybe, I would enjoy what Dominican Republic offers right now, but not anymore. I mean, now that I have seen outside the box, I do not see myself back there. I have nostalgia from what it used to be, which is not anymore …. But actually where I feel the best is in Holland. Now this is what I call home. I go to the Dominican Republic, but after two or three weeks, I already want to be back in Holland.

Mercedes tells about where she feels home is since migrating to the Netherlands. Her answer highlights several dimensions of attachment to one's country of origin and feelings of home. Firstly, home has a dynamic nature: the Netherlands has become home because she has changed and on the other side the Dominican Republic has changed as well. Secondly, her quote highlights home's dual character: a home in one's mind differs from a home in one's heart. She feels love for the Dominican Republic, but her mind is in the Netherlands, where she can do what she finds important for the current stage of her life. She has come to appreciate aspects of the Netherlands: opportunities for growth, enrichment and broadening horizons. And thus home, thirdly, is related to certain qualities of a country and activities which can be carried out there. Fourthly, this quote also points to a lost home: the Dominican Republic *Mercedes* knows does not exist anymore; there is a certain longing for a bygone time, nostalgia. In sum, *Mercedes'* quote

---

Post-Migration Experiences, Cultural Practices and Homemaking:
An Ethnography of Dominican Migration to Europe, 39–66
Copyright © 2023 by Sabrina Dinmohamed
Published under exclusive licence by Emerald Publishing Limited
doi:10.1108/978-1-83753-204-920231003

40 *Post-Migration Experiences, Cultural Practices and Homemaking*

shows that attachment to a place and feelings of home can change and 'that there is elasticity to how we think about home; aspects of home are not fixed, rather fluid or even ambivalent' (Wiles, 2008, p. 123).

This chapter focuses on what home means for Dominicans after migration. Departing from the idea that home is not necessarily in one's country of origin although it may remain important for its familiarity, the question arises: where is home after migration, and what makes a place feel like home? I argue that immigrants have attachments that go beyond the standard two options of country of origin or receiving country. Furthermore, attachments to country of origin and feelings of home are not static and they change due to migration.

Using Perez Murcia's (2018) categorization of the different attachments migrants have with their place of origin, I examine Dominicans' attachments to the Dominican Republic in terms of home and why the country does or does not still feel like home. Perez Murcia (2018) describes four groups with different relationships to places of origin and receiving contexts: (1) community, culture and identity are rooted in one single place, which is the country of origin, and home is there; (2) home is experienced while on the move; it can be anywhere, thus also in the receiving context, depending on the presence of family and the lives one constructs in the receiving context; (3) home is in the context of origin as well as the receiving context because both places have certain characteristics which make it home; and (4) home is nowhere; negative memories of the country of origin and the struggle to develop a sense of home after migrating stand in the way of the sense of home in the receiving context and in the context of origin. To gain insights into why a certain place is considered home, I take into account the following elements of home (Boccagni, 2013; Duyvendak, 2017; Hage, 1997):

- familiarity: a sense of 'knowing' customs and practices;
- community: recognizing people as one's 'own' kind and feeling recognized by them as such, a feeling of shared symbolic forms, values and language and the feeling that at least some people can be morally relied on for help;
- opportunities: opportunities of a better life, to develop capacities and skills, of personal growth and for advancement (upward social mobility, emotional growth or in the form of accumulation of symbolic or monetary capital).

In this chapter, home and processes related to the change of home are described in three sections. The first section describes how the first flows of Dominican immigrants recreated practices, spaces and places from the Dominican Republic in the Netherlands. It shows efforts by Dominicans to recreate some familiarity. The second section moves from specific recreation actions to Dominicans sharing their experiences and opinions of the Netherlands' unfamiliar characteristics. This section is meant to show the context in which Dominicans settle and how they deal with unfamiliar characteristics of a place. The third section then deals with attachment to the Dominican Republic and the Netherlands, following the efforts Dominicans have made to create a life in the Netherlands. It shows where Dominicans' homes are, but also why, and revealing that location of home may change and be connected to certain characteristics of a country. These stories

Dominicans' Culture and Home **41**

about encounters with unfamiliar cultural and social characteristics and sense of home enable delineation of elements of home for the Dominicans in this research. Knowing what these elements of home are is important to, as the next chapters focus on, determining whether food practices are indeed homemaking practices. This chapter ends with a reflection on attachments, place of home and feelings of home.

3.2 The Creation of Quisqueya in the Netherlands

Quisqueya is the name for the island of Hispaniola in the Taíno language. It means 'mother of the earth' and is also used to refer to the Dominican Republic, one of the island's two countries (the other being Haiti). Dominicans everywhere might use this word to refer to the Dominican Republic and everything related to the country. For example, Washington Heights, a neighbourhood in New York City with the largest Dominican population outside the Dominican Republic and where Dominicans have recreated a 'little Dominican Republic', is often referred to as Quisqueya Heights. So how is *Quisqueya* recreated in the Netherlands?

3.2.1 The 1980s: The Beginnings of a Dominican Social and Cultural Infrastructure

After arriving in a new country people seek ways to start a new life. These initiatives can be economic, such as finding a job, and structural, such as learning a language. However, a new life is not only about taking such necessary steps, but also daily practices, for example, re-creating cultural elements of the country one has emigrated from. As Collins (2008) says about post-migration practices of immigrants (p. 166):

> The purpose of such acts is to overcome the splitting of memory and lived experience that is so common for individuals who migrate, even temporarily, across borders. These acts of remembrance serve to overcome the estrangement of migration by remaking the relations with spaces that appear to be unfamiliar through the process of re-inhabiting such spaces by reprocessing practices and experiences.

Recreation of familiarity and customs is thus a way of dealing with the new situation. On the topic of a material infrastructure and home specifically, Law (2001, p. 277) notes that 'the absence of familiar material culture and its subtle evocations of home is surely one of the most profound dislocations of transnational migration'. For Dominican immigrants, the migration from the Dominican Republic has caused a rupture in familiar social and cultural practices. These immigrants therefore recreate familiar spaces, places and practices in the Netherlands. They do so in several ways, living within a new society shared by people with other customs and practices. These include Dutch natives and well-established immigrant communities comprising people from Suriname, the Dutch

42 Post-Migration Experiences, Cultural Practices and Homemaking

Caribbean islands, Morocco and Turkey, all whom have resided in the Netherlands for approximately three generations.

From the 1980s, a 'Dominican infrastructure' emerged (consisting of people offering services and of specific places) fostering different activities and practices such as (1) maintaining contact with family in the Dominican Republic; (2) getting hold of Dominican commodities; and (3) the recreation of cultural elements. By carrying out these specific practices, Dominican immigrants recreated *Quisqueya* in the Netherlands.

Maintaining contact with family in the Dominican Republic was not easy in the 1980s and 1990s. *Leydi, Carlos* and *Isabel*, who arrived during these decades, described their effort to maintain contact with family the Dominican Republic. *Leydi*, born in the capital city of Santo Domingo, came to the Netherlands in 1995, when she was 14. Her mother came first and she followed with her brother. She mentioned how maintaining contact with family in the Dominican Republic was costly, but that she and her family in the Netherlands would make the effort:

> In that period it was really expensive to call to the Dominican Republic. We would make appointments like calling every two weeks, that day, that time. Yes, yes, yes. Or we would buy a calling card to call once a week or once a month. But after that it became easier, and now it is totally easy with WhatsApp.

At the time there was also the existence of *el teléfono negro* ('black phone'). Those within the community who possessed this phone charged lower rates than the regular phone company. *Carlos* tells me about this telephone. He arrived in 1986, during his mid-20s. He tells about how the Dominican community was able to set up a cultural and social infrastructure in the Netherlands and how nowadays it was easy to communicate with the Dominican Republic, send money and keep up to date with what's new there. In the 1980s, it was different, however. He continues about the 'mafia' telephone (*teléfono de mafia*). This was a portable car telephone, an AT2. He would go from window to window offering his portable telephone services. He tells how he made a lot of money with his telephone services. *Carlos'* story shows how he not only helped his compatriots by offering his services but also turned his community's needs into a business and source of income. *Isabel* also told me about experiences with keeping contact with family members in the Dominican Republic. She arrived in the Netherlands in the 1990s at age 21. She came with her husband (who is Dominican, but has a Dutch passport through his mother, who lived in Curaçao) and left her parents and siblings in the Dominican Republic. She explained what they were willing to do to get hold of such a telephone:

> I remember, for example: now you can call with your telephone, but in the past you had to search for a telephone, we called it the 'black telephone'. You had to walk so far, we were living in Kraaienest and there was a Dominican woman in Gein who had this black telephone. I remember that it had snowed a lot. We struggled, but we got hold of a black telephone.

Isabel shows the effort made to maintain contact (walking from the Amsterdam neighbourhoods of Kraaienest to Gein takes 45 minutes) and the value of this illegal option to maintain more affordable contact.

Along with maintaining contact with family in the Dominican Republic, getting hold of Dominican commodities in the Netherlands was important. When asked what defines Dominican culture, food was mentioned as one of the primary pillars. Recreation of a cultural element, such as Dominican food, was not always easy because it was hard to access ingredients (Chapter 6 elaborates on how receiving context characteristics influence food practices). Many Dominicans would bring back products from their holidays or would rely on holidaying compatriots to bring them back some ingredients (e.g. oregano and condiments) from the Dominican Republic or Madrid, where the largest Dominican community in Europe resides. The transnational traffic would provide the Dominican community in the Netherlands not only with ingredients for food preparation but also other commodities. *Carlos* and *Leydi* acknowledged the importance of other countries to get hold of Dominican commodities:

I would go to the United States, to New York, buy clothes, buy necklaces with names, rings. Dominicans like bling bling, it is part of our culture. We like rings, chains and things like that. Every Dominican you meet will wear a watch, a chain, a ring, and back then four or five. There was a time of rings with names. – Carlos

So, a lot of people went from here to Madrid, did the shopping and brought stuff to the Netherlands. Or you could place an order and those persons would bring something for you for a small commission. You know, like, yes, I am going to buy hair products. – Leydi

Carlos' and *Leydi's* quotes reveal several points. Firstly, again, products' unavailability or limited accessibility opened up business opportunities within the Dominican community. Secondly, transnational communities were important for facilitating the recreation of social and cultural elements.

Apart from food, several cultural elements were cited as defining Dominican culture. They included music, dance and *ambiente*. According to all Dominicans in my research, *ambiente* is a defining characteristic of Dominican culture. It can be defined as an atmosphere of cheerfulness, talking, laughing and that which is conducive to music and dance. *Carlos*, for example, exclaimed: 'Dominican culture is food and *ambiente*'. *Ambiente* is at the heart of 'Dominicanness' and a need for it seems to run through Dominicans' veins. While food practices were not always easy to reproduce in the 1980s and 1990s in the Netherlands, cultural elements such as music and dance were. Salsa, merengue and bachata are important music genres in many Dominicans' life, with the genre depending on region of origin and social class. Writing about music as a medium for expressing migrant experiences, Gill (2012) emphasizes that migrant populations are composed of a variety of people from many different regions and classes and with varying gender – factors of which are all crucial to a more nuanced understanding of

44 *Post-Migration Experiences, Cultural Practices and Homemaking*

migration practices and listening preferences. This cultural element of music has different meanings within the Dominican migrant population.

Merengue is considered the Dominican Republic's national music and dance, though has not always held that distinction. Since merengue has strong African roots, the music and dance were initially rejected by the upper class and those with European roots. Merengue nevertheless prevailed, and President Trujillo aided in spreading its acceptance and popularity. Bachata has long been considered by Dominicans as a marginal music genre, performed and listened to by the lower classes (Pacini Hernandez, 1995). Bachata is related to bolero, and in the songs, mostly sorrows and heartaches are expressed. It is considered a 'people's music' wherein the experiences of poverty and urbanization shape musical practice and all its various aesthetic and social functions: dancing having fun, feeling good, forgetting, lashing out, fighting back and hearing the sound of one's own voice (Pacini Hernandez, 1995, p. 239). According to Pacini Hernandez (1995), bachata eased the transition of poor rural migrants to shantytowns, expressing social outrage about the circumstance of the lower classes and revealing gender conflicts aggravated by economic crisis and social dislocation. From the 1980s and 1990s, bachata became more popular among other social classes and internationally. Juan Luis Guerra was one of the first artists who gave bachata a place in the international music scene. This opening also made it easier for traditional bachata musicians to access the media and other social classes who had previously repudiated them and their music.

In the Netherlands, music became an important way for Dominicans to create some *ambiente*. *Carlos* explained how he was the first Dominican deejay and one of the first persons to organize parties for Dominicans in Amsterdam:

There were two places to dance salsa: Huis 88 and discotheque Chic. There I was working as a deejay on Sundays, the first Dominican deejay. We paid 75 guilders to be able to play some music. And I organized everything with and for the Dominican community. The first Dominican night that was organized in the Netherlands, in 1988, was organized by me. At that time, there were not many Dominicans here, but enough to fill a discotheque. There were the women who were working, all those women, and some Dominican men. There were some women who were married to Curaçaoan men. And some Colombians also began to visit. The discotheque was beginning to fill up. In 1989, I was already familiar with this scene, and I met Harold, a Hindustani, who had a place named Starsky, in the Red Light District. There were two places there: Santo Domingo Bar and Salsabar La Esquina. And these were the meeting places for Dominicans. And afterwards in the 1990s, there was a place named Bugatti Bar, where I also was to first the play music on Sundays. A lot of Dominicans were coming there. In that time, you would play music from cassette tapes: I would mix them at home, merengue and bachata. That is when the boom started. Dominicans kept on coming to the Netherlands, and the Dominican population in the Netherlands kept on growing in that era and never stopped.

Dominicans' Culture and Home   **45**

Carlos' quote highlights several aspects about the setup of the social and cultural infrastructure. Firstly, discotheques were meeting places for members of the Dominican community including, as *Carlos* also explicitly mentioned, those 'working' women in reference to prostitutes in the Red Light District. Secondly, these discotheques served as a home outside one's home as well as a piece of the Dominican Republic available in a public space in the Netherlands. *Carlos'* story reflects what Sansone (2009) shows in the case of the first Surinamese in Amsterdam and how the 'pleasure circuit' produced

> an atmosphere (*surinaamse sfeer*) in which the large Surinamese population could revive memories of their tropical homelands – that is, relaxed, feel at ease and forget that they were in fact in a foreign country …. (p. 173)

Thirdly, the Dominican infrastructure also connected to the needs of other immigrant communities and served as a bridge.

3.2.2 After the 1990s: A Growing Community With an Expanding Infrastructure

From the 1990s, the Dominican community began growing. Consequently, the needs of the community increased, as did the availability of services. Maintaining contact with the Dominican Republic, getting hold of commodities and re-creating Dominican cultural elements remained important practices. However, the end of the 1990s ushered in some visible shifts. Maintaining contact with the Dominican Republic had become easier due to social media and cheap communication apps, including WhatsApp. Furthermore, due to more contacts with culturally similar communities, such as the Surinamese and the Curaçaoan, commodities, including hair and food products, became available on the Dutch market, for example, at Surinamese 'tropical' stores. Also, more Dominicans in the population meant Dominicans could help each other with finding jobs and housing while at the same time earn something for themselves. To this day, many Dominicans sublet a room in their home to another Dominican. This is seen in, for example, Amsterdam's Zuidoost neighbourhood (also referred to as 'Bijlmer'), where concentration Dominican immigrants lives. They charge between 300 and 400 euros per month for a room. This lets recently arrived Dominicans find housing quickly. Announcements about who has a room available come by word of mouth. Often the person cannot register at the address so a third party is sought with whom to register on paper and, for this service, to pay approximately 100 euros monthly.

With regard to the recreation of cultural practices, the arena has become bigger. There are more places to dance, eat and celebrate Dominican festivities. In Amsterdam, for example, Dominicans go to Picalonga, El Punto Latino and El Molino, venues where one can eat Dominican food, play bingo on Sundays, dance to the sounds of bachata, merengue and dembow, commemorate La Independencia Dominicana, celebrate Dominican Mother's Day and drink Brugal (Dominican rum) and Presidente (Dominican beer). *Carlos* summarized how the different needs were fulfilled by an infrastructure all within a couple square metres in

46 *Post-Migration Experiences, Cultural Practices and Homemaking*

Amsterdamse Poort, a shopping centre in Amsterdam's multicultural borough Zuidoost:

> To our luck, there are Dominican and Latin bars and cafés. At this moment, for example, we are now in a Dominican pizzeria—the owners are Dominican. Listen to the music in the background: salsa, merengue, bachata. Around the corner there is a Dominican bar, Picalonga. There is place here, a travel agency, where you also can send money to your country, buy an airplane ticket, get information. When your people in the Dominican Republic need some calling credit, you can pay for it here and help your family there. Do you want to play the Dominican lottery? Here they sell the Dominican lottery.

While Dominicans became entrepreneurs and set up restaurants, barbershops, beauty salons and bars to serve the Dominican community, not all enterprises offering Dominican-focused services are owned by Dominicans. Discotheques, restaurants and bars show an especially interesting picture. Some are run by Dominicans for Dominicans. Then there are barbershops and beauty salons that are run by Dominicans but aimed at everyone. And there are bars and discotheques run by native Dutch or other immigrant communities aimed at Dominicans.

Dominican immigrants also have organized themselves in different areas. With regard to social assistance, the *Fundacion de Emigrantes Unidos en Holanda*, for example, offers help to the Latin-American community and in particular to Dominicans, focusing on financial problems, outpatient support, project-based activities and information about socio-economic themes. They also organized themselves through religious organizations in different cities of the Netherlands, including Amsterdam, Rotterdam and The Hague. With regard to sports activities several baseball clubs have been formed. With regard to dance and music *Grupo Ritmo Dominicano* aims to bring Dominican culture and rhythm in very corner of the Netherlands. *Comparsa Sabor Dominicano* celebrates the origin of Dominican folklore and the magic of its rhythms, dances and traditions. *El Vacilon Musical Amsterdam Latino* is one of the radio stations which brings news and music to Dominicans in the Netherlands and other parts of the world.

This section showed how Dominican immigrants recreated familiar social and cultural practices in the Netherlands. This infrastructure of practices and places provided feelings of home for some Dominicans, but not for all, which will be elaborated in Chapter 5 about the co-ethnic communities' role in homemaking.

3.3 The Encounters With Dutch Contextual Characteristics

Thus, Dominicans were able to recreate a little bit of the Dominican Republic in the Netherlands. But which unfamiliar elements did they encounter in daily life?

3.3.1 Ambiente

Ambiente is something Dominicans missed in daily life and during festivities. According to the Dominicans I spoke, the Dominican Republic is a country where enjoying life is central. Part of that is *ambiente*, music, being together. *Mateo* gave an example of a Dominican birthday and emphasized the importance of having a good time, which involves food, music, dance and rum:

> Look, Dominican culture is, like we call it, a cool (*chevere*) culture, because everybody celebrates you. For example, on someone's birthday, people decide to have a party. Maybe not everybody will bring you a gift and maybe the ones who do will bring you bottle of rum, two or three beers or something that would help create *ambiente* for a party. We make *sancocho* [meat stew/soup], we dance, everybody happy. *Ambiente*.

Mateo explained how being together and *ambiente* had an important place in his past. His life in Santo Domingo was different. In the evenings, in the weekends, he would go out. He mentions how he would take a shower, go to the disco, get together with friends, drink a couple of beers or play a hand of dominoes. He does not have that in the Netherlands. And while he misses his routine in the Dominican Republic, he does not seek it out in the Netherlands. He has learned to live without it and knows that when he is the Dominican Republic, he can have it again. He says: 'those are things that you miss, but also things that wait for you over there. When I go there, I can play dominoes. Now it is important to be with my wife and son'. *Margarita* offered a kind of scientific explanation for the lack of *ambiente* in Nordic countries:

> The structure of northern Europe, to which the Netherlands belongs, is different from the structure of my country. Our cheerfulness is in our blood. In theirs also, but is located in two different poles. When we look at scientific research, we see that in a country with a cold climate, people turn inward. You create another kind of personality due to environmental characteristics. And in countries with warm climates, as Dominicans would say it, the energy bursts from your pores. It just happens. Do not even talk about dancing, that occurs without you wanting it. And in these [northern European] countries, the structure is different. Society is not like that.

According to *Margarita*, differences in 'cheerfulness' can thus be explained by differences in climate.

Part of *ambiente* is music. And music is an essential part of every Dominican; according to many respondents, it's in their blood. *Valentina* gave an example of how *ambiente* was maintained after migrating to Aruba and afterwards to the Netherlands:

48   Post-Migration Experiences, Cultural Practices and Homemaking

While cleaning, radio [turned on] sky-high. Everybody is welcome. A party here, a party there [is how it was] then in Aruba, and now still, my parents' house is always full of people. You know, that also helped us …. The first thing that I did when I arrived here was going to Mediamarkt and IKEA. With my savings and the money my parents gave me, I wanted to buy everything at once. And I needed a good radio. CD player, cassette recorder, everything. I brought all my CDs from Aruba. And I was always pumping those speakers, but I was also aware that I could not do that too often here.

The central place of music, *ambiente* and hospitability also came to the fore during my fieldwork. It was especially clear in my interview with hairdresser *Emilia*, which turned into a five-hour event consisting of small talk, *ambiente* and a haircut. She migrated from San Pedro de Macoris, in the southeast of the Dominican Republic, to the Netherlands. After sending a message to *Emilia* about my research, she immediately called and expressed willingness to cooperate. We agreed on 5 p.m. on a dark, cold late December day at her beauty salon in the eastern part of Amsterdam. Entering the place, I was met by high-volume bachata music and *Emilia*'s request that I wait because she was still busy. I took a seat and someone who identified as *Emilia*'s little brother (he in fact was not, I discovered later) started to talk with me. He asked whether I wanted a beer, but I expressed my preference for some tea. I saw three people working: *Emilia* was busy giving a woman a haircut; her female colleague was shaping another woman's eyebrows; and a male hairdresser was giving a young man a haircut.

While waiting, a client addressed me after noticing that I spoke Spanish. He said that I do not look like a *hispana* (someone of Spanish-Caribbean or Latin-American descent), to which I responded that I am not. He immediately asked for my phone number. I declined by lying, saying that I have a boyfriend. He said that he does not mind, adding 'a person always needs a spare tyre'. He also asked why I should be monogamous because it is not as though I know what my boyfriend is doing. Our conversation continued, covering the nationality of my imagined boyfriend and my interlocutor's migration from the Dominican Republic to Puerto Rico onto the United States and then the Netherlands, where he had been for six months, living in Ganzenhoef, not far from *Emilia*'s salon.

After two hours, I finally began the interview I came for. *Emilia* and I spoke in a room in the back, and afterwards, I again took a seat in the salon section. All kinds of conversations concerning different topics took place between the staff and between them and the clients including a group of Spanish boys. I observed this while letting *Emilia* try her hand at cutting my hair. The Spanish boys left and one of them gave me his phone number through the male hairdresser. After finishing with me, *Emilia* asked when I would come visit her again and invited me to one day visit her at home.

The hours spent at *Emilia*'s salon revealed how a place that from the outside may look like a small establishment on a street corner in eastern Amsterdam is a world in itself on the inside. This world has a typical Dominican atmosphere, playing Dominican music and serving Dominican beer. The world teems with

Dominicans' Culture and Home   **49**

typical Dominican hospitability. It is also a world with typical first-encounter behaviours between Caribbean men and women.

3.3.2 Living Inside

Living inside is something many Dominicans mentioned having difficulties with. *Oscar* and *Arturo* showed how life in the Dominican Republic occurs outside the home, where your friends are, and how continuously living inside the home can cause feelings of isolation.

Oscar was 14 when he came to the Netherlands, arriving in Amsterdam. His mother was already in the Netherlands and let him and her two other children follow. When asked what he found difficult upon arriving in the Netherlands, *Oscar* said:

> The atmosphere surrounding me, my friends. Friends, mainly the atmosphere, because [in the Dominican Republic] life occurs on the streets. We were living on the streets; you taste the street, the atmosphere. And that vanished [in the Netherlands]. You were isolated between four walls. Living outside did not exist anymore. The fact that I could only speak Spanish at home was frustrating.

Arturo echoed *Oscar's* experiences, noting that even when people in the Netherlands tended to be more outside in the summer, the atmosphere was still not the same. He compared Dutch with Dominican outside life and mentioned how in the Dominican Republic you see people on the streets, talking, laughing and playing dominoes. He also questioned if he should adapt:

> In the Dominican Republic, every moment of the day you can cut your hair in the streets, boys and girls are playing, there's a game of dominoes, people have a good time. Well, Dominicans suffer from talking loud. Where there are Dominicans, you will recognize them by their voice. So you see, these are things that you miss. When you go out, you are in a different place, like on a different planet. I do not know if I am the only one who feels this way, and maybe I should adapt to the situation here. Mostly in the summer people enjoy [outside life] here. When there is some sun, everybody goes to the square, everybody is sitting but they do not know each other; everybody [stays] on his own side. Here, where I work in the Bijlmer, there is a little square in the mall. Everybody is sitting there isolated. Maybe two people talking to each other, but not all with each other. Dominicans, when they know each other, and also when they do not know each other, make conversation with other people, talk and create *ambiente*.

Oscar's and *Arturo's* quotes point to feelings of home found outside the house and challenge the prevailing western European conception that home can only

50 *Post-Migration Experiences, Cultural Practices and Homemaking*

be in the private, domestic space. They not only show that a home's four walls are associated with unhomely elements, like isolation, but also that home is outside with others. Boccagni and Brighenti (2015) note that the fixation with sharp home/not-home boundaries is simply unknown in many contexts of emigration as well as in different civilization patterns. The private/public divide (where the location of home begins and ends) is not that rigid; there are no boundaries, 'but smooth, porous thresholds' (p. 4).

3.3.3 Individualism

Individualism is another trait that Dominicans mention struggling with in the Netherlands. The individualistic lifestyle is cited as a constraint to feeling home and making a home. Individualism in the Netherlands is tied to closedness, lack of contact with neighbours and lack of togetherness, which includes 'hanging out' with friends and family. They mention that in the Dominican Republic you can always pass by a friend's house, you are welcome at any time of the day, but in the Netherlands you need to schedule in advance, even with friends and family.

Many Dominicans mentioned that in the Netherlands they did not know their neighbours or, for that matter, if they were even alive. Contact with neighbours was expressed by many as an important part of daily social contact. *Martha*, living in the Netherlands since 2007, reported getting accustomed to many Dutch cultural elements though still missed more neighbourly contact:

> I like the [Dutch] culture. The only thing that I sometimes find strange is the [lack of knowing my] neighbour. I have been living here for 11 years and I do not know him. There is no contact. I miss the contact, the warmth, a coffee, going outside and talking.

Some respondents mentioned how in the Dominican Republic, neighbours help each other with all kinds of household-related activities, and these points of contacts also provide warmth. In *Mariasela's* words:

> I miss the food. I miss people dancing on the street corner. I miss the neighbour who brings everything to life. Where I live now, you do not know your neighbours. The ones on both sides I do know, but it would never occur to me to ask them for an egg if I would need one. In my country, this is very normal: you go to your neighbour asking for an egg or a little bit of milk. I miss that. Here people are dehumanized.

With regard to the individualistic lifestyle in the Netherlands, spending time together, with others, instead of being alone, is mentioned as important and the lack of it a difficult aspect of Dutch life. *Laura* said that in the Dominican Republic she felt good. There she had her family, and people would look each other up. In the Netherlands, she found that everybody lived within four walls and when people did not plan activities, they stayed within those walls, not seeing others.

Dominicans' Culture and Home   *51*

In the Dominican Republic, people visited or received visitors, so there was always something to do. *Mercedes*, who said that now she was perfectly fine living a more 'individualistic' lifestyle, and *Casandra* both mentioned the normalcy of constant togetherness and found it difficult to miss that:

> At the beginning, that's what I missed, always having my friends around; it was always fun. After work, every day I would have a plan. From Monday to Monday .... There is no spontaneity [in the Netherlands]. In the Dominican Republic you just pass by, no one would be offended if you ring the bell. You can plan the same day actually to go to the beach. You can plan the same day to go out for dinner. I used to miss that a lot. That's part of the lifestyle I was mentioning to you at the beginning. I mean, I would always be with people, because I would leave my work, and one of my friends would tell me: 'Come pick me up at my work and then let's just go home and order some beers and let's just drink there, in my living room'. So nothing special, but it was something social to do. It was very fun. So, not even those little things [happen here], it is difficult to arrange. – *Mercedes*

> In the Dominican Republic you are never alone. There is always a party. I would always have a lot of contact with my friends. And when I arrived here, the first thing that I felt was the coldness, the coldness of the people. People here are not like people there, where you have lots of neighbours who would say: 'Hello, how are you? Come over and have something to eat'. This is what I missed a lot in the beginning. – *Casandra*

Mercedes' and *Casandra*'s quotes show not only that in the Dominican Republic being together with others is the norm but also that meet-ups are arranged differently than in the Netherlands: you do not make appointments. Furthermore, being together does not mean doing something in particular, but rather is a kind of 'hanging out'. The Dutch way of structuring daily life is what Boccagni (2013), calls the 'staying-at-home/going-to-work/back-home' routine from which Ecuadorian immigrants in Italy could escape by spending time with other Ecuadorians (p. 283).

Consciously or unconsciously, the motive for meeting up with other Dominicans was that mutual understanding. *Marcos* expressed this, highlighting how fellow Dominicans would understand situations from the Dominican Republic, jokes and migration experiences:

> I really need to meet my people often. We cook, we make jokes. We have a group of people who are 40 years old and up, and we share these old jokes or old ways of speaking Spanish, which you almost never hear, and we laugh .... When we meet, we hug each other and feel that there is true brotherhood. [We ask:] 'Oh my love,

52   Post-Migration Experiences, Cultural Practices and Homemaking

how are you?' and we give each other a strong hug—this is what we miss. It is like a battery that you recharge. I do not know how I would feel if I would not have these contacts with Dominicans. These meetings with my own people nourishes your love, your love for your country, you get to know more about your culture .... [It means that] one is not bitter, does not have a bitter life. That is why it is of utmost importance to communicate with my fellow countrymen. There are of course limits—I do not hang out with everybody.

Marcos' quote shows how spending time with his 'own' evokes feelings of nostalgia, familiarity and human warmth and helps maintain connection with the Dominican Republic. His quote also shows how not all Dominicans want to hang out with each other, which will be elaborated in Chapter 5. Dominicans may miss being together, but that does not necessarily mean they want to meet up with every random Dominican; there is selectivity.

Valentina also describes this selectivity, but at the same time mentions the importance of having contact with other Dominicans. She told me that in the past she mingled with all types of Dominicans, including those of, what she referred to as 'lower' economic status. After she became successful in her career, she was often 'accused' of having changed. She felt that she was not accepted by other Dominicans, although she had lost connection to them because her life took another route. At a certain point, she said that she chose to stop mingling with 'certain' types of Dominicans in order to 'stay out of trouble'. She missed contact with other Dominicans, with whom she had shared experiences and memories, for example, of the typical Dominican mom:

In the Dominican Republic or in Aruba, it does not matter where they live, their mom is the same. The typical Dominican mom with the same personality, it makes you laugh. Or when someone tells about services, like water, that you have to walk 10 blocks to get some water. Or when everybody applauds when the electricity returns. You know, those are the things that only a Dominican would understand.

These stories about the difficulties encountered within the individualistic Dutch lifestyle show how spending time together is an important means for feeling at home, but that at the same time people are selective about whom they spent time with. Feelings of home are thus not felt or shared with every Dominican.

It is important to note that 'the Netherlands and its culture' does not exist. Also, within the Netherlands, there are differences in social atmospheres and how people interact with each other. For example, lifestyles in cities and rural areas differ; Dutch people from outside the Randstad – the Netherlands' interconnected urban centres including Amsterdam, Rotterdam, The Hague and Utrecht – may also perceive those large cities as individualistic.

Dominicans' Culture and Home 53

3.3.4 Coldness

Coldness of people is another characteristic of the Netherlands according to the Dominicans in my research. They related it to a lack of empathy, indifference, lack of concern and robotic manner of interacting with others. Respondents mentioned how in the Dominican Republic there is human warmth and people care for each other. Many Dominicans said they missed *el calor humano*, human warmth. A Dominican was generally described as a loving, sociable, helpful and cheerful person. *Monica* explained what this warmth looks like:

> We are cheerful people. In the Dominican Republic you laugh about anything. People are more loving, they always invite you into their homes. [They say:] 'Come and have something to eat'. These things I really miss. What I really miss from the Dominican Republic is the human warmth we have. Nothing can replace that. You can go to any country in Latin America and you will not find it. Not in Chile, not in Peru, nowhere. We Dominicans are very loving people.

Human warmth is thus expressed in being cheerful, hospitable, helpful and sociable.

An afternoon at *Margarita*'s house showed me this warmth and hospitability. When making the appointment for the interview, *Margarita* indicates that she will pick me up from Leiden station because that would be easier for me. When we arrive at her house she says right away: this is your house too. She gives me a tour of her house. I see two typical Dominican paintings hanging. One in the front room and one in her bedroom. When we get to the guest room, she says I can come stay anytime. I get to sit in the kitchen and she makes me tea. Already in the car she started telling herself about her migration process, how she arrived in the Netherlands. She continues at the table in the kitchen. *Margarita* was born in Santo Domingo and migrated to the Netherlands because of her ex-spouse. She never intended to migrate as she was very satisfied with her life in the Dominican Republic, where she studied political science, worked as a teacher and was involved in politics. And with a vibrant social life, her life felt complete. I had brought Toblerone chocolate for her, she opens it, takes a few for herself and puts five on a plate for me. We start the interview and remain talking for hours. At one point she says she cannot let me go without eating. She will get something ready soon. Normally she cooked early on Sundays, but yesterday she was home late. She pulls out ripe plantains and Dominican cheese. She bought the cheese yesterday in a Dominican restaurant. There is a lady who sells cheese and *longaniza*. I think I know who it is. She cooks the plantains and fries the cheese. *Platano con queso*. She asks if I would like an egg too. I see that she takes olive oil to fry the cheese and that doesn't seem very Dominican to me. I ask her if that's normal. She says Dominicans mainly cook with corn oil. While the plantains are boiling, she fries the cheese. After a while there is a pan with boiled ripe plantains in front of me, a plate of fried cheese and fried eggs. She says about the bananas that they

54   Post-Migration Experiences, Cultural Practices and Homemaking

were probably picked green and only ripened later. She serves herself her share and leaves extra for me. I have to eat everything, that is, all for me. She has put a glass of water on the table for me and asks if I would like some extra juice. And if I want fruit I can take that too. Whatever I want. *Margarita*'s ways reminded me of my own Caribbean family and being with her felt like home. When we finished eating, we notice that it is already late and she takes me to the station. Before I get on the train, she gives me a tour through Leiden and shows me the places that are meaningful to her. Before I leave the car she tells me that we have to keep in touch.

Yet many Dominicans in the Netherlands learned to live with a lack of this typical warmth and also saw a positive side to Dutch ways of socializing. *Sofia* missed the warmth, but noted how the Dutch have mastered the 'first-degree encounter':

> I am not saying that the Dutch are the warmest people, but I could say that they have mastered the first-degree encounter. Like, when they randomly meet you in the street or at a party or at a bar, you know what I mean? ... For example, me coming from the Dominican Republic, seeing people that open, I was interpreting that for a while as: well, these people are really open. It's not that they are totally open to you. It's that, first of all, there is a culture that people don't have to be really ashamed of anything. So they can just tell you anything they want, because they are not afraid to be judged. And yes, like at the beginning, I misunderstood that. But now I see that there are degrees, but that this first encounter can be very intense. You know, you can meet somebody who is Dutch, end up having a party at their house and never talk to them again. Have a great time, they were your best friends for a night. I like that because not everybody is going to be your friend forever.

Sofia's quote shows how the encounter with what she considered a Dutch way of socializing opened up a new form of being in contact, in which she also saw value. *Isabel*, however, was critical. She expressed missing the human warmth of the Dominican Republic, but also noted that in the Netherlands this does not exist even among Dominicans themselves, who change after arriving. She mentions that the people here are not like in Santo Domingo. Here no one greets you on the streets and even between Dominicans themselves you will not find this human warmth of Santo Domingo. She explains it by saying that people change after having lived in the Netherlands so many years.

These experiences of coldness and human warmth reflect what Meijering and Lager (2014) wrote about how social structures – seen, for example, in the categories of cold and warm people – affect a sense of home for Antillean migrants in the Netherlands. These migrants expressed how the individualist nature of Dutch society and lack of human warmth stood in their way of feeling at home.

Dominicans' Culture and Home **55**

However, the Dominican respondents in my research also showed how feelings can change over time and new ways of socializing could be appreciated.

A different experience of coldness is the literal one, the climate. Some respondents experienced the Dutch climate as difficult and called it *demasiado horrible* ('too horrible'). Many mentioned being so shocked by the weather; they almost returned to the Dominican Republic. It was not only the cold temperature that was difficult, but also the wintertime darkness. *Petronila* recalled how her first winter coloured her feelings about the Netherlands:

> I arrived in January and that killed me. It was a crucial point, which left a mark on me because I am a person who suffers from the cold. I believe it was one of the heaviest snowfalls ever—there was a lot of snow here. And my father-in-law wanted to go walk in the woods and that put me to be in a bad mood. And that is when started to feel something like hate for this country.

For *Irvin*, it was the reason he would eventually leave the Netherlands and return to Aruba:

> The weather here drives me crazy. December was grey, the whole month. It drives me crazy. And my children too, they say: 'If the weather would be better, I would want to stay'. So, I do not say that we will return, but it is our dream. That is what we want, but only well prepared.

3.3.5 Overregulation

Many Dominicans mention appreciating how organized the Netherlands is, but their stories also show criticism and dissatisfaction. They cited street cleanliness, social security, medical insurance, a reliable justice system and punctuality (e.g. experienced when taking public transportation and appointments with public services). However, that very organization also led to conflicts. *Emilia* expressed a certain duality:

> I like Holland because of its organization. It is really quiet here, but it is organized .... I do not like the Belastingdienst [Dutch tax authority]. The taxes. I do not like these things; I think nobody likes it. But I am not going to say that I do not like Holland. I am in Holland, and I do not want to look a gift horse in the mouth ['*aceptar una buena chaqueta*']. I think that the taxes are really exaggerated. I do not like it, but I respect it. I like the organization, and this is part of it. Holland is Holland.

Emilia's quote reveals an understanding that enjoying the benefits of organization also means putting up with the negative consequences of it. Some respondents

56 *Post-Migration Experiences, Cultural Practices and Homemaking*

mentioned appreciating the organization, yet struggling with the rigidity of systems and finding that if they did not fit into a certain category, they seemingly did not exist.

In general, Dominicans found a lack of flexibility in Dutch society, which undermined their feelings of freedom and humanity. *Margarita* explained how 'the Dominican' is wired and mentions that a Dominican always wants to show when he is happy and wants to feel free. She has noticed that when the Dominican is somewhere with a lot of structure, he loses a little bit of that spontaneity. According to her this confrontation damages the Dominican. They cannot maintain that spontaneity; there are other values. For example, you have to schedule in advance to socialize with others. She concludes with: 'the Dominican, wherever he is, does adapt, but these changes always are a shock'.

3.3.6 Language

One of the activities I engaged in while doing fieldwork was working as a representative for the Dominican Republic Tourism Office for the Benelux at holiday fairs. There was a fixed group of people whom I would meet a couple of times a year at holiday fairs in the Netherlands and Belgium. My ability to speak Dutch came in handy in promoting the country to Dutch speaking visitors. Most of my colleagues were born in the Dominican Republic and had been living in Europe for a couple of years. *Benjamin* was 14 years when he left the Dominican Republic to live in Spain. At the time we spoke he had been living in the Netherlands for two years. He tells how he misses the atmosphere in the Dominican Republic, *ambiente* and the human warmth. In his life in the Netherlands he feels the *ambiente* and human warmth when he is with other Dominicans, but 'once you are outside, in real life, it is all gone', he mentions. When I comment that he speaks Dutch very well, he explains that the past two years learning Dutch was his main focus. He wants to speak 'ABN Nederlands' (Algemeen Beschaafd Nederlands – proper Dutch) because he believes that that will provide opportunities to achieve things in the Netherlands.

Language was mentioned by almost all respondents as a challenge. Many said that they thought they would never learn Dutch (because it being a difficult language to learn), though understand that mastering it was important for maintaining social contacts, finding a job and expressing who they were. Dominicans had different ways of dealing with the language difference. Some said they did their utmost to learn Dutch by taking courses. Others who followed their mothers to the Netherlands said that their mothers would prohibit contact with other Dominicans because it would stand in the way of learning Dutch. Some also mentioned how good it felt to speak Spanish with other Dominicans and Latinos, although they knew that socializing only within their own community stood in the way of learning Dutch.

After having examined encounters with new and unfamiliar social and cultural elements, I now turn to Dominican immigrants' locations of home and feelings of home.

Dominicans' Culture and Home   57

3.4 Where is Home After Migration?

I love this land,
the land where I was born.
love it and carry it deep
inside of me.
I come from deep within the
heart of my land
and my country is
where all of the most beautiful things come from.

(Translated by the author)

The majority of the Dominicans I spoke express what Poncho y su Cocoband sing in 'Mi Tierra': deep love for the Dominican Republic. Still, Dominicans expressed different attitudes towards the Dominican Republic and its relation to where they considered their homes were. In this section, the relationship with the Dominican Republic and the Netherlands is explored in relation to home.

3.4.1 Home Is in the Dominican Republic

The stories of Dominicans who consider the Dominican Republic their home show that what and where home is has to do with several aspects. Firstly, the presence of family is important. *Laura* had been living in Bani, in the south-eastern Dominican Republic, and came to the Netherlands in 1993 seeking a better future. She left her two children there and started a life in the Netherlands. She appreciated how the Netherlands offers a lot of opportunities if one makes the effort to integrate, but said that the Netherlands never could be her home. It is *un país de acogida*, a phrase other Dominicans also used to refer to a place where you are merely received – nothing more – whereas in the Dominican Republic, *Laura* is surrounded by her family and human warmth.

Secondly, birthplace and cultural identity seem to be decisive. *Mariasela* arrived in the Netherlands in 2003 when she was 29. She studied marketing in La Vega and decided to come to the Netherlands with her husband, whom she had met six years earlier, married and lived with in the Dominican Republic. She had to get accustomed to the Netherlands and the Dutch, but had since found her place. She was proud to be Dominican and visited the Dominican Republic every year. *Mariasela* referred to the Netherlands as her second home. Because she is Dominican and always will be Dominican, she said, the Dominican Republic was her first home. *Margarita* said she appreciated the Netherlands and mentioned how, without being conscious of it, she changed and adapted, but her dream was to return to the Dominican Republic. Her association of home was a place where you can fully be yourself, and *Margarita* felt fully herself in Dominican Republic:

I love my country, I like it there, I identify with it. I feel me, I feel at home. I feel good in the Netherlands, I adapted myself, but I

58   Post-Migration Experiences, Cultural Practices and Homemaking

feel that I am missing something all the time because I know I do not belong to this play of dominoes [this country, this way of living]. You know in a game when one or two pieces are missing. You know it is missing and it is never going to be complete because the piece disappeared. I have to die and be born here or something like that, but this is not my culture.

Thirdly, feeling accepted seems to be important for feeling at home. *Luis*, born in Santo Domingo, migrated to Sint Maarten when he was three months, returned at 18 and arrived in the Netherlands at 21. He said he appreciated the Netherlands. He likes that it is clean and organized. People are very open and well-informed. There are a lot of job opportunities here and you can create a future here. He considered the Dominican Republic home despite having lived more years of his life in Sint Maarten:

I do not feel at home [in the Netherlands] because I do not feel that I am accepted—I am tolerated. You know, actions speaker louder than words .... So, I have noticed that I am tolerated, but not accepted. And this continuously reminds me of the fact that I am here, but that this is not my country. You are from the outside. I love Sint Maarten, it is a home, but I prefer the Dominican Republic .... Look, in my mind, my home is in Sint Maarten because I was raised there, I have my memories there, memories of happiness, memories of sadness. But my heart is Dominican. I am Dominican.

Similar to *Mercedes* at the start of this chapter, *Luis* also pointed to differences between mind and heart: Sint Maarten should feel like home because of its familiarity, his family and memories there, but the Dominican Republic is still the real home in his heart. Other Dominicans also relayed experiences of discrimination and racism and how these affected their feelings about the Netherlands. *Yasmin* said she always feels like an outsider in the Netherlands. When asked whether the Netherlands was home, she expressed ambivalence:

Yes and no. You always feel like a *buitenlander* ['foreigner']. I personally feel that I have to show that I am a good citizen and that automatically means that I do not feel fully at home here ... Yes, I feel at home there [Dominican Republic]. You belong to one place, that is one thing, but whether you feel at home there is something else. I feel that I need to be here with regard to mentality, but feeling at home is there. I have always had the feeling that I should not be there. Strange. I fit in here, there not. Our system [Dominican Republic], they way we treat each other, I totally disagree.

Yasmin's quote showed how feeling accepted is important for feeling at home. And again, like *Luis* she underscored a certain duality albeit in a different way: belonging to a place with regard to mentality, but feeling at home in another.

Dominicans' Culture and Home **59**

While the importance of family and identity resonates with other studies about the immigrant home (Blunt, 2005; Lam & Yeoh, 2004; Nowicka, 2007; Wiles, 2008), being accepted by the receiving society is one aspect yet to be explored in home studies as a determinant or element for feeling at home.

3.4.2 Home Is in the Netherlands

For some Dominicans, the Netherlands had become home. Three reasons or combinations of reasons emerged. Firstly, some mentioned how they have changed due to being exposed to and appreciating aspects of Dutch society, such as organization, quietness and equality. Since becoming accustomed to this level of organization, some said that they would have to readapt to the Dominican system, and if they compared it with the Dutch system, internal conflicts would arise. *Camila*, born and raised in Santo Domingo, came to the Netherlands when she was 25. She had married a Dutch man and lived with him, his son and her son in Rotterdam. She mentioned how she got accustomed to Dutch organization and how the lack of it frustrated her in the Dominican Republic:

> I will never say 'never'. If I have to, I will return. It is my country, but I do not want to live there … because I am used to the organization. For example, the traffic. People here drive better than people there. Oh my God, you cannot drive there. Those kinds of things, details. It is more organized here. Every time I go there I get frustrated, because I notice the difference.

Many Dominicans also mentioned how in the beginning, they would miss street noise: busy traffic, music on every street corner and people talking loud. They found it so difficult to get accustomed to the silence in the Netherlands; they discovered that even silence has a sound. However, after years in the Netherlands, they appreciated this *tranquilidad* ('peacefulness') and missed it when holidaying in the Dominican Republic. This mechanism also emerges in research by Meijering and Lager (2014) and Gram-Hanssen and Bech-Danielsen (2011), finding how migrants visiting their country of origin miss the life they constructed in the receiving society. Dominicans also mentioned liking the Netherlands' sense of equality. According to them, there was no (visible) gap between rich and poor, and institutions were more likely to treat those with less money and the rich equally. *Carlos* explained how many Dominicans live to eventually return to the Dominican Republic, but stay. He found that the Netherlands provides for its citizens basic needs, including a roof over one's head, clothing, food and healthcare. In the Dominican Republic, when you do not have money, you have nothing, *Carlos* said. When you are sick, you cannot count on good services, whereas in the Netherlands your economic situation does not matter, found these respondents. *Martha* also mentioned how she disliked inequality and how that caused her to feel totally disenchanted with the Dominican Republic:

> I have had a bad experience which made me feel different about my country. Before that, I would miss everything: my job, my sister,

60 Post-Migration Experiences, Cultural Practices and Homemaking

the sun, the beach ... because I am a person who considers everybody equal. But there, it is like whoever is well-off or has better social contacts has more, which I hate. This is what I like about the Netherlands: equality. I love that. It is like my mother used to say: 'Those who have more saliva eat more puff pastry'. You also have that here, but here there is more equality. This disenchanted me completely. I, who was always saying that I would retire in Santo Domingo, no, not anymore. I can stay there for six months, but my home is here in the Netherlands.

Martha's quote exposed a change in feelings towards her county of origin, caused by negative experiences there and positive experiences in the receiving society. With regard to Dutch characteristics, *Anthony* was one of the few Dominicans I spoke to who mentioned how the community-focused lifestyle of the Dominican Republic did not suit him. He liked the anonymity, as he puts it, of the Netherlands:

Here I go out and I am [just] a number; I like feeling like a number. I like knowing that I am at a train station and that nobody knows me. Very individualistic. I like it. There you go somewhere, everybody knows who you are, where you are from, who your parents are, who your family is. That does not suit me. If you work there, this is what you have to deal with, because we Dominicans, culturally, are like that. And I have a particular lifestyle; I am a very practical person.

These stories showed the open and flexible nature of home, which shifted from the Dominican Republic to the Netherlands due to getting to know other ways of living.

Secondly, for others, the Netherlands became home because they had houses in the country, achieved things in the Netherlands, created friendships and partook in activities. They still felt a connection with the Dominican Republic and the houses they grew up in, but the Netherlands was where they created a life for themselves and their children. This idea of having built a life in the Netherlands had different dimensions. *Bryan* mentioned that he grew up in a dangerous Santo Domingo neighbourhood, and his memories are mostly of poverty. When he was 20, his mother, who was already living in the Netherlands, urged him to come. He mentioned the importance of the fact that everything he achieved was achieved in the Netherlands:

I am the kind of person who adapts fast. I feel like the Netherlands is my country. Half of my life I have been here. I have my children here, my mother, my friendships. I made my life here. Everything I achieved, I achieved here. I do not feel Dutch, but I do feel that the Netherlands is my home. I have achieved everything here.

Dominicans' Culture and Home   **61**

Leydi highlighted a different reason for staying: children. She always thought she would go back to the Dominican Republic, she said, but the Netherlands was her children's home and thus also hers:

> For a holiday, it is nice. I see my family, but I do not feel at home there anymore. Yes, in the beginning I did, the first years that I went for holidays, I really felt at home. And I always wanted to return; [I thought that] when I would finish my studies, I would rent a place there and live there. Or if I had the possibility to buy a second house, it would be there. And now I do not have the need anymore. What has changed is the fact that I have children now. They were born here, and this is home for them. They do not feel at home there; it is a holiday for them.

Bryan's and *Leydi's* quotes show that feeling at home is influenced by practicalities (a house, a job) as well as family ties, and that even if formed in a foreign country, the ties can strengthen attachment to a place which once was foreign (Lam & Yeoh, 2004). *Pedro* also placed value on having built a life in the Netherlands. *Pedro* was living with his wife and child in Santo Domingo when he was offered the opportunity to come to the Netherlands. He accepted and arrived at age 24. Even though he had a difficult start because of the weather, missing his family and having to learn a new language, he reported feeling good in the Netherlands nowadays. He said that what the Dominican Republic lacks the Netherlands provides, and what the Netherlands lacks the Dominican Republic provides. He expressed loving his life and simultaneously wishing to build a house in Paraiso, a village in the southern part of the Dominican Republic, where his family was from. His story shows that becoming accustomed to the receiving society is a process. This process could eventually lead to considering the receiving society home as well as appreciating the society's characteristics and opportunities offered:

> In the beginning, one is half in the Dominican Republic and half in the Netherlands. You are thinking of there because you have a child and your mother, you have family [there]. And I was alone in this country. So that is hard. But with time, you become aware that this country offered us a lot; it is country where there is freedom. You can walk in the street any time of the day without any problems. It is not like our country. And I lost some friendships in the Dominican Republic: some have died, others have families. It is not the same anymore. I have created a life here. You saw me at the radio station last night. In 1992, I started as a DJ here.

Thirdly, for other respondents, the Netherlands had become home, but it did not have to do with appreciation for the country, constructing a life in it or any achievements. Rather, it was because the Dominican Republic had changed or appeared not to progress, economically or politically. Many mentioned safety,

62 *Post-Migration Experiences, Cultural Practices and Homemaking*

no longer feeling free to walk the streets. Dominican politics also irritated some Dominicans in the Netherlands, and many admitted detesting Dominican politics. Interesting with regard to political change is that there are Dominicans who from the Netherlands remain active in the politics of the Dominican Republic. In this way they, as they mention, hope to create a country to which they can return.

The stories of this second group show how home shifted to the receiving society due to a place's essential qualities (Lam & Yeoh, 2004) and the construction of lives therein (Lam & Yeoh, 2004; Perez Murcia, 2018), but also due to the situation in the country of origin.

3.4.3 Home Is in Both Countries

For some Dominicans, both countries were home. Some mentioned that both countries have different functions, which was mostly the case for those living in the Netherlands for many years. *Casandra* said that after having lived for so long in the Netherlands, the country became part of her:

> I feel like the Netherlands is my home, because I came here when I was young and I arrived in a period of my life when I was becoming an adult. The Dominican Republic will always be my home, forever. It is my country where I was born, and everything I am is due to my country. I do not owe the Netherlands anything. Yes, it helped me a little bit in my formation, but my formation as a person occurred in the Dominican Republic and that is why I am thankful to the Dominican Republic .... But I feel home here in another way. The adult way. I do not know how it is to live in the Dominican Republic as an adult because I have never done that. But I know how my childhood and youth were there. And here is where I became an adult. So, how do I say it, I feel like both [are home].

While *Casandra* expressed great appreciation for her upbringing and personality formation in the Dominican Republic, she equally valued the Netherlands for her formation as an adult. Consequently, both countries felt like home. *Emilia* also described the different roles of both countries:

> It would be difficult to leave the Netherlands or stay away from the Dominican Republic. I will stay here as long as I can. And when I retire in Santo Domingo, I will always visit the Netherlands. It is like your father and your mother. I was born in the Dominican Republic, but was raised in the Netherland. I mean, 30 years here is not nothing.

Casandra and *Emilia* expressed a certain duality about home as a place and a feeling. Home is here and there. This resonates with what Perez Murcia (2018, p. 7) refers to as 'ambivalent homes':

Dominicans' Culture and Home **63**

a tension between 'here' and 'there' .... not only because people have strong cultural and emotional attachments to the abandoned place and miss their way of life 'there', but also because they have refashioned ideas of identity, belonging and home on the move.

3.4.4 Home Is in the Dutch Caribbean

The previous chapter described how some Dominicans have lived in the Dutch Caribbean islands before migrating to the Netherlands. For some, the Dutch Caribbean islands were home. *Francisco* showed a deep love for Curaçao, which he moved to at age 14 due to his mother's job. He expressed love for both Curaçao and the Dominican Republic, but revealed he would choose Curaçao as a place to spend his life:

> So, that is where I was raised, where I developed myself. Curaçao is my little fatherland. It is my first country, because half of my life I have lived there, since I was 10 years old. So they call me, like they do there, a *bon yu di korsow* ['a good Curaçaoan']. One never loses this shine, this Dominicanness. This way of thinking one never loses. But when I commune with my heart, I identify with Curaçao. When I go to Santo Domingo, I identify with Santo Domingo. I adore Curaçao, and when I retire and have to choose between one of those, I would choose Curaçao. In Curaçao, I have three children and my mother. I have nieces, nephews and my sisters living there. My best friends I have in Curaçao. I wish for the second period of my life to be in Curaçao. The most beautiful memories and satisfaction were in Curaçao.

Curaçao is *Francisco*'s home because he grew up there, achieved much in his career and still has a lot of family living there.

Many mention that experiences of discrimination and not feeling welcome stood in the way of feeling at home in Curaçao or Aruba. However, they considered these islands home, often because their families still lived there, which points to what Lam and Yeoh (2004) call a family-centred definition of home as opposed to a place-based notion. *Valentina* was eight years old when she left the Dominican Republic, due to her father accepting a job in Aruba's hotel industry. After migrating to Aruba, she used to visit the Dominican Republic annually with her parents. In Aruba, she was raised 'Dominican', with Dominican food, music and friends. When she was 21 he moved to the Netherlands to continue her studies, as many Aruban youngsters choose to do. She explained that home was where her parents were, Aruba. However, she identified as Dominican, not as Aruban. *Irvin* also migrated to Aruba due to his mother accepting a job in Aruba's hotel industry. He described his teenage years in Aruba:

> I was 16, 17, and I was between two worlds. I was not enough Aruban and not enough Dominican. All my Dominican friends would

64 Post-Migration Experiences, Cultural Practices and Homemaking

> say that I was Aruban because I was raised there; I would not know the [Dominican Republic]. And all Arubans would say that I am Dominican. So it was real difficult to identify with something or someone. So then I created my own identity: I am a Dominican who has been raised in Aruba, who did not forget where he is from, but knows where he is going.

Experiencing not being accepted by Arubans or Dominicans, *Irvin* created an identity in which both countries were present. He identified as Dominican, but Aruba is his home because he grew up and has memories there. The majority who had lived on the Dutch Caribbean islands felt more connected with Dominican culture than to the Dominican Republic as a country.

Interesting is that Dominicans who had lived in Sint Maarten before migrating to the Netherlands mention that they did feel at home there. It would be good to further explore whether certain characteristics of receiving contexts are more conducive to home feelings of immigrants. In the case of the Dutch Caribbean islands, it would not be strange, as the Leeward and Windward islands differ from each other linguistically, culturally, climatologically and possibly socially. *Sandra*, for example, lived in Curaçao as well as Sint Maarten. She did not feel at home in Curaçao, but did in Sint Maarten.

The stories of these Dominicans who came to the Netherlands via the Dutch Caribbean show that home is related to family, familiarity, childhood memories and achievements.

3.4.5 Home Is Anywhere

There is a small group for whom home was not related to a geographic location. When asked where their home was, they answered that it was anywhere and everywhere. The cases of *Claudette* and *Victor* show that the home is related to activities.

Claudette grew up in Santo Domingo and before the Netherlands, had lived in Barbados, Curaçao and Bonaire. She was 37 when she arrived to the Netherlands, having been in the country for 20 years when we spoke. She said she feels at home anywhere because the activities that she can participate in are what make a place home.

Victor came to the Netherlands with his mother when he was six. After joining the Dutch army, he went to study law. One of his career aims was to help Spanish-speaking immigrants participate in and integrate into Dutch society. His connections with the Dominican Republic were strong as he often visited for holidays or to attend to the social project he set up in his town of birth. When asked where his home was, he answered that home is there where he has a mission. For the moment that was in the Netherlands. He said: 'I am not here to enjoy the weather, to watch television. I am doing something here'.

Sergio's story shows something else: a certain kind of detachment from culture and location. Due to his mother, *Sergio* came to the Netherlands when he was 13. After spending 15 years in the Dutch army, he began working as an audio-visual technician. He reported visiting the Dominican Republic regularly and about culture and home said:

> Culture and customs, I do not how to look at that, because I feel home everywhere. I lived in Suriname for four months and I felt Surinamese. I have lived three years of my life in Curaçao and I was an Antillean, you know .... Of course I am proud of the Dominican Republic .... But also when the Netherland wins the World [football] Championship, I am proud .... You know, in the end, I do not have a home. I want my children to have a home, and their home is here in the Netherlands.

Sergio's quote also shows a certain duality. On the one hand, he does not need one country to be home; home is everywhere. On the other hand, he does want that for his children.

These stories of Dominicans for whom home is not necessarily attached to a place show that they do consider the Netherlands home because there is where they are now.

3.5 Conclusion: Attachments, Place of Home and Feelings of Home

The guiding question in this chapter asked: for Dominican immigrants in the Netherlands, where is home and why? To contextualize their feelings of home I showed how Dominicans tried to recreate social and cultural practices in the Netherlands. These were at first, in the 1980s, primarily aimed at maintaining and facilitating contact with family in the Dominican Republic, obtaining Dominican commodities and the reproducing a Dominican atmosphere in public through dance and music in nightlife. In the 1990s, the community began to grow, and the social and cultural infrastructure extended to other types of initiatives including restaurants, churches, bars and radio stations. These activities not only maintained connections with the Dominican Republic and its cultural elements but also created connections with the Netherlands.

I also showed the challenges Dominicans encountered while setting up a life in the Netherlands. The lack of a cheerful atmosphere (*ambiente*), living inside, the individualistic lifestyle, perceived lack of human warmth, climate, language and organization were challenges when settling in the Netherlands. But these feelings were not fixed: one could become accustomed to certain characteristics of a country and even appreciate them to the point that they became an element of home.

Using Perez Murcia's (2018) categorization to explore the relationship with the Dominican Republic and the Netherlands in terms of home showed a varied picture with regard to attachments to these two places. Some considered the Dominican Republic home; others considered the Netherlands home; and others considered both places home. There was also a group who considered the Dutch Caribbean home. And there was another group for whom home was anywhere and everywhere. The results are similar to those of Perez Murcia (2018),

66 Post-Migration Experiences, Cultural Practices and Homemaking

but depart when it comes to her nowhere category. Those results may look similar to my last category, but differ because this anywhere and everywhere category was experienced positively by the Dominicans, while the nowhere category was experienced negatively in Perez Murcia's Colombian case.

But what makes a place home? Why is something home? Several themes emerged as defining features of home. Home is related to *birth soil and national identification*: being born in the Dominican Republic means that home is there, irrespective of appreciating aspects of the Netherlands or disapproval of aspects of the Dominican Republic. Furthermore, *social relations* (family and friends) make a place home. A family-centred definition of home can lead to both strengthening and weakening attachments to place (Lam & Yeoh, 2004), and these social relations can be in the Dominican Republic, the Netherlands and even the Dutch Caribbean islands. Therefore, these countries can each be considered home. Also, *certain characteristics of a country are related to home*. The Netherlands is related to individualism, tranquillity, safety and independence, which some considered key to feeling at home. The Dominican Republic is related to certain ways of socializing, wherein spending lots of time with others, human warmth and *ambiente* are key. Many mentioned missing human warmth, *ambiente* and being together with others (community-based ways of socializing) and the lack thereof as standing in the way of feeling home in the Netherlands. Last, home is related to certain *lifestyle needs*: the Netherlands was associated with progress, growth, development and financial security, and thus home was defined by the practicalities of immigrants' life courses (Lam & Yeoh, 2004).

So what home feelings emerged for Dominicans in my research? I started by considering the elements of home mentioned in home literature (Boccagni, 2017; Duyvendak 2011; Hage, 1997). While familiarity and nostalgia were important elements, this was not always something all Dominicans wished to recreate. Moreover, in some instances, the absence of certain familiar customs and values of the country of origin can cause immigrants to feel at home elsewhere (Philipp & Ho, 2010), as was expressed by Dominicans who found some Dutch traits to be a relief. Individualism and quietness, for example, were appreciated characteristics of the Netherlands. This not wanting to recreate familiarity also had a temporal component; over time, aspects of the receiving country came to be appreciated. Furthermore, the element of community emerged as an element. Belonging to a local or transnational community evoked feelings of home. Also, Hage's (1997) element of hope/opportunities seemed relevant, as expressed in the importance respondents ascribed to broadening one's horizons, financial security and having or owning a home somewhere. To existing categorization of home, my research adds *ambiente* and human warmth as important elements. These elements are created with others, inside the home, but more often outside the home, which shows that the private/public divide (where home begins and ends) is not that rigid (Boccagni & Brighenti, 2015).

Chapter 4

The Differentiated Meaning of Dominican Food After Migration

4.1 Introduction

> Well, the food mainly. And our music. The Dominican Republic
> is a country that is open for everyone, we are a happy country.
> Although we are an underdeveloped country, but we are a happy
> country. We are always laughing, we are always smiling. We let
> things go. We are not going to stress about it, we always think that
> life goes on. – Pedro

In exploring the meaning of cultural practices in post-migration life and its relation to feelings of home, I asked Dominicans what they considered typical Dominican cultural elements. Like *Pedro*, others mentioned food, followed by music, dance, *ambiente*, cheerfulness *(alegria)* and human warmth.

The previous chapter showed Dominicans' very different attachments to the Dominican Republic in terms of home and showed that feelings of home are related to feelings concerning cultural origins, sense of community, opportunities, *ambiente* and human warmth. The value of opportunities, especially, showed that Dominicans are not always and only attached to their country of origin, but could also appreciate newly encountered ways of living and broadening horizons. However, this differentiation in orientation does not come to the fore in prior studies of homemaking – that is, ways in which people create a home post-migration (Dinmohamed, 2023). In the majority of immigrant homemaking studies, immigrants are portrayed as people needing to recreate practices from the country of origin. Accepting the idea that immigrant communities are heterogeneous in their attachments to the countries of origin, I am curious about how this is expressed in the practices with which they create home after migration.

This leads to the question: *Do cultural practices from the country of origin constitute feelings of home in the receiving society?* I argue that immigrants have different relationships with practices from their country of origin and are not

---

Post-Migration Experiences, Cultural Practices and Homemaking:
An Ethnography of Dominican Migration to Europe, 67–91
Copyright © 2023 by Sabrina Dinmohamed
Published under exclusive licence by Emerald Publishing Limited
doi:10.1108/978-1-83753-204-920231004

68 Post-Migration Experiences, Cultural Practices and Homemaking

only orientated around the country of origin in making home. This differentiation is caused by individual and migration-related characteristics. Furthermore, I argue that what is familiar depends on the economic, social and cultural context from which an immigrant has migrated.

This chapter and those that follow use food to explore processes of homemaking. By connecting the elements of home examined in the previous chapter to the meaning of food Dominicans cite in this chapter, I show whether food practices from the country of origin are indeed homemaking practices. Up until now, Rabikowksa's (2010) study has been the only to show immigrants' varied relationships with food practices from the country of origin. Their practices are categorized on a continuum from maximal to minimal exchange with the receiving society. This categorization comes in handy to explore the differentiation in meaning of Dominican food. To explore the differentiation in relationships and attitudes, I created two sets of factors: migration-related characteristics and personal characteristics. By shining light on how these factors relate to immigrants' cultural practices, I also explore whether it is true that so-called 'low-skilled, poor' immigrants are less open to unfamiliar practices and heed Marte's (2008) call to examine the connection between food practices maintenance, education and/or income level of Dominican immigrants.

The first section focuses on the idea of differentiated familiarity. The second section describes the food consumption of Dominican immigrants after migration to the Netherlands and the importance of these practices and meaning *vis-á-vis* feelings of home. This leads to a categorization of Dominicans' different food practices. The third section explores which migration-related and individual characteristics correlate with the variation in practices. This chapter ends with a reflection on immigrants' cultural practices and feelings of home

4.2 'Typical' Dominican Food: La Bandera, Sancocho or Something Else?

Dominican cuisine is predominantly a combination of Spanish, indigenous Taíno and African influences. In exploring the meaning of Dominican food in Dominicans' post-migration life, I first needed to know what Dominicans in my research consider Dominican food. Different dishes were mentioned when I asked them what they considered typical Dominican food, varying from different rice dishes with meat, to plantain dishes and sweet dishes. *La bandera* (rice, stewed beans and meat) and *sancohco* (stew/soup with different kinds of meat) were considered by many the most important Dominican dishes.

As for ingredients, they cited rice, yucca, plantain, salted cod fish, eggplant, salami, cheese, pigeon peas, avocado, beans (red, brown, black), meat (chicken, pork, goat), fish, plantains, chayote, okra and *mondongo* (beef or pork tripe) as typical. Seasoning and herbs were also considered essential and defining of the Dominican taste. Oregano was the most important herb to give food that special Dominican taste. Others were cilantro, culantro *(cilantro ancho)*, garlic, salt, pimiento, *bija* (an orange-red condiment and food colouring derived from the seeds of the achiote tree), tomatoes, onions and parsley. Typical seasoning

Meaning of Dominican Food **69**

also came in bottles, for example, *salsa ranchera* and *sopita* (Maggi meat bouillon cubes). For an overview of dishes, ingredients and seasoning mentioned by respondents, see Appendix.

Also characteristic of Dominican foodways are certain food customs related to specific holidays. Two holidays are especially important. During the festivities of *Semana Santa* (Holy Week), food is central. In the Dominican Republic, the festivities begin with Palm Sunday and continue throughout the week. The three most important days for the Dominican Republic's practising Christian population are Holy Thursday, Good Friday and Holy Saturday. Special food is prepared for *Semana Santa*, usually in large quantities for extended family and visitors. Dominicans traditionally abstain from meat during this week, so seafood is eaten a lot. Christmas is another important food festivity, celebrated on 24 December (*Noche Buena*), with leftovers to be eaten on 25 December. Dinner on the 24th is meant for sharing, and eating with a group of people is important. Typical dishes are *puerco asado* (roast pork), *ensalada rusa, verde, de papa* (all types of salads), *moro de guandules* (rice with pigeon peas), *pavo relleno* (stuffed turkey), *pastel en hoja* (plaintain and beef pockets) and *pollo al horno* (roasted chicken).

Another characteristic of Dominican foodways is consuming a warm meal at midday. Dominicans usually eat three times a day: in the morning, around noon and in the evening. *Anthony* explained when meals are consumed and what these meals consist of:

> We have three meals: breakfast, main meal (*comida*) and dinner (*cena*). Between 12 and one at midday, people have lunch consisting of a normal meal. And between seven and nine, people have dinner. Breakfast and dinner can consist of tubers, sausages, cheese, salami or stews. Lunch is rice, beans and different types of meat, which can be chicken, pork or beef with salad. Everything depends on the economic level of the family, but this would be typical.

In conveying what is 'typical', *Anthony* said something provocative: if 'everything depends on the economic level of the family', can I speak of 'typical' Dominican food practices in my research?

Before exploring the differentiated attachments to Dominican food practices, I focus on the idea of familiarity. In homemaking studies, it has been identified as being one of the elements of home feeling: engaging in familiar practices would lead to increased feelings of home. As said, I suspect that not only all immigrants do not wish to recreate the familiar, but what is considered familiar is also differentiated. The stories about food reveal two points (Dinmohamed, 2023). Firstly, differentiation in familiarity is particularly shown in specificities of the region one is from as every region has its own distinctive dishes. While *la bandera* and *sancocho* are considered national dishes of the Dominican Republic, what a Dominican in the Dominican Republic considers Dominican and consumes also depends on the region where one was raised (see also Marte, 2008). The Dominican Republic is divided into El Cibao (in the north and middle), the southwest and the southeast. These regions can be further divided into 31 provinces,

70 *Post-Migration Experiences, Cultural Practices and Homemaking*

155 municipalities and 231 municipal districts. When asked what typical Dominican food is, *Sofia* (from Samaná, in the north, where dishes have French influences) and *Rafael* (from the region of El Cibao) answered differently, reflecting
regional variations:

> That is an interseting question, because it depends on where you
> come from. We don't eat *chenchen* in Samaná. That's the [eaten in
> the] south. Or, for example, *pescado con coco* is something more
> usually on the seaside. In Santo Domingo, maybe once in a while,
> but I would not say its habitual diet. You don't eat *yaniqueque* in
> Santo Domingo. If you go to Boca Chica, you eat *yaniqueque.*
> If you leave Santo Domingo, it will be different, even the sur-
> roundings. People have access to other thing. Yes, when you go
> to Samaná you eat *gateau*. It's like a sweet potato cake. Even the
> bread we eat, it's different in different places. In the north, like
> Samaná, people will eat more bread made with coconut milk, you
> do not eat that in Santo Domingo. – *Sofia*

> In the south, they have other ways of eating, which in El Cibao are
> not common, for example, *chaca, chenchen*. In El Cibao, people do
> not know that. This mountain chain did not permit for this tradi-
> tion to reach us. What separates the south from El Cibao is this
> mountain chain. It is difficult crossing it. – *Rafael*

Sofia's and *Rafael's* stories show how some dishes are considered almost foreign,
for example, some typical dishes from the south, such as *chenchen* (corn pilaf
dish) and *chaca* (corn pudding). It also illustrates that this regional culinary variation is the result of access to certain products. For example, in the country's
interior less fish is eaten, but on the coast, more seafood is consumed. It furthermore shows how geographical circumstances (mountains) can stand in the way
of spreading some culinary traditions. There are also differences in preparation
between regions. *Anthony*, originally from Navarrete, a town 25 kilometres north
of Santiago de Los Caballeros, the country's second largest city, elaborated on
preparation styles. His story shows not only regional variation and how Dominicans visit and associate regions with certain kinds of preparations but also how
dishes have become Dominican over time. This shows the dynamic and open
nature of food practices. For example, *yaniqueque* ('Johnny cake') was brought
by labourers from the English Caribbean islands and is only consumed in the
southeast of the country:

> There are other areas with a lot of people with African roots and
> they have a dish named *dumpling*, in San Pedro de Macoris, in La
> Romana. These are dishes which are not Dominican but with time
> have become Dominican. We, los Santiagueros in the north, we do
> not even know how to prepare this food. It is not part of our menu,
> but it is a Dominican dish. The same counts for the Southwest or

Montecristi. They prepare goat in a certain way, and people from other cities go there to eat the goat prepared in that specific manner. It does not matter that they also prepare goat in their own city; they go specifically there to eat goat prepared in that specific way. The same counts for Puerto Plata. There is an area which is called Maimón, where they sell fried fish and people go there to eat that. Every city has its own culinary touch and characteristics, and people associate certain dishes and flavors with certain regions.

Secondly, income of households also influences what is considered familiar. About the relationship between economic resources and food consumption *Sofia* mentioned that her family is well-off and continues 'I am not sure if somebody who is not well-off can buy fish in Santo Domingo. You know what I mean, with that facility to buy fish'. In her book about food practices of three immigrant communities in the United States, Diner (2001) described how in their countries of origin, immigrants experienced internal variation with regard to food consumption. In the case of Italian immigrants, for example, in Italy there was a distinction between the food of the poor and the food of the rich. Interestingly, in the Dominican case, rice and beans were considered by many as the national dish; by others, it was considered as inexpensive food for 'poor people'. *Julia*, coming from a middle-class family mentioned that in her parents' house they consumed finer foods and not the typical rice and beans. A 'poor' Dominican, according to *Julia*, was used to eating a lot of rice, eggs and beans. However, while being well-off increased the possibility of consuming more diverse food, it did not necessarily exclude the typical rice with beans. *Petronila*, from well-to-do circumstances, mentioned that in her grandmother's home, where she was raised, 'the holy rice, beans and meat' combination was consumed every day. This dish, as she described it, is something typical to be proud of rather than something related to income.

San Pedro de Macoris, 2019. The story of 'my' Dominican family is an interesting case of both intra-regional Caribbean migration and differences within the Dominican Republic regarding food practices. *François*, originally from Aruba and of Surinamese descent, was working in Curaçao when he met *Luz Teresa*, who in 1989 decided to go work in Curaçao, following her three sisters who were already there. In one of our many conversations she tells me that it was the most difficult time of her life; having to leave her children behind in the Dominican Republic was heart-breaking. After *Francois'* retirement they decided to go live in San Pedro de Macoris, near Andrés, where her children were living. While assisting *Luz Teresa* in preparing *sancocho*, I learned there are very different ways to make dishes. She explained how her daughter had a different way of preparing meat before adding it to the *sancocho* and that she was going to give it a try that day. I also came to hear certain food ideas: the stewed beans known as *habichuela* are good when they are *cremoso* ('creamy') and not having meat or fish in your dish is uncommon. I realized that 'Dominican food' does not exist. There are changes in what one consumes due to temporal changes (meat was a luxury in the old days); circumstances such as internal migration from rural areas to cities; and

72   Post-Migration Experiences, Cultural Practices and Homemaking

last but not least, taste. *Luz Teresa* gave a telling example while we were eating. She had made rice, meat and eggplant, but the neighbour (mid-30s), who also was invited to join, had no eggplant. When I asked him why, *Luz Teresa* (mid-60s) answered for him, saying:

> Children in this era do not eat eggplant. We are accustomed to eating that because when I was little there was not always meat available. When they would slaughter an animal in the village, then there would be meat. This generation does not know that.

As these accounts testify, I cannot approach Dominican food from an essentialist or static view because what is considered Dominican varies according to regional, income-related and even generational differences. However, for practical purposes, I needed a word for foods that Dominicans brought from their country to the Netherlands. Thus, variations exist in what is considered Dominican food, but there is consensus about typical dishes, ingredients, celebration food and customs, so I will continue using 'Dominican food' to refer to what is consumed 'typically'. While a slippery one, I make the distinction between typical and traditional, the first referring to what is common and the second to what is part of traditions (e.g. in celebrations).

4.3 Dominican Food and Feelings of Home

> For me, Dominican food is very important. I like other foods, for example, Chinese or Surinamese. But every day in my house it is Dominican food. – *Sandra*

> I like it, I love it, but I do not need Dominican food to feel good. I cook, but it does not necessarily need to be Dominican food, I prepare what I feel like that day. – *Bryan*

Sandra and *Bryan* were already introduced at the start of this book. Their stories show different attachments to Dominican food, though both were born in the Dominican Republic. For *Sandra*, Dominican food had an important place in her life in the Netherlands. While she also ate food from other cultures, in her house, she cooked Dominican. *Bryan*, despite expressing appreciation for Dominican food, was open to including food from other cultures in his daily menu. He really did not need Dominican food in his daily life in the Netherlands; it was just one of the many dining options he had. These quotes raise questions about the meaning of food from the country of origin in the immigrant experience and how a cultural practice can have such different meanings after migration and in relation to feelings of home. This section explores how food practices from immigrants' country of origin are related to feelings of home.

I did not only wanted to know whether Dominican food was important in daily life but also which feelings it evoked and whether it was necessary to create

Meaning of Dominican Food   **73**

a home post-migration. Rabikowksa's (2010) study shows immigrants' varied relationships with food practices from the country of origin. Their practices are categorized on a continuum from maximal to minimal exchange with the receiving society. Instead of focusing on identity, as Rabikowska did, I focus on the meaning of home. The first type of food ritual that Rabikowska (2010) refers to is 'orthodox': a category that is closed off from exchange and influences from the host culture. The second type is 'porous': a category in which 'normal' food is implied as food from the country of origin, but some influences from foreign cultures are accepted; the practices of exchange are accidental or coincidental. The third type is 'alternate': a category in which food exchanges are consciously accepted, with effort made to initiate and repeat it. While this categorization describes rituals and practices, it still provides a starting point from which to explore different *categories of persons* with certain practices. The following subsections show the variety in meaning of Dominican food.

4.3.1 'Dominican Food Is Important'

4.3.1.1 Human Warmth. It was a November afternoon, one of those days in winter when it gets dark at 4 p.m. After wandering around in Zoetermeer, a small city near The Hague, dealing with a frozen face, I finally find Casandra's apartment building. When I entered she and her children welcomed me with hugs. Our appointment was at 5 p.m. and she assumed that after a long day, I would be hungry. *Casandra* showed me to the dining table and my plate, which she had set for me. *Casandra* finds it important to receive other people with warmth, which offering food was part of. Later she mentioned that Dominican food is important to her because that is what she brought with her from the Dominican Republic. It connects her to a place that is so important to her. This was not the first time that I was offered food. Sometimes food was prepared for me, or respondents mentioned how there was no time to cook an extensive dinner for me and bought some cake instead. Others mentioned after the interview that they would soon invite me to a good Dominican meal. *Casandra* emphasizes that I should serve myself enough and that I certainly should not feel ashamed to eat a lot. This is something that was told to me often when eating at a Dominicans' house: do not feel ashamed, please eat as much as you want. It also reminded me of my own Surinamese family, where food is also a way to show hospitability.

For those in this category, which I will call 'category A', Dominican food had a prominent place in daily life. The stories of these Dominicans show how they engage in Dominican food practices to recreate home post-migration. They show similarities to other studies about immigrants' homemaking and the importance of recreation of practices from the country of origin. My research shows which particular feelings are evoked by Dominican food. *Mateo* and *Analisa* showed how preparing Dominican food connected to human warmth, something they find important.

Marrying a Dutch woman brought *Mateo* to the Netherlands. He was born and raised San Juan de la Maguana and moved to Santo Domingo, where he had a managerial position at a factory. He never intended to migrate; he was

74 Post-Migration Experiences, Cultural Practices and Homemaking

very satisfied with his life in Santo Domingo. After living in the Netherlands for three years, at the time of our interview, he had found a way to navigate all the country's cultural, social and weather-related differences. For *Mateo*, Dominican food was important, and he prepared it as regularly as possible. Similar to Casandra, it also connected him to hospitability, *ambiente* and human warmth. After finishing my interview with him *Mateo*'s words revealed the importance of hospitability for him and how it is connected to preparing food for guests. *Mateo* said:

> You know that we are here, you should feel at home here. You can come whenever you want. You just call me [saying]: 'Mateo, I am coming to your house. I want us to cook something, prepare me this. And I'll do it, no problem'. I always have told my wife: 'When my friends come to my house, I want them to feel good'. Because they also make me feel good. We have good time, it can be here or we can drink a coffee somewhere else, but it is important having a good moment together, with people you like .... You know that we are here, you can come whenever you like. I put on some bachata, every music genre. And I always have some rum here.

For *Analisa*, hospitability, human warmth and sharing were important elements of home. A day at *Analisa*'s house showed me how this is expressed through Dominican food. Wanting to serve my guests Dominican food and knowing about her catering services, I asked *Analisa* to cook for my birthday. Afterwards, I needed to return pots in which she gave me the stewed chicken and rice with beans. I called her to schedule a time and she immediately asked me what I wanted to eat on the day I returned the pots. I did not expect her to cook for me and joked that I like *pastelon de platano maduro* (plantain casserole). She told that it had been a while since she prepared it, but that she would surely make it for me. She asked me how I wanted it. I did not understand her question because I never had it with something on the side, but then she explained how normally it is eaten with rice or salad. 'OK', I thought, 'maybe that is how Dominicans from San Juan eat it'.

It was a nice and sunny summer day in September, when I rang the bell of the terraced house in IJsselstein, a suburb near Utrecht. *Analisa* opened the door and welcomed me in with that smile always on her face. As I entered her home, the smell of oregano greeted me. *Analisa* had already started cooking. I took a seat and we started talking about work. I saw she was indeed making the *pastelon* I asked for. The minced meat was on the stove, seasoned with garlic, cilantro, oregano, three colours of bell peppers and celery. I expressed surprise that she had taken my wish seriously. She said: 'That is what you wanted, right?' We talked about the regional variation of Dominican food. In the meantime, she mashed the nine plantains she bought, buttered an oven dish and spread the plantain mash in it, creating the first layer of the *pastelon*. Then she added a layer of minced meat and another layer of plantain mash. She grated some slices of cheese and spread it over the *pastelon*. She used typical Dutch cheese (*jong belegen*), though in the

Meaning of Dominican Food **75**

Dominican Republic would use 'the one in the red package, the Parmesan'. She put everything in the oven. Then she asked whether I wanted white rice or *locrio* (a mixture of rice with meat or vegetables, to which colour is added with tomato sauce or annatto). I told her that I do not want to give her extra work, and she told me that nothing is too much work.

Then she got some salami and pork chop from a freezer in the garden barn. The salami was from the Dominican Republic. She always would bring products back from the Dominican Republic, she explained. Salami is also sold in the Netherlands, but it was too expensive. Plantains were also expensive, especially at Plus supermarket, where they sold for one euro a piece. At the Surinamese market, she bought them for two euros a kilo. She started making the *locrio* and then the salad. We continued talking about Dominican food. It was important for her, but *Analisa* said she also should be open to Dutch food, not least because of her husband, and on Mondays, she always made *stamppot* (Dutch potato and vegetables mash). While we kept talking as the food cooked.

Analisa's son and daughter-in-law arrived for a visit and then the whole group, myself included, sat at the dining table. We enjoyed the *locrio, pastelon de platano maduro* and a salad. We talked about the Dominican Republic, identity, differences between socializing in the Netherlands and the Dominican Republic and careers. The dinner concluded with coffee and cake. On announcing I was about to leave, *Analisa* gave me two containers: one with leftover *locrio*, one with leftover *pastelon*. So I would not have to cook tomorrow, she said. *Analisa* accompanied me to my car and wanted to make sure I had a nice evening. I confirmed and gave her a hug.

This afternoon and evening with *Analisa* and her family exposed different aspects and functions of food. Firstly, it showed how she deals with her new context and limitations therein (Dutch cheese and Dutch partner). Secondly, it showed how warmth and hospitability could be expressed through food. Third, it showed the importance of transnational space to recreate food practices.

4.3.1.2 Cultural Pride. For others, preparing and consuming Dominican food had to do with staying connected with the Dominican Republic and being proud of Dominican food. *Emilia* said she appreciates the Netherlands as well as the Dominican Republic and identifies as Dominican. She mentioned that Dominican food is important in her daily life. And even though she is open to other foods, in her house – and especially for visitors – she would always prepare a Dominican dish.

> It is what I like the most. I am open to everything, but in my house, where I am free to do what I want, I am going to cook Dominican for my guests. Also, to let them taste how good the food from my country is.

Eva's story goes one step further: she almost never consumed Dominican food, but still considered it the best for guests. She was born in Santo Domingo and migrated with her mother, sister and brother to Venezuela when she was three. She lived there up until age 17 and then moved to the Netherlands. Her identification

76   Post-Migration Experiences, Cultural Practices and Homemaking

underwent some shifts, from Venezuelan, to Dominican to, at the time of our interview, 'Latina'. She has two sons and a Dutch husband. Her husband does not like too much seasoning, so she said she adapted to what he made because he loves cooking. However, when her own guests would visit, she was sure to prepare Dominican dishes. Others also mentioned how on important occasions, Dominican food was the only 'real' and 'good' food to offer your guest.

These accounts show that apart from the special feelings that Dominican food can evoke in someone, it is also used to show others the food's greatness. Being proud of one's country and culture of origin and expressing that in food consumption also come to the fore in many studies about the role of food from the country of origin in the post-migratory experience. These stories, however, are different from what other studies reveal about inviting guests and food. Mehta and Belk (1991) and Vu and Voeks (2012) show that immigrants adapt their food for American or Canadian friends for fear that they will not like their foods. This was not the case in my research, with the Dominicans expressing pride in their dishes.

4.3.1.3 Taste. Others mentioned that Dominican food was important because of its taste. While they also consumed other types, though Dominican food held a special place because of its taste. Unlike others for whom eating Dominican food was connected to home feelings of national or cultural pride and human warmth, these Dominicans emphasized liking the taste of it.

For *Olivia*, home was in both the Dominican Republic and the Netherlands, and home for her meant human warmth. She expressed really liking the taste of Dominican food and that's why it is important for her. When asked whether she needed it in her life, she replied: 'It is super tasty, and I grew up with it. I eat food from every culture, but my rice, beans, my things, are always present'. She invited me to her birthday party, which she celebrated together with her husband, who is of Chilean descent. In the invitation, she added that it might be good for my research to attend a Dominican birthday party. With my preconceived ideas about Dominicans, their food and the interview with her on my mind, I expected a whole different experience. I expected to be met with Dominican smells and sounds. Instead, I did not smell oregano when I entered the home and heard something that sounded like a Mexican band (or was it Chilean?), singing boleros and ballads I knew from my time in Curaçao. I saw people wearing sombreros: Chilean people, Dominican people. I looked at the dining table and saw bread and fruit, and thought: where are the *gaundules*, where is the *arroz moro* with *pollo guisado*?

I saw *Olivia* turning on the stove, moving some food here and there. I saw empanadas, tacos and paella. Because she had expressed such great appreciation for Dominican food and its taste during the interview, I expected Dominican food. When I asked her about it, she said: 'I told you that we eat everything here. We have Spain, Chile and Mexico'. To my question about why there was nothing Dominican, she shrugged her shoulders as though it was of no importance. I told her that I saw a bottle of *mamajuana* and she answered that 'every self-respecting Dominican has a bottle of *mamajuana*'. We started to laugh.

Meaning of Dominican Food 77

The evening unfolded and people began dancing. The band played 'Guantanamera' and some songs by Cuban singer Compay Segundo as everybody danced. In the garden, there were piñatas, one for children and one for adults. Both were smashed to pieces. After that, everybody took turns deejaying, and the party continued with sounds of dembow and reggaeton, followed by a typical Dominican birthday song. After that, the cake appeared and everybody sang a Dominican birthday song and a Dutch birthday song. I asked Olivia whether this was a typical Dominican cake. She answered yes, but that it was also Chilean – she learned it from her mother-in-law. After cutting the cake, some Sergio Vargas merengue classics and some palos were played. *Olivia* said she always played palos (sacred/spiritual music) on her birthday because we should always remember the *santos*, the holy spirits. Around 12:30 AM, I decided it was time to go home. I was escorted to the door with all the warmth imaginable. While driving home from De Meern to Amsterdam, I concluded: Olivia is proud of her Dominican identity, of the Dominican Republic, and liking and finding Dominican food important does not mean that is has to be a daily practice.

Analysing these particular stories, I could not find an equivalent category in Rabikowska's (2010) food rituals. These Dominicans' practices might be slightly similar to what Rabikowska considers orthodox rituals, though even those for whom Dominican food was important and feelings of home were evoked showed they were open to exchanges and influences from the receiving society. These people would come closer to rituals described as porous, where 'normal' food is food from the country of origin, but influences from foreign cultures are accepted. Furthermore, with regard to feelings of home, those in this category who said Dominican food was important in their lives show that it did not necessarily evoke feelings of home (*Olivia*). In those for whom it does, food was related to human warmth, sense of community (sharing) and connection to the Dominican Republic (cultural origins).

4.3.2 'Dominican Food Is Very Appreciated, But I Do Not Need It'

A limited number of homemaking studies have shown how immigrants welcome receiving society influences and considering it a way to broaden their horizons (Bonhomme, 2013; Philipp & Ho, 2010). Exploring the food practices of Dominicans allowed to show some nuance. The Dominicans in this category (B) show that what makes something feel like home was related to other foods. They mentioned that they had been eating Dominican food all their lives and that being in the Netherlands provided the chance to try other cuisines. They mentioned being open to Italian (pasta), Thai, Surinamese, Indian, Persian and Mexican food. However, while the persons in this category consciously accepted and sought exchanges, this does not mean that they disliked Dominican cuisine, but rather did not need it in their daily lives.

4.3.2.1 Broadening Horizons. *Mercedes, Leydi* and *Sofia* showed their appreciation for Dominican food, but broadening their horizons was more important.

78 Post-Migration Experiences, Cultural Practices and Homemaking

They mentioned that they had been eating Dominican food all their lives and that being in the Netherlands provided the chance to try other cuisines. *Mercedes* lived in Santo Domingo until age 22. For her work with the Dominican government, she has lived in London, Brussels and Denmark and finally ended up in the Netherlands, where she was living for five years at the time of our interview. She identified as Dominican, but said she did not need Dominican food in her daily life. As she put it: 'I love all Dominican dishes – all of them – but I do not need them, just to make it clear'.

Leydi came to the Netherlands at a young age and mentioned liking the international atmosphere of Amsterdam and the possibilities to get to know other cultures. She gave an example of what she made for herself, her Dominican husband and two children:

> A mix of sometimes Dominican, then pasta. Or what I also prepare is roast chicken, with those little potatoes, because they like that. Roast chicken with some salad. A mix. And then sometimes we order pizza. So, no, it does not need to be Dominican. I also prepare rice with chicken or beef with whatever, but it does not need to be Dominican.

Sofia left the Dominican Republic at 18 to study in France, where she lived for six years. She finished her second master's degree there, after which she was offered a job in the Netherlands. She expressed pride to be Dominican and a great love for Dominican culture and the Dominican Republic. However, while she said she liked it, she did not need Dominican food in her daily life:

> No, I don't need it. There are other things to enjoy. And I am eating Dominican for, like, a long time .... We are, we cannot just be Dominican, you know. It's like there are more things that make you a person than just the cultural aspects.

Besides showing the importance of broadening horizons, the stories of *Mercedes, Leydi* and *Sofia* also revealed that they came from very different walks of life. *Mercedes* always had an international outlook on life. *Leydi* came to the Netherlands at a young age, following a mother who came to the Netherlands to provide a better future for her children. *Sofia* ended up in the Netherlands because of work. An openness to other cultures thus may originate in personality and personal preferences rather than some kind of intellectualism (caused by high levels of formal education and income) that would cause a cosmopolitan attitude. In Section 3.4, I will elaborate further on the relationship between cosmopolitanism and openness.

Taste and preferences are not fixed, however. *Martha*, born and raised in Bonao, located in the centre of the Dominican Republic, came to the Netherlands after marrying a Dutch man. Dominican food was and remained important for her, but she did not need it daily anymore. She used to serve Dominican food on

Meaning of Dominican Food **79**

three days and Dutch food on three days, also taking into account her Dutch husband:

> When the children were living here, I had everything organized. Mondays: rice with beans and chicken. Tuesdays: pasta or my daughter or me would cook *locrio de fideo con carne* and vegetables inside. Wednesdays: I would make *moro* with different kinds of beans, black beans, for example, or *asopao*. And the other days: pork chop, fish, like two times a week, fish with potatoes or potato mash and vegetables.

Martha became accustomed to Dutch food (potatoes, *karbonade, speklapjes*) and said she would not want to eat Dominican food every day. Also, things had changed: only one son was left at home, her husband came to cook more than she did and she took life easier now; if she had to eat Dutch food for an entire week, that would be no problem. *Mercedes*, on the other hand, mentioned how she came to like Dominican food after migration and shows how a post-migration re-encounter with Dominican food led to her appreciation for it:

> I have always liked pasta. I mean, to tell you the truth, I started liking and loving Dominican food when I left. When I was living there, I hated it when they did a *moro*. My first question always when my mom picked me up from school: 'What's for lunch today? Oh *moro*. Whyyyyy!?' I would always love *pastelones de yuca* or *platano maduro*, but rice and beans for me was horrible. I started liking it when I moved. Precisely because I missed it, or I started liking it – I don't know what happened in my head. I never missed it when I was in London. It was when I moved to Brussels because I had more Dominicans there, like my friend Ruben .... So because of him, I started liking *arroz con habichuela*. He started bringing *habichuelas* that his mom used to make and then every time he would bring it. And I was like: 'It's good, it's really good'. But before that, I could eat pasta and anything else, like international food.

4.3.2.2 Health and Lifestyle. Certain lifestyles led Dominicans to look differently at Dominican food. Some respondents had health issues, which does not allow them to eat 'Dominican food', as they would call it. Others chose to follow a fitness-focused lifestyle that did not accommodate 'heavy' Dominican food. They mentioned how their food consumption was related to conscious choices about health and lifestyle, which Dominican food did not fit in. Dominican food, for example, was seen as unhealthy and heavy. *Anthony* and *Petronila* mentioned lifestyle decisions as reasons to cut Dominican food from their regular menu.

Anthony, born and raised in El Cibao region, left the Dominican Republic when he was 28 to do his master's degree in Spain. He also completed his PhD there and

80   Post-Migration Experiences, Cultural Practices and Homemaking

was offered a job representing the Dominican government in the Netherlands. He strongly identified as Dominican, but did not feel the immediate need to return. He said he would like to explore Europe. He consciously chose a fitness-focused lifestyle in which rice, lots of meat and beans do not fit. He liked Dominican food, but consumed it sporadically and made a conscious decision about how to do so:

> Sometimes, because of my diet, I limit the consumption of rice. I eat very varied. Sometimes, when I go out or something, I can eat some Dominican food. I eat the rice then at midday, eat light at night and then go out.

Petronila also chose to follow a health-conscious diet in which Dominican food did not fit. She was born and raised in Santo Domingo and left the Dominican Republic with her husband to explore the Netherlands for working opportunities. She was attached to Dominican culture and food. She mentioned how rice with beans was mandatory in her parents' home and for a long time also in her home in the Netherlands. However, that stopped when her husband and sons took up a fitness-focused lifestyle and when she was diagnosed with fibromyalgia.

The stories of *Anthony* and *Petronila* show how Dominican food can be appreciated, but still cut from a daily diet. While Dominican food for those in the previous category was the only worthy food to give guests, for this group it was considered unhealthy. These findings contradict studies wherein food from the host society is considered unhealthy and thus cause immigrants to prefer to eat the foods from their country of origin (Brown, Edwards, & Hartwell, 2010; Brown & Paszkiewicz, 2016).

4.3.2.3 Celebration Food. These Dominicans, however, regularly consumed Dominican food during celebrations. An example was preparing of *habichuela con dulce* for Easter. *Oscar*, born and raised in Santo Domingo, came to the Netherlands when he was 14. He identified as Dominican, but would not want to live in the Dominican Republic anymore, he said. He liked Dominican food, but did not need it in his daily life. However, at Easter he did:

> Some salads on festive days, or what is very traditional are pies. We make yucca pies, which are very difficult to make. But it is something that I really want to learn because it is so tasty. It is something my grandmother would make and then my mother learned it from her. And on Easter, for example, we eat a traditional dessert made from beans. Beans, I do not know if you know that, but *that* is holy for us. These are things that I eat a lot in the month of April.

Also, at *Mercedes'* mid-December birthday, the table looked 'European', with cheese, chorizo and wine and typical Dutch meat ragu balls (*bitterballen*), but there was also *pastel en hoja* served, which is a traditional dish consumed in December. At her Christmas celebration, there was a mix of traditional Dominican and non-Dominican dishes. The traditional included *ensalada rusa, arroz moro, pastel en*

Meaning of Dominican Food **81**

hoja and turkey; the less traditional included lasagna, smoked salmon and shrimp cocktail. *Petronila* noted how on Christmas and Easter, Dominican food practices are the only option and her words not only show the importance of 24th December as festive day, but also that it should be accompanied by typical Dominican dishes. The same goes for Easter:

> The 24th is holy for us. We celebrate the 24th of December. For us, the 25th is to rest and the 26th does not exist [as a holiday the way it does in the Netherlands]. So here we make stuffed turkey, roasted pork leg, *moro de guandules* and, when I am up for it, I make *pastel in hoja*. I make those, but I also buy them from a lady who sells them. So, I have my traditional meal. This day we eat everything .... And in *Semana Santa*, yes, *habichuela con dulce*. I had a friend, may she rest in peace, every year when the date of *Semana Santa* would near, she would call me: 'When can I come and pick up my *habichuela con dulce*?' I prepare a pot and all friends come and pick up their *habichuela con dulce*. This is something sacred.

Thus, while these people chose a daily diet free of Dominican food, for celebrations it was the only real and worthy food.

The food practices of these respondents resembled those of Rabikowska's (2010) alternate food rituals, in which exchanges are consciously accepted and efforts are made to initiate and repeat. The persons in this category did identify as Dominicans and were proud of their culture, but also liked to explore other ways of life and consciously accepted and sought exchanges. Food practices were motivated by desires to broaden horizons, keep healthy and/or maintain a certain lifestyle, but Dominican food remained important for celebrations.

4.3.3 'Dominican Food Is Not Important'

In immigrant homemaking literature in general and immigrant food literature specifically this category is still underexposed. Dominican food had little importance in the lives of Dominican respondents in this category (C). While those in the previous category expressed their appreciation for it, despite not needing it in their daily lives, for this group, Dominican food did not evoke anything.

Yasmin left the Dominican Republic when she was 33. When we spoke, she lived with her son and strongly identified as Dominican. She was on her way to becoming a full vegetarian and said that she could go without Dominican food for months and never made it. She mentioned how even in the Dominican Republic, typical Dominican dishes were not important to her although at her mother's house there would be typical Dominican dishes. She explains by saying 'this has to do with myself, I am the one who is different compared to everybody there'. In her daily life, she consumes a lot of vegetable soups, potatoes with vegetables, vegetarian meat and omelettes. She also mentioned liking the Curaçaoan *saté ku batata*, which she got to know through her Curaçaoan ex-partner.

82 Post-Migration Experiences, Cultural Practices and Homemaking

Josefina, born and raised in the countryside, was also raised with all typical Dominican dishes. However, she suddenly felt that she could not eat meat anymore, in a country where meat has a prominent place:

> When my children were little, I started to consume less meat. I do not know, I could not eat it anymore. I tried it, but I could not. In the past, with my cousins, when we wanted to eat a little snack, we would always go to the Chinese shop (*el Chino*), but suddenly I could not eat it anymore. And then I stopped eating meat. But I was always difficult with meat. We would eat a lot of pork, chicken. I can try it now, I will not die, but I do not like the taste, it tastes like soap. When I was living with my sister, she could not imagine me not eating meat. I would always tell her not to save any meat for me. I would eat bread.

A couple of months after our first interview, *Josefina* invited me to eat at her home. Her three (grown-up) children also were there to visit. At the table, they spoke a mix of Dutch and Spanish. When *Josefina* had her children follow her to the Netherlands a couple years after she arrived, she made sure to let them learn Dutch as soon as possible. Strikingly, she spoke the most Dutch of all of them. *Josefina* described the food she was serving as *la bandera* but without meat. I saw white rice, white beans, okra, grilled bell peppers and a cabbage and tomato salad. She told me several times to have as much as I wanted. This was the first time I consumed the typical *la bandera* in a vegetarian variant.

Jorge mentioned how due to his mother's marriage to a Dutch man (his stepfather), he was already accustomed to Dutch food while still in the Dominican Republic, and that this affected his food practices in the Netherlands. In his life in the Netherlands, Dominican food he was really not important for him, he said, though he consumed a combination of Dominican and Dutch dishes. He described a typical week as follows:

> For example, we make potatoes with garden peas, vegetables and pork chop cutlets. Tomorrow we make salmon with potatoes, but then fried potatoes and a green salad. But the day after that, we make *locrio de pollo* or white rice with beans and stewed chicken, a salad and fried plantains.

Jorge's case shows a dynamic I also observed in other Dominicans: they said that Dominican food was not important, but still regularly ate it out of custom. *Marcos* felt really connected to the Dominican Republic and identified as Dominican, but said that he is very diverse when it comes to food choices. He mentions that he does not want to limit himself by only consuming Dominican food. However, he prepares Dominican food very often because this is what he learned to prepare. He mentions that he would like to learn to prepare other foods. *Marcos'* and *Jorge*'s cases show Dominican food can be a custom, albeit without really evoking special feelings.

Also for these Dominicans, Dominican food remained important for celebrations. The custom of eating Dominican dishes at Easter (*habichuela con dulce*) and Christmas (*pastel en hoja*) stayed intact, together with the joint consumption and the sharing of these delicacies during celebrations. The stories of *Camila* and *Delia* underscored that importance.

Camila never made Dominican food, but ordered a HelloFresh box (a meal subscription service that delivers ingredients for recipes) every week. However, for Easter, she maintained the custom of eating *habichuela con dulce* together with Dominican friends at the home of the friend who prepared it.

Delia, born in Mao Valverde in El Cibao region, came to the Netherlands when she was 31. She had married a Dutch man and came to the Netherlands seeking a better future for her children. She visited the Dominican Republic regularly, not least because her mother still lived there. However, she would not want to live there anymore, finding it too dangerous and feeling that the Dominican Republic she left does not exist anymore. She said that Dominican food had no particular importance in her life. She liked all kinds food including typical Dutch food. However, when I entered her home on Easter, I felt I had been transported to the Dominican Republic. On her doorstep, I was already met by the sounds of *merengue tipico* and smells of Dominican seasoning. I was invited that day to get to know *habichuela con dulce*. I got seated at the big dining table, where I was served my first bowl of *habichuela con dulce*, with the mandatory biscuit, which was of course 'not as good as the Dominican one' (Fig. 3). After some talking about *Delia's* migration to the Netherlands and her experiences, dinner was served. We ate white rice, stewed pigeon peas, roast chicken, fried plantains, avocado and cabbage, tomato and cucumber salad; on the side was some Surinamese *sambal*.

Fig. 3. *Habichuela con dulce* With a Dutch Biscuit.

84 Post-Migration Experiences, Cultural Practices and Homemaking

Again relating these practices to Rabikowska's (2010) categorization, I found that the Dominicans in my research fall into another category altogether. This would be an additional category of persons who are not only fully open to practices from other cultures, but who in a way reject practices from their country of origin.

4.4 Explaining Dominicans' Attitude Towards Dominican Food

What was I thinking when I started this research? That Dominicans with a lower levels of formal education would be more attached to Dominican social and cultural practices and that people with higher levels of formal education would be more open to other practices. I also thought that people who come from poor neighborhoods in the Dominican Republic would be more attached to their cultural and social practices.

This quote is an excerpt from my fieldwork notes and shows my reflections about cosmopolitanism and social class. When starting this research, I suspected that differences in immigrants' attachment to social and cultural practices of their country of origin could be explained by their economic situation in the country of origin. I hypothesized that immigrants from poor backgrounds, with low education levels and who were forced to leave their country, for economic reasons or otherwise, would be more attached to their country of origin and its practices and be less cosmopolitan. This idea was fed by literature about immigrants' economic status in relation to openness towards other cultures – cosmopolitanism. The ability to switch from one cultural milieu to another has long been associated with elite ways of life (Pécoud, 2004). According to Friedman (1997), immigrant intellectuals are able to adopt multiple cultural identifications, and 'working class fellows' are not concerned by such discourses, being confined by their 'local ghetto identity'. True cosmopolitanism has been seen as only possible among the elite who have the ability to travel, learn other languages and absorb other cultures.

Applying this literature to an analysis of immigrant homemaking, category A should comprise of people who were forced to migrate for economic reasons, have low educational levels and few economic resources and therefore are strongly attached to practices from the Dominican Republic. By contrast, people for whom Dominican food was not a homemaking practice should have migrated out of free will, have higher educational levels and sufficient economic resources, which would foster their cosmopolitan tastes. But was this true for the Dominicans in my research? The stories pointed towards a more nuanced reality.

The idea of economic background as a determinant of cosmopolitanism is being challenged. Studies have documented non-elite migrant cosmopolitans and refer to them as ordinary cosmopolitans (Lamont & Aksartova, 2002) or working class cosmopolitans (Werbner, 1999), referring to migrants with low levels of formal education, but who are cosmopolitan. These studies show how

Meaning of Dominican Food **85**

non-elite immigrants use cosmopolitanism strategically to facilitate their work as street vendors (Kothari, 2008) or entrepreneurs (Pécoud, 2004). Kothari (2008) is very explicit in her criticism towards 'the largely Eurocentric, urban-centred and often elitist assumptions about who has the potential to be cosmopolitan and the characteristics that constitute a cosmopolitan sensibility' (p. 500). She finds that travel, production of cross-cultural interactions and sensitivities of poor migrants are never acknowledged as cosmopolitanism, but instead 'interpreted solely as a survival or livelihood strategy' (p. 501). Kothari demonstrates how adopting a cosmopolitan identity is indeed a resource and strategy required to survive in conditions of social and economic vulnerability, discrimination and exclusion. However, even if poor migrants use cosmopolitanism strategically – being cosmopolitan 'at work' and parochial 'at home' – these skills and talents are not necessarily acquired and used only as an economic strategy, but with time and in daily life cosmopolitan attitudes and behaviours can and do become embedded in the lives of non-elite migrants.

But, if differences in practices are not (only) outcomes of differences in economic characteristics, what factors can explain those differences? To be clear, the aim of my research was not to assess the relation between economic characteristics and homemaking, but to explore whether so-called deprived economic migrants really are more orientated towards their country of origin in making home.

The following section examines the various traits of Dominican immigrants in the Netherlands. I created two sets of factors to explore reasons for differentiation in immigrants' homemaking practices. I distinguish these factors as either migration-related characteristics (migration motive, length of residence, identity and orientation towards adaptation) and personal characteristics (education, income/occupation, intermarriage and pre-migration food traditions).

4.4.1 Dominicans' Economic Status and Unfamiliar Practices

Economic characteristics, migration motive and pre-migration traditions seem to influence the importance given to Dominican food practices. Economic characteristics refer to income, formal education and occupation. I asked no questions about income, believing it would be too intrusive, though used occupation as an indicator for income. Occupational backgrounds were diverse. The Dominicans in my research were government employees/diplomats, nannies, taxi drivers, managers, hotel employees and teachers in the Dominican Republic. In the Netherlands, they were diplomats; unemployed or in between jobs; logistic employees; managers; hairdressers; cleaners; small business owners handling clothing, photography, a fitness centre and a hair salon. Due to language barriers and 'diploma devaluation', a large share of Dominicans in my research were engaged in a type of occupation requiring a lower education level; for example, some who were teachers in the Dominican Republic were doing cleaning jobs in the Netherlands.

As mentioned earlier what is considered 'familiar' depends on the economic context one is from. The first thing that stood out is the fact that persons coming from middle- or high-income contexts mentioned that in the Dominican

86   Post-Migration Experiences, Cultural Practices and Homemaking

Republic they were already accustomed to consuming non-traditional Dominican food, referring to pasta and seafood. However, although Dominicans with high-income levels showed that they consumed a broader variety of foods in the Dominican Republic, this did not mean that after migration they were necessarily more open to 'new' foods. It is crucial to keep in mind the difference between the consumption of international foods before migration and openness to new cultural practices after migration. Dominicans from high-income contexts were not necessarily more open to typical Dutch food, for example. A second result was Dominicans' openness to non-Dominican food practices among those who climbed up the income ladder after migration. Migration brought not only more economic resources but also exposure to different kinds of food (which Dominicans coming from high-income contexts already had in the Dominican Republic). *Irvin* mentioned that having more economic resources meant that his family in the Netherlands could diversify their consumption:

> You know it is cheap, beans, rice, chicken. So in the Dominican Republic, for what you earn there, you are forced to eat that every day. But due to our current lifestyle and what we earn here, we can vary now. We do not need to eat the same every day anymore.

Burns (2004), in her research about Somali immigrants in Australia, also shows that migration from a low-income to a high-income country leads to increased income, which then leads to increased availability and range of products immigrants can purchase.

The level of education of Dominicans in my research varied from high school (which some did not complete) to PhD level, with high school and bachelor's degrees predominating. Data indicate that education level did influence attitudes towards Dominican food. Dominicans with lower levels (primary and high school) more often found Dominican food important in their lives. Respondents with higher levels (bachelor's, master's) also appreciated Dominican food, but more often said that they were also open to getting to know other cuisines and broadening their horizons.

Examining the relationship between migration motive and attitude towards Dominican food, I found that half of economically motivated migrants considered Dominican food important. For those who came to the Netherlands to broaden their horizons, Dominican food was important but not necessary. Almost one-third of the respondents came to the Netherlands because of a spouse, and for more than half of them, Dominican food remained important post-migration. The picture is thus mixed, and my findings do not fully correspond with Bonhomme's (2003) observation that migrants who migrate for economic reasons or who are forced to leave, stay more attached to the practices of their origins. However, my findings do show that all migrants who consciously chose migration as a mean to broaden their horizons were more open to adopting other cultural practices.

Pre-migration food traditions affected the attitude towards Dominican food after migration differently. *Mercedes'* and *Jorge's* stories show that food practices

Meaning of Dominican Food **87**

in the household where one grew up have a strong influence on post-migration food practices. *Mercedes* mentioned how her father always prepared different, sometimes Dominican-inspired dishes and that up until now she did not need them for homemaking:

> At my father's house, they would do some sort of a Dominican fried rice, *chofan*. But Dominican-style with the pork, and I used to love that, so that was the rice they would do and the *platano en caldera*. So it was like more, not 100% Dominican, there would always be something Dominican, like *tostones* always or *platano maduro frito* or *platano maduro en caldero*. But then with something that I would really like, like c*hofan* or pasta …. They were divorced since I was four. I always had two houses. My mother's house they would cook whatever, even if I did not like it, like Dominican, very Dominican, but in my dad's house it was always like: 'Oh let me see what you want eat today'. So I never, by choice, I never had the *arroz con habichuela*, I did not like it at all. But at my dad's house it was always chilli con carne, I used to love that. I do that lentil soup. We used to eat that a lot in my …. that are some of the things that I cook. Like one day, chilli con carne, one day, lentil soup and then simple pasta.

Jorge mentions how already being accustomed to Dutch, due to his mother's marriage to a Dutch man (his stepfather) affected his food practices in the Netherlands:

> If you have been raised 100% Dominican, yes. But my upbringing was not 100% Dominican, let's say half-half. In my house, we used to eat three times a week Dominican food and four times a week Dutch food. So, potatoes or *erwtensoep* [pea soup] or something like that is fine for me. I do not have any problems with that. For example, my father, if he does not have his warm meal at midday, he feels like he has not eaten; if you do not give him is rice, beans and meat and you give him just rice an meat, he feels that there is missing something, because there needs to be beans or pigeon peas or something like that.

Jorge's specific case resonates with what Fontefrancesco et al. (2019) have shown in their research about different cultural adaptation strategies *vis-à-vis* food from the country of origin. Their research shows that Albanian migrants in Italy were already accustomed to consuming Italian food in Albania and, as a result, consumed much more Italian food than Moroccans migrants in Italy.

Mercedes' and *Jorge*'s experiences also shine light on the difference between typical and familiar. Collins (2008) in his research about Korean immigrants' food practices after migration to Australia shows that people engage in familiar

88   Post-Migration Experiences, Cultural Practices and Homemaking

food practices, but that this familiarity does not always or only have to do with 'typical' practices from the country of origin. For example, South Koreans go to Korean restaurants and make and eat Korean food together, but they also go to Starbucks because they were used to going to Starbucks in Korea. Similarly, I distinguish between Dominican food and pre-migration food practices from the Dominican Republic. The latter does not necessarily refer to what has been considered 'typical' Dominican dishes. Thus, recreation of familiarity is not about re-creating pure national cuisine, but about recreation of everyday life as people knew it before migration (Collins, 2008). In this way, Collins (2008, p. 165) underscores that food in a post-migratory context is not always about 'culinary essentialism' – that is, re-creating 'a "pure" national cuisine connecting migrants to homelands'.

4.4.2 Intermarriage, Length of Residence, Identity and Adaption: No Correlations

Several studies show that the longer one stays in the host culture, the greater the occurrence of adopting the host culture's food practices (Mehta & Belk, 1991; Săseanu & Petrescu, 2010; Verbeke & Lopez, 2005). My study contradicts these findings. While the studies I am referring to involve larger data sets than my qualitative study, I believe that my Dominican case does give some indications. *Pedro*, for example, arrived in the 1980s and still preferred to eat Dominican food, while *Sofia* who had been in the Netherlands for five years had a preference for trying other cuisines. I found no correlation between length of residence and food practices. The findings show that Dominicans who lived in the Netherlands for more than 20 years still might prefer to eat Dominican food; on the other end of the spectrum, recently arrived Dominicans did not necessarily prefer to eat Dominican food.

Having a partner of a different cultural background may affect food practices, but not how much importance is ascribed to them. While partners could influence what is prepared and consumed, Dominicans with a non-Dominican partner did not find Dominican food less important in their lives. It remained important, but there were different ways of dealing with partners' preferences from non-adaptation to total adaptation. Some said that they adapted entirely to the partners' wishes, but cooked Dominican food on special occasions. *Eva* shared that her husband does not like too much seasoning as he is 'typically Dutch', her words. However, when her people come to visit, she cooks and then she cooks Dominican. *Monica* also adapted to her partner's wishes. She was born in Salcedo, in the northern part of the Dominican Republic, and left for Italy when she was 30. At 44, she decided to move to the Netherlands because of her partner, with whom she lived along with their daughter. She said she adapted to her husband's preferences and made Dutch food at home and also mentioned for that reason, never cooking on 24th December at home herself, but seeking a solution elsewhere, going to her friend's house. *Mateo* said that he would cook and eat Dominican food every day if it were just for himself, but being married to a Dutch woman made him adapt. The following quote shows the negotiations

Meaning of Dominican Food **89**

Mateo made in adjusting to life in the Netherlands and, as part of that, balancing his tastes and those of his wife and her children:

> After you arrive in a place where you do not have everything you want and where you have to deal with different kinds of people, you have to find balance. I am going to cook what I like, but I am also going to cook what you like. I think I am getting into a different routine now, and I also do not want to eat the same thing every day. I mean, in Santo Domingo, there is not as much variation in food as here ... But what can I tell you: I feel good here. I miss my customs, but I am getting accustomed. I need balance. I came, and found a Dutch family, and we need to balance the food, as well as the customs.

Rabikoskwa (2010) finds that having a partner from the host culture can make one accept food exchange from that culture. *Mateo's* specific case shows nuance: he accepted the exchange though would still rather eat Dominican food. His quote also revealed his attitude towards adapting to his new situation: he accepts it and makes the best of it. Yet another way of dealing with cultural food differences is not taking into account partners' preferences at all, as *Aurelia* noted:

> When my husband has this urge to eat his Dutch food, when he misses his delicious juicy food, let him go to [Dutch supermarket chain] Albert Hein and buy his little dish and heat it up in the microwave. That is how we solve this problem.

Contrary to many studies about homemaking and about immigrant food practices food was not related to the (re)production of identities; the two practices could be separated from each other. The majority of Dominicans identify as Dominican. However, how they identified culturally showed no correlation to whether they found Dominican food in daily life important or if they consumed/prepared it. *Bryan* said that Dominican food did not have importance in his daily life and he did not need it to feel at home nor any other Dominican cultural practices. However, he was undoubtedly Dominican, or to use a phrase Dominicans used, *Dominicano mil por mil*. In *Bryan's* own words about himself: 'Dominican, always, always. Nothing has changed. I feel at home here, but I will always be a Dominican, *mil por mil*'. *Claudette* was very engaged in promoting Dominican culture. One of her goals was to show the Netherlands more about Dominican culture through organizing cultural events. She expressed love for the Dominican Republic and all aspects of its culture, though did not have to have the food to feel at home:

> I do not need it. I like variety in gastronomy, that is really important for me. I have a way of cooking in which, with leftovers from yesterday or the day before, I make a better dish for the next day after tomorrow. So, I create my own recipes. For me, food is the most important thing in life, besides love .... I never separate myself from my roots, from my essence. I am Dominican, and I will always show that I am a Dominican wherever I am.

90   Post-Migration Experiences, Cultural Practices and Homemaking

Food practices may change due to an orientation towards adaptation to the receiving society. Fontefrancesco et al.' (2019) observed that that migrants who tended towards cultural adaptation were more open to the receiving society's food practices, whereas migrants who were trying to preserve their traditions are less open. However, my research shows that the reality is more differentiated. Every Dominican I interviewed found adapting to the Netherlands important. Their answers ranged from the value of learning the Dutch language to embracing the attitude of adapting wherever you are and from equating adaptation with progress to fully maintaining Dominican culture. However, with regard to maintaining Dominican food practices there is differentiation. Some specifically mentioned preserving Dominican culture in their lives, but did not necessarily give importance to the food. In the group who stressed adaptation to Dutch society there were some who adapted their food practices, while others still found Dominican food important. *Isabel* revealed how an orientation towards adaptation to the receiving society was expressed in food practices. She expressed missing the Dominican Republic every day, but also appreciated the opportunities for progress the Netherlands offered, even if getting one of her favourite food products in the Netherlands was difficult:

> For example, salami, this was a problem. I had to bring salami from the Dominican Republic to here. Or buy it via someone who came back from a holiday there, buying it expensive. Until I discovered a salami that is sold in Venserpolder. Everything is question of adaptation, to be aware: I am not in Santo Domingo. For example, hair products, they really need to be from there .... I adapt and accept where I am. You are now here, and you have to learn the language, for example. Even if I do not agree with some things here, I have to adapt.

Isabel's story reveals the importance she attaches to adaptation and accepting the salami from a shop in Venserpolder, a neighbourhood in Amsterdam Zuidoost, was part of adapting.

However, orientation towards adaptation was not always expressed in a positive attitude towards typical Dutch food practices. This often had to do with taste. *Camila*, for example, stressed the importance of learning the language and hanging out with Dutch people to progress in Dutch society, but she did not like Dutch food. She said she could eat it, but it was not her favourite simply because she disliked the taste. She also mentioned being open to other cuisines other than Dominican. *Aurelia* attributed importance to learning the language and how to live without things you miss, instead staying in the present wherever she was. This, however, was not expressed in making Dutch food, though she liked other cuisines. Similarly, *Sandra* found it important to learn Dutch and to always adapt to where she was, but did not express that in an appreciation for eating or making Dutch food.

4.5 Conclusion: Cultural Practices and Feelings of Home

Homemaking literature shows mainly how immigrants recreate practices from their countries of origin, which then evoke feelings of home, primarily feelings of familiarity and connectedness to the country of origin. What remained under-researched

Meaning of Dominican Food   **91**

are immigrants and their practices that are not directed towards the country of origin. I examined this chapter's principal question – *Do cultural from the country of origin constitute feelings of home in the receiving society?* – by studying Dominicans' relationship with food from the Dominican Republic and its meaning.

I used Rabikowska's (2008) categorization as a point of departure to explore this relationship. The exploration leads to a categorization of homemakers, which shows (1) the different relationships with Dominican food practices; (2) the differentiated feelings these food practices evoke; and (3) what makes Dominican food a homemaking practice. The findings show three orientations of Dominicans towards Dominican food. For respondents in category A Dominican food was a homemaking practice, evoking feelings of home, like human warmth, sense of community and connection to the Dominican Republic. However, they do not resemble Rabokowksa's orthodox rituals. Practices of those in category A showed rather similarities to Rabikowska's porous rituals: the respondents preferred Dominican food and at the same time were open to other food. Respondents in category B found Dominican food important, but did not need it in daily life. For them, feelings of home related to broadening horizons, which led to consuming different foods. The results of my research produced another category: those who did not find food from the country of origin important. Respondents in category C did not attach value to Dominican food; it had no specific meaning for them, and when consumed, it was out of habit or custom. Some even consumed it very often, showing that frequency of consumption is not necessarily a reflection of being a homemaking practice. An interesting finding was that for celebrations and festivities, Dominican food was important for all categories.

The categorization shows that immigrant practices are not only orientated towards the country of origin, as the majority of homemaking studies tend to show, but that there can also be orientations towards the receiving society or both the country of origin and the receiving society. It is important to take into account that while basic patterns can be distinguished, the categorization emerging from the data is not strict, but fluid. The fluidness is exemplified by the case of *Mercedes*, who liked to try a lot different cuisines (she still appreciated Dominican food, placing her in category B), but maintained the custom of eating a warm meal at midday and would travel throughout the Netherlands to get quality plantains or avocados.

Part of exploring these variations in practices also meant exploring the reason behind the variation. This exploration revealed how identity, intermarriage, length of residence and orientation towards adaption do not influence practices, but education level, income/occupation, pre-migration household traditions and migration motives do influence them. Thus can we conclude that lower-educated, lower-income immigrants, who were forced to migrate for economic reasons were more attached to Dominican food practices? No, but two points stand out. Firstly, immigrants with higher formal education levels did make more conscious choices about food, which could lead to less consumption of Dominican food. Secondly, Dominicans with lower formal education or income levels showed interest in new foods after migration precisely because they did not know or were not exposed to these foods prior to migration. Migration and more economic resources allowed them therefore to consume a broader variety of foods.

Chapter 5

Habichuela con Dulce and *Noche Buena*: The Role of Dominican Co-ethnics in Homemaking

5.1 Introduction

> I bring the sauce for the roasted pig
> I come with happy vibes my dear
> Christmas Eve arrived and we need to celebrate
> Forget your sorrow my brother and come dance
> I bring the sauce for the roasted pig
> I come with happy vibes my dear
> We shall eat roasted pig
> *Pasteles en hoja* my friend and a good stew
> Let the party begin
>
> (Translated by the author)

In his song 'Salsa pa' tu lechon' Johnny Ventura sings about Christmas Eve and how this night will be celebrated in a typical Dominican manner: with lots of music, dance and food. But how do Dominicans celebrate special occasions after migration? Building further on the idea that immigrant practices 'are never developed in isolation as a result of exclusively individual experiences and memories' (Parasecoli, 2014, p. 419) but are enriched by the opportunities provided by others who share the same background (Abbots, 2016), this chapter shows how immigrants' practices are embedded in co-ethnic structures and opportunities. Co-ethnics in my research refer to people with the same country of origin living in a new receiving society. As mentioned earlier, I do not assume homogeneity and acknowledge possible differences in terms of educational background, income, region and ethnicity, affecting their relationships with the Dominican Republic and cultural and social practices. However, I am interested in how a shared country of origin is related to engagement in cultural practiced and the creation of home post-migration.

Post-Migration Experiences, Cultural Practices and Homemaking:
An Ethnography of Dominican Migration to Europe, 93–117
Copyright © 2023 by Sabrina Dinmohamed
Published under exclusive licence by Emerald Publishing Limited
doi:10.1108/978-1-83753-204-920231005

94 *Post-Migration Experiences, Cultural Practices and Homemaking*

Immigrant homemaking studies mention how the presence of co-ethnics facilitates material practices (access to products, objects, ethnic clothing) (Philipp & Ho, 2010; Wiles, 2008) and social practices such as familiar ways of socializing or re-creating familiar activities from the country of origin (Boccagni, 2013; Hondagneu-Sotelo, 2017; Meijering & Lager, 2014). However, it remains unclear how opportunities provided by co-ethnics evoke feelings of home. Moreover, we do not know which home feelings these practices evoke. This leads to the following principal question guiding this chapter: *How do co-ethnics and the opportunities they provide affect cultural practices and feelings of home?* This chapter argues that a co-ethnic community not only facilitates the recreation of material and social practices, but that this recreation also cements the bonds. The recreation of these practices, furthermore, not only occurs in the private sphere of the home, but also in communal spaces, which are experienced differently by members of the same ethnic community.

I take several steps to show this. Firstly, I explore what the presence of co-ethnics means with regard to feelings of home. Doing so, I keep in mind that immigrant groups are not only internally heterogeneous but also they themselves have opinions about their compatriots. Scandone's (2018) strategies of distinctions ('hanging on to hierarchies of value' and 'self-distancing') within ethnic communities come in handy to indicate the dynamics. Second, I explore the food-related opportunities co-ethnics offer and how they are related to feelings of home, while distinguishing between opportunities in the domestic as well as communal spaces. In the former, I distinguish between material practices (ingredients and products) and social practices (commensality and celebrations). Outside the domestic space, in communal spaces, grocery stores, for example, provide ingredients, but are also important places which enable a reconstruction of the country of origin and identity (Mankekar, 2002; Philipp & Ho, 2010; Sandu, 2013).

The first section describes Dominicans' feelings of home in relation to co-ethnics. As such, it provides an entry point into understanding the different attachments to and functions of the community. The second shows how co-ethnics provide opportunities to keep familiar Dominican food practices alive and, in so doing, play a role in making home. The third focuses on food institutions in communal space such as restaurants and grocery stores, and how these institutions evoke different kinds of home feelings or none at all. The last section reflects upon how co-ethnics and the opportunities they provide affect practices and feelings of home.

5.2 Feelings of Home in the Dutch-Dominican Community

This section describes how other Dominicans evoke feelings of home as well as the divisions within the community. With regard to the latter Scandone (2018) shows two strategies of distinctions within ethnic communities: hanging onto hierarchies of value and self-distancing. The first refers to retaining ethnic and class stereotypes and taking a contraposition *vis-á-vis* a certain segment of the co-ethnic community. The second refers to distancing oneself altogether from the co-ethnic community and adopting cultural features of

Habichuela con Dulce *and* Noche Buena   **95**

the dominant society. While there are several gradations in between, this distinction is a starting point for exposing differentiation and dynamics within ethnic communities.

5.2.1 *I Need Other Dominicans to Feel Good*

Co-ethnics enable immigrants to recreate social activities and forms of recreation they were used to in their country of origin (Hondagneu-Sotelo, 2017; Meijering & Lager, 2014). *Arturo* mentions that he likes his life in the Netherlands and that spending time with other Dominicans contributed to that as it provided feelings of familiarity, belonging and a sense of comfort. Their presence enabled the practice of activities from the Dominican Republic or carrying out activities in a 'Dominican way'. He finds home in a Dominican initiative La Comparsa Sabor Dominicano, which promotes Dominican culture. He mentioned that it consists of marvellous persons, persons who have been living in the Netherlands for many years. For the last couple of months he spent lots of time with them and he mentions that it has been a great relief for him. He has difficulties getting accustomed to life in the Netherlands, but thanks to them he has had some pleasant moments and he feels that he is part of a family. The preparing of food together, their way of talking, the stories, the jokes – typical Dominican expressions with double meanings; it all helps to feel better so far away from everything that is familiar. He says 'they are good people, they treat you well, they are honest people and because of them, I have had some great moments. I thank God (*le doy gracias a Dios*)'.

    Arturo's story shows that co-ethnics not only contribute to the recreation of familiar practices but they also enable immigrants to inhibit space and time in a familiar way (Boccagni, 2013). Chapter 3 showed how Dominicans perceive the Dutch as being individualistic and how this individualism is a trait that Dominicans mention struggling with in the Netherlands. The individualistic lifestyle is cited as a constraint to feeling at home and making a home. Individualism in the Netherlands is tied to closedness, lack of contact with neighbours and lack of togetherness. This togetherness has been defined by Dominicans in my research as 'hanging out' with friends and family: not doing something in particular, but 'just' being together. *Analisa* had been living in the Netherlands since 1986 and was active in Dominican social and cultural events and like *Arturo* was part of La Comparsa Sabor Dominicano. Asked whether it was important for her to maintain contact with other Dominicans to feel good, she said that she experienced the Netherlands as a very solitary country. Other Dominicans used words such as *deprimente de naturaleza* ('depressing by nature') or *un país muy triste* ('a very sad country'). Engaging with other Dominicans helped *Analisa* counter feelings of loneliness. Her words also reveal her perception of the Dutch as individualistic and Dominicans as very sociable:

> It is not obligatory, but it helps, to stay in contact with people, because this is a real lonely country (*un país muy solo*). For them [the Dutch] not, because they are like that, but we are not. We

96   Post-Migration Experiences, Cultural Practices and Homemaking

are very much together, very together. I have never been without Dominicans, I always have had friends, I have always been surrounded by Dominicans.

Being with other Dominicans furthermore provided the opportunity to share migration experiences. Co-ethnics can understand where their compatriots are from and what they are going through, including the 'highs and lows' of migration and life in the Netherlands, as some mention.

The centrality for Dominicans of spending time together, in a Dominican way, came to the fore in the Christmas celebration of the Dominican radio broadcasting station in Amsterdam. *Pedro*, who set up the broadcasting station, had already invited me in October to first come to his house to eat and afterwards go to *la radio*, where his radio programme started at 7 p.m. It was a cold and misty December afternoon when I picked up my mother, who came to appreciate the Dominican atmosphere and food through my extensive involvement in the community, to go to *Pedro*'s house. When *Pedro* opened the door he greets us with hugs and kisses. In my round of greeting everybody inside I also entered the kitchen and see two women washing meat in the sink and lots of *guandules* on the kitchen counter. On the menu today is: *moro de guandules, pollo guisado* and carne de *cerdo guisado*.

In the meantime, the guests in the living room, other Dominicans and a Dutch man, were chatting with each other while the television channel was set on a World Cup soccer game, Morocco-Portugal. The television was muted and on the background a radio broadcasting station from the Dominican Republic was playing salsa, merengue and bachata. Then the discussion arose about why some Moroccans in the Netherlands have chosen to play for the Moroccan team instead of the Dutch one. The opinions were divided: one Dominican man and the Dutch man believe that they are Dutch and should be loyal to the Dutch team. The others believed differently and one Dominican had clear ideas regarding this matter: 'no matter which nationality you hold, you always feel connected to where you are originally from. Not the least because we are also not considered Dutch by the Dutch'!

Then we heard: 'food is ready!'. *Pedro* invited us to the kitchen to serve ourselves. The kitchen table was full of food. Two pots with meat, one pot with *moro de guandules*, one plate with *ensalada rusa* and one with green salad. The approximately 30 guests started to stand in line. While eating, my mother, a Surinamese woman who has been living in the Netherlands for over 50 years, mentioned how this gathering reminded her of family gatherings in Suriname: everybody busy cooking, talking, cheerfulness. At the same time she recognized the closeness of friends (as if they are family) from the time she had just arrived in the Netherlands from Suriname. Not having family members in the Netherlands, she and my father created tight bonds with others from the Surinamese community, with whom they could 'be together in a Surinam way': eat Surinamese food, listen to Surinamese music and dance to Caribbean sounds.

After having reassured that everybody had eaten more than enough, coffee was served by *Pedro*. Then suddenly it is almost 7 p.m. and we needed to go *la*

Habichuela con Dulce *and* Noche Buena   **97**

radio. Arrangements were made to make sure that this whole group of people arrives there. We arrived at the radio and the place had been transformed (the day before) from a common radio station interior to a cosy little disco with lots of Christmas lights. Chairs were arranged, everybody sat down, the radio programme started. Somewhere on the side the dance floor was created. I saw people dancing, laughing, making jokes and hugging each other.

It was freezing outside, but here it was warm, with cheerfulness, *ambiente*, food and drinks. I recognized this scene from somewhere – oh yes, from all the times I have been to the Dominican Republic.

Dominican co-ethnics thus fulfil several roles. They are considered providers of a warm haven (a sort of social refuge), partners in countering feelings of loneliness and fellow migrants with similar migration experiences. Being with other Dominicans permitted recreation of activities they were used to in the Dominican Republic and inhabit space and time in a Dominican manner, which evoked several feelings such as nostalgia, familiarity and human warmth.

5.2.2 'I Am Not Like Those Other Dominicans'

While many miss being together, not all have the desire to look up other Dominicans. There was a certain kind of perceived homogeneity by some Dominicans with regard to 'other' Dominicans from whom they self-distanced. This finding recalls the process Scandone (2018) describes where immigrants hang on to stereotypes about their own community and take a contraposition towards a segment of the co-ethnic community. Many seemingly saw one type of Dominican and/or they looked through the eyes of others whom they think see one type of Dominican. Many said: 'I am not like those other Dominicans'. Speaking to me as a researcher, some would say: 'I am not like the other Dominicans you have met', as if they knew whom I had met and what I thought about them.

The stories revealed a differentiation in outlook along lines of economic background. *Rafael* was sent by the Dominican government to work at the Dominican consulate. Prior to the Netherlands, he lived in New York, where there is a big Dominican community comprising almost one million Dominicans. Unlike in the Netherlands, he felt at home there. One of the reasons was the existence of a more heterogeneous Dominican community consisting of people from different Dominican regions and socio-economic backgrounds. He explains his hypothesis about the differences between the Dominican community in the Netherlands and the United States:

> I have a hypothesis about the United States. The majority of the people in the United States come from El Cibao due to economic and political reasons. And here [the Netherlands], the majority is from the south. People from El Cibao are farmers, very productive. When I arrived here, I was shocked a little bit because the New York community is very advanced. There are doctors, lawyers, there are all kinds of professionals over there. The food market is

98 Post-Migration Experiences, Cultural Practices and Homemaking

dominated by Dominicans, the bodegas, the supermarkets, almost all are Dominican. And here, the only type of stable businesses are beauty salons [owned by] a woman married to a Dutch man. I tell you, the people, the way they socialize, is different. It is like a marginalized neighbourhood in Santo Domingo. They reproduce the behaviour of these neighbourhoods here. This is why it was difficult for me to adapt. I went to visit the Dominican community, but sporadically …. In the United States, you have all social, educational and economic levels. Here the majority or the core pertains to the working class or the unemployed, social-benefits people. So the needs and priorities of these kinds of people are different. Also, people from El Cibao are white. The majority in the Netherlands is brown (*morenitos*).

Rafael's story reflects a differentiation of Dominicans by social class, regional descent and skin colour. Mostly, he focused on the lack of variation in education level and occupation type, which recalls Slootman's (2014) finding about university-educated people of Moroccan and Turkish descent in the Netherlands. Highly educated Moroccans and Turks in the Netherlands felt more connected to other highly educated co-ethics. The lack of diversity in types of Dominicans in the Netherlands caused *Rafael* to not socialize with Dominicans because he felt many did not share his values and beliefs. Therefore, he chose to socialize in a neutral setting (*ambiente neutral*).

Other mentioned attitude towards progress as something differentiating them from 'those' other Dominicans. *Camila* stressed the importance of personal progress, which she has not observed in most Dominicans in the Netherlands. She came to the Netherlands in 2008 after falling in love with and marrying a Dutch man. In the Dominican Republic, she did a bachelor's degree in advertising and worked as a radio and television producer. In the Netherlands, she worked as an independent photographer. Asked whether she needed contact with Dominicans to feel good, she replied that Dominicans in the Netherlands are different from those she would socialize with in the Dominican Republic. *Camila*'s story shows that being from the same country was not to base a friendship on:

I think that most Dominicans who have come here, are from a very low …. [did not complete sentence]. They are not the kind of people whom I would call my friend and would sit down with in the weekends for a cup of coffee. Being Dominican is not sufficient. But it is not that I would never do that, I mean, I can hang out with everybody. But I do not have time, I want to move on, I do not want to go back, you know what I mean? And that's with everything in life. Not only Dominicans. It is about people who are not positive or do not want to grow. And if you only hang out with those kinds of people, you also will stay there.

Habichuela con Dulce *and* Noche Buena   **99**

Bryan's view on adaptation underscored *Camila*'s. For a long time, he would only hang out with Dominicans, but then decided that he wanted to grow and chose to hang out less with Dominicans. But for him, progressing did not necessarily mean losing his culture. He mentioned that he has good Dominican friends and that his girlfriend is also Dominican. He finds that the majority of Dominicans in the Netherlands do not absorb the good things. He expresses his lack of understanding for people who come from a tough situation in the country they left behind and after migration do not make the effort to progress. He attributes that to the fact that life in the Netherlands s easy:

> They make life easy for you over here. They give you money. They see that things are easy here, so they do not have to change their mentality and lifestyle. So, they do not adapt, thinking that when you adapt to a country, you will lose your culture. But it is not like that. Look, I used to walk around with my sunglasses and chain on. People see you in a different way and doors close for you.

Bryan's story reveals several points: his ideas about the perceived fear of Dominicans losing their culture if they adopt a more future-orientated lifestyle; the fact that the Netherlands makes it easy to maintain this attitude; and his own efforts to change.

Yasmin expressed a duality about co-ethnics. She came to the Netherlands in 2010 at age 33. She finished a degree in industrial engineering studies at the Universidad Autonoma de Santo Domingo and worked as a shop manager in one of the Santo Domingo's largest malls. Asked whether contact with other Dominicans was important for her to feel at home, she answered that it helps once in a while to be in contact with other Dominicans. It helps in post-migration life: it is important and it creates balance in her life here, a life of a Dominican abroad. According to *Yasmin* there is no such person who does not want to be with their own people. And she mentions: 'Even if you do not like to be with them all the time, you still miss them. You cannot remove that feeling from yourself; it is human'. However, her words also reveal an ambivalence towards other Dominicans. Similar to *Camila*, the Dominicans she met in the Netherlands are not ones she would hang out with. She finds most Dominicans in the Netherlands superficial, materialistic and lacking progress. She attributed the differences between her and the majority of the Dominicans she meets to educational level, culture and lifestyle:

> Yes, there are Dominicans here [in Delft]. But unfortunately, most of the Dominicans who migrate are not the ones I would like to invite into my home. I do not want to sound negative, but they are not the Dominicans I would normally hang out with in Santo Domingo. It does not necessarily has to do with where you have lived, but with educational level, culture, lifestyle .... No, we do not attract each other. In general, the younger ones, they are busy

100　Post-Migration Experiences, Cultural Practices and Homemaking

> with other things. We do not deal with each other .... There is one of whom I think: yes, with you I can talk about normal things. We do not talk about the latest shoes we bought, do I go on holiday to Santo Domingo bringing boots or not, because I have to show that I am from abroad. Damn, I have to go to the hair salon. You are gone 20 years, living in another country and you still have this chip from Santo Domingo in your head, hello! This not specifically Dominican. It also occurs in other immigrant communities, Turkish, Surinamese.

Camila's, *Bryan*'s and *Yamin*'s words made me wonder about successful migration and its relation to 'progress'. Progress for them seems to be about achieving a better economic status, being open to other cultures and participating in different spheres of the receiving society. Then migration could be considered successful. However, what progress and successful migration are might be more nuanced; migration motive and maybe even the level of poverty in the pre-migration context should be taken into account. Graziano (2013) mentions that the goal for most poor Dominicans is not to climb socially but rather to live more comfortably post-migration and being able to provide for basic needs like shelter and food. He mentions that (in the case of Dominicans in Puerto Rico) it is about the search of basic economic stability. It is not about the 'American dream', but

> they are motivated more by a Dominican dream: the alleviation of the struggle for subsistence, acquisition of a decent home, improvement of the situation for the next generation and a modest share of disposable income for functional and luxury consumer goods. (Graziano, 2012, p. 14)

This search for basic economic stability might also be applied on segment of the Dominican community in the Netherlands; this same segment who is being considered by other Dominicans as not wanting to 'progress'. Progress seems to have a different definition for them. A distinction should also be made between progress in the receiving society or the country of origin. Oso Casas (2009), in her study about social mobility of female Dominican migrants in Spain, mentions that whereas these women might suffer downward mobility (due to working beneath their educational level or labour sector), their remittances would lead to social mobility for family members in the Dominican Republic.

In Chapter 3, I showed how many Dominicans, like *Valentina* and *Marcos*, appreciate contacts with co-ethnics to counter the individualistic lifestyle in the Netherlands, but are at the same time-selective. *Marcos* elaborated on differences in lifestyle and mentioned different ways to reach goals. He came to the Netherlands to seek a better future. He said it was really important to socialize with fellow Dominicans and being together provided feelings of warmth. However, he also cited a conscious choice not to hang out with certain people because of their

Habichuela con Dulce *and* Noche Buena   *101*

choices. While his story reflects his choosiness about friendships, it also reflects his respect for other lifestyles:

> They have another lifestyle than I have. Their perspective is different than mine; it is not the same vision. We do not walk the same path. And if we do walk the same path, we do not use the same methods. Yes, we share the music and the food. But the train they use to reach their goals is not the same as mine. Maybe they use the Intercity [fast train], and I a Sprinter [slower train with more stops]. I take the Sprinter, enjoy the view and, when I want to go back, I take another one. I prefer my Sprinter. I have come to know a lot of people since I arrived here, but they are not my friends. They see me and we greet each other.

5.2.3 We From Rotterdam Are Serious Dominicans

Two other forms of differentiation also concerned lifestyle, originating in differences based on place of residence and migration trajectory. Some respondents noticed a difference between Dominicans living in Amsterdam and Rotterdam. *Francisco*, who lived in Rotterdam, tells that when you compare those who live in Amsterdam with those who live in The Hague or in Rotterdam, you will notice that they behave differently. He mentions that when you are in Amsterdam and you go to Picalonga, it is full of Dominicans playing bingo, but that the Dominicans in Rotterdam are serious: they go out at night, but work during the day. *Francisco* shows how Dominicans in Rotterdam were perceived not only as hardworking but also as having more style. *Rafael's* and *Sandra's* stories suggest that Dominicans in Rotterdam are more united and organized, while those in Amsterdam are ready to party but less interested in cultural activities:

> I feel that those in Rotterdam are more motivated to organize themselves, participate as a group, carry out activities within the community. Here [in Amsterdam] they are more individualistic; people tend to isolates themselves. For example, last week we celebrated Independence Day. It was a family-like atmosphere. There were children and families. I mean, there was no alcohol, the bling bling and the showing off. It was beautiful. You do not see that in Amsterdam. – *Rafael*

> Yes, I have heard from people in Amsterdam that things are different there. As an organizer of Dominican events, I am happy with the response we get here. If you organize the same kind of event in Amsterdam, the room would be empty. Here [in Rotterdam] people crave their culture. Going to a bar, dancing and eating are different than going to a cultural event. A different

102 Post-Migration Experiences, Cultural Practices and Homemaking

atmosphere. Sometimes we go as a group to activities in Amsterdam. Those from Amsterdam do not respond to activities like those from here. – Sandra

The second form of differentiation related to lifestyle was migration trajectory. Respondents expressed opinions about those who arrived directly from the Dominican Republic, via the Dutch Caribbean islands or via Spain. Dominicans who came to the Netherlands from Spain were seen as lacking manners and education. *Carlos* characterized them as people from marginalized neighbourhoods, without education, without basic concepts of culture. He mentions that in Spain they have the same needs they had in Santo Domingo. In the Netherlands, however, things are different because the Netherlands is a rich country and everybody has access to education and food. In *Carlos'* view, these Dominicans from lower walks of life had not progressed much post-migration nor had the chance to. *Victor* emphasized how Dominicans who arrived in the Netherlands via Spain overestimated their knowledge of Europe. *Victor*, just like *Carlos*, said that Dominicans in Spain live a similar life to that of life in the Dominican Republic and that settling in the Netherlands was a much bigger effort than expected:

Look at those people from Spain who come here. They think that they also come from a European country, so it will be easier to integrate. Nonsense, because Spain is actually also a bit of a third-world country. And the language is also very different .... so there is not a very big difference, because they simply lived in Spain the way they lived in the Dominican Republic.

I also observed differentiation in the opinions about Dominicans who came via Curaçao. *Francisco*, who had lived in Curaçao for many years before coming to the Netherlands, compared them with those who came directly from the Dominican Republic:

We can divide the Dominicans in the Netherlands in two groups. Those who came via the Antilles, thus Curaçao, Aruba and Bonaire. The majority in the Netherlands come from there. Then the ones who came here via Spain or directly without knowing the Antilles. We Dominicans who came via the Antilles, we feel that we are Dutch, we have a Dutch passport and we come here and get the same treatment as those with a Dutch passport who were born in Curaçao, Aruba and Bonaire. We come here thus like the owner of the house, because we are at home. We know a little bit about Dutch culture, we are familiar with it. Dominicans who come directly from the Dominican Republic arrive here without a parachute BAM!

Francisco's quote, which he punctuated with the sound of a crash landing, shows how it can be easier for those who lived in the Dutch Caribbean to adapt to

Habichuela con Dulce *and* Noche Buena   *103*

the Netherlands because they have already come into contact with Dutch structural and cultural elements there. Others mentioned that those who have lived in Curaçao and then migrated to the Netherlands did so for the country's social services. *Sandra's* story highlights different perspectives on progress and work ethic between the three Dominican groups. Again, the Dominican Republic and Spain seem to be considered similar not only because of a shared language but also because of social and economic context. *Sandra* described the three groups as follows:

> Everybody comes with a different rucksack. For example, those who come from Curaçao come for the social benefits. They say: 'I am tired of working in Curaçao. I am going to live in the Netherlands for free'. They have worked hard in Curaçao and now want to go to rest in the Netherlands. Those who come directly [from the Dominican Republic] come with a hunger to work, to study, because there they did not have the opportunity and now they want to grow. Those who come from Spain also. Very different from those come via the Antilles, they come to sit here and do nothing, regrettably.

Now that I have given a glimpse into internal dynamics in the Dutch-Dominican community, it became clear that I cannot speak of *the* Dominican community in the Netherlands or similar needs and expectations. In the next sections I look to how these dynamics are translated into food practices in domestic sphere and communal sphere.

5.3 Food Practices, Business Opportunities and Dominican Sociability

5.3.1 The Story of Ingredients: Business Opportunities and Recreation of Authentic Taste

> Plantains, avocado, in the 1990s, it was really difficult to get these ingredients. Do you know what's *verdura*? They did not sell *verdura* here. I remember that in these times when prostitution was booming, there were a lot of Dominican women in Nieuwmarkt. And there they start selling products. Those prostitutes brought them and sold them here.

Isabel's quote reflects a time when Dominicans had just a small presence in the Netherlands and co-ethnics were essential for getting Dominican ingredients. Her story not only shows the importance of the Dutch-Dominican community for obtaining products but also of transnational relations maintained through, in this case, women working in Amsterdam's Red Light District who often travelled to the Dominican Republic.

104 Post-Migration Experiences, Cultural Practices and Homemaking

In the past, Dominicans found different ways to get their products. One way was via holidays. After a visit to the Dominican Republic, Dominicans would bring suitcases full of products into the Netherlands. Travelling to Spain was a second way. Due to the large concentration of Dominicans in Spain, it was easy to obtain products there and Dominicans living in the Netherlands would bring everything they needed back. *Leydi*'s story shows that the scarcity of products in the Netherlands became a business opportunity for some Dominicans travelling frequently to Spain, as Dominicans living in the Netherlands would pay them a small fee to bring back ingredients and products. As *Leydi* recalled:

> There are a lot of South Americans in Spain, so they sell a lot. So when you go to Spain, you think: 'I want this and this and I can buy it there'. ... So a lot of people went from here to there, bought what they needed and brought it here. Or you could order via people who were going on a holiday, who then bring you the things you need, for a small commission.

A third way was through frequent travellers to the Dominican Republic who would bring back ingredients for others in the Netherlands. An interesting phenomenon was the Dominican prostitutes who would do this. *Isabel*'s quote in this section's introduction showed how difficult it was in the 1990s to obtain ingredients and how prostitutes who travelled frequently to the Dominican Republic brought ingredients and sold these to other Dominicans. There still is a large number of Dominican prostitutes who work in Amsterdam's Red Light District.

Dominican prostitutes in the Netherlands are a reflection of the ties between the Dominican Republic and the Dutch Caribbean islands, as described in the previous chapters. Since the 1970s, there has been an increase of Latin-American and Caribbean women in the Netherlands' sex sector. Of the 25,000–30,000 women working in this sector nowadays, it is believed that half are immigrants and 5,000–7,000 are from Latin America and the Caribbean (Barajas Sandoval, 2008). As discussed in Chapter 2 many Dominican prostitutes got to know the Netherlands from their time spent in Curaçao, where many Dominican women also work in the sex industry. The women have a pattern of circular migration, where they spent, for example, eight to nine months working and a period of two or three months back in the Dominican Republic during Christmas time, to rest, to be together with family (Janssen, 2007).

On a local level, it became easier to find products due to the presence of other immigrant communities and their need for similar products. In Chapter 6 on food practices and the characteristics of the Dutch society, relationships with other immigrant communities will be elaborated upon. However, ingredients directly from the Dominican Republic were still considered to be of better quality and tastier. As a consequence, Dominican immigrants kept bringing ingredients back to the Netherlands after their holidays. They brought back Dominican salami, biscuits, Dominican seasoning in bottles by the Dominican brand Baldom (*sazon completo, sazon criollo*), oregano, Dominican cilantro and coffee. Several studies have traced the practice of bringing food from a country of origin despite

Habichuela con Dulce *and* Noche Buena   *105*

availability of the products in the receiving society (Christou & Janta, 2018; Fontefrancesco et al., 2019) and all show how quality and tastiness are reasons for keeping up the circulation. *Sandra*, living in the southern part of Rotterdam, where ingredients can be readily found, she would still take a 'supermarket' back when she returns from a holiday in the Dominican Republic. Good prices and freshness products are main reasons:

> I bring *mama gallina*, oregano, I bring my salami, I bring *bija*, I bring tamarind, fresh *guandules*. It is fresh and cheaper. For example, here you see the cans of *guandules*, but there you see the fresh ones, things like that. And then you think: I cannot go back without *guandules*. All those seasonings you have there. Once a Colombian friend told me: 'But you bring a supermarket back every time you go'.

Others mention another important point: only products from the Dominican Republic create an authentic taste. They bring back bags of oregano because 'without this Dominican oregano, the food does not come out Dominican'.

The stories about ingredients show how other Dominicans facilitate the recreation of familiar cultural practices and consequently feelings of home. The stories echo other studies that describe how transnational space and relations offer opportunities to get hold of commodities from the country of origin, in this case ingredients (Christou & Janta, 2019; Fontefrancesco et al., 2019). They underscore what Abbots states (2016): 'food cannot be considered in isolation but has to be situated in a wider context of movement, travels and flows across of spaces' (p. 24). This highlights the fact that it is not only immigrants' agency *vis-à-vis* the receiving society but also that other actors are involved outside this dynamic between immigrants and the receiving society.

5.3.2 The Story of Sharing and Celebrations: Re-creating Dominican Sociability

Apart from help in the area of ingredients, the presence of other Dominicans also enables the continuation of social aspects of food: sharing food and celebrations.

The sharing of food is important and seems to be a way to maintain the more community-centred way of life Dominican immigrants were accustomed to and appreciated (Giovine, 2014). *Analisa* noted how normal it was in the Dominican Republic in her younger years on *el campo* ('the countryside') to share food with neighbours or family members. And even though Santo Domingo was bigger and not everybody knew each other, there was still a 'culture of unity':

> Yes, in the capital city it is different. Less, but still united. I have my neighbour in Santo Domingo and whenever she wants, she comes up to my house, we drink coffee, we cook together. She gives me this, I give her that, do you understand? Even though everybody is different and does not live together, there are people who still have this tradition of sharing.

106   Post-Migration Experiences, Cultural Practices and Homemaking

The custom of sharing food was a practice fostered by other Dominicans in the Netherlands. *Roberto* rented a room from a Dominican woman, who also rented another room in her home to another Dominican man. The two men had neighbouring rooms. *Roberto* said he always left food for his roommate when he cooked, and that his Dominican roommate did the same. He said that taking care of each other was important.

One night I had gone out with some Dominicans, and they decided that 3 a.m. was too early for the party to stop. The decision was made to go to *Pedro*'s house and continue to dance and hang out there. As soon as we arrived, the host led us to the kitchen. First, we were going to eat! Plates of *tostones* (fried plantains), *chicharrón* (deep-fried pork rind), *picapollo* (deep-fried chicken) and seasoned yuca were put in front of the group. Being the only non-Dominican and relatively new to the group, I was urged to eat as much as I wanted. While eating, all sort of topics were discussed. One person shared words of gratitude for being together and said that being and eating together like this made his life in the Netherlands more pleasant.

The presence of other Dominicans also enabled them to maintain their way of celebrating festive days. The preparation of specific food as well as customs related to celebration were transplanted to the Netherlands. One of the most popular dishes during Holy Week was *habichuela con dulce*, which is a mixture of red beans, condensed milk, spices and other ingredients served in a cold pudding style. Sharing it was important, as *Sandra* explained:

> When you make *habichuela con dulce* in Semana Santa, it is for sharing. It is no use making it and eating it alone in your house, it is for sharing. You make the *habichuela con dulce* and call everyone you know and say: 'I have *habichuela con dulce*. Are you coming to pick it up, or shall I bring it or send it to you?'

In celebrations, eating together was of great importance. Dominicans emphasize that everybody is welcome to join, especially those who do not have a place to celebrate. *Analisa's* story shows how other Dominicans provided the possibility to maintain the practice of commensality on the 24th December. In order to celebrate the festivities in a familiar manner, they depended on others who shared the same tradition:

> Everything depends on what others want. I always used to get together with my friends on the 24th of December, but with time that changed and they wanted to celebrate it the way it is celebrated here. I used to plan the 24th and the 25th so that I would go to a friend. We are always together, they not [the Dutch]. When I go to Santo Domingo, I invite all my brother and sisters for *Noche Buena*.

Cooking together on festive days is another food practice fostered by the presence of co-ethnics and that, at the same time, evoked a sense of community. *Margarita* mentioned how on her birthday her friend from Amsterdam would come to her home in

Habichuela con Dulce *and* Noche Buena *107*

Leidschendam and together they would prepare a meal. She tells how on birthdays or any other celebration, there is an overflow of food and she says 'we make everything we like: *moro de guandules*, roast chicken, how we Dominicans like it, with our flavor'.

The stories about sharing food and celebrations underscore how the recreation of cultural practices from the country of origin is not only facilitated by the presence of co-ethnics, as was exemplified by the case of ingredients, but that it also cements bonds between them. These food practices were a way to connect with the Dominican Republic and to help create familiarity, sense of community and human warmth post-migration.

5.4 Contested Homes in Communal Spaces

This section explores food-related initiatives that Dominicans set up in the Netherlands. In doing so, I show the opportunities these initiatives provided to other Dominicans and the different meanings they evoked. This is done through case studies of a restaurant and a grocery store. I chose to anonymize these because particularly the restaurant always has been controversial, and I did not want my research to add to any stigmatization. First though, I give an overview of Dominican food initiatives.

5.4.1 Dominican Food Initiatives in the Netherlands

As will be presented in the next chapter, Dominicans have always had access to their products through other Caribbean communities who have set up stores selling similar products. More recently, Dominicans have set up stores, selling Dominican products (Fig. 4). Plaza Latina, MJ Tropica and J&J Embutidos Company sell products online as well as in physical stores. The stores do not only sell products but often also are spaces for and organizers of cultural activities. J&J Embutidos, for example, has been involved in organizing several cultural events in Rotterdam including the celebration of Dominican Independence Day (Fig. 5).

Dominicans have also set up restaurants in different parts of the Netherlands. Several respondents cited the well-known restaurants El Merengue in Amsterdam and El Fogon in Rotterdam, which were popular in the 1990s but no longer exist. In the last 10 years, Dominicans set up several restaurants in Amsterdam, The Hague and Rotterdam, including El Palacio de Chichacharon, El Caseron de Cacha, Casa del Mofongo and Buen Provecho. Outside the large cities, initiatives have also popped up, for example, Pura Vida in Deventer. Dominicans noticed how some restaurants had short lifespans. The biggest problem, they said, was that restaurant owners were unfamiliar with how the Dutch system (*el sistema holandés*) worked when it came to entrepreneurship. *Margarita* shared how she saw the situation and her words suggest that many who start businesses do not know what they are getting into:

> Sometimes I feel very sorry that there is not a list of good Dominican restaurants. You have to understand the system, because

108   Post-Migration Experiences, Cultural Practices and Homemaking

Fig. 4.   Dominican Condiments and Seasoning.

Fig. 5.   Flyer for the Celebration of Dominican Independence Day.

Habichuela con Dulce *and* Noche Buena   *109*

sometimes they start but don't know the system, and after two years you don't see it [the restaurant] anymore .... It is more that you should know how the system works. And there are a lot of persons who fail. Speaking about this, it is not for nothing that the economy of this country is so good. You have to know everything very well from the beginning or else better not get involved. And if you get in, be careful, otherwise you will be in it up to here.

Dominicans have different attitudes about visiting Dominican restaurants. Some do not go to restaurants because they can make everything at home or have a family member who cooks for them. Others do visit restaurants, even if they can prepare Dominican dishes themselves, going for the ambiance or to try somebody else's hand at cooking. As *Sandra*, a very frequent visitor of Dominican restaurants in Rotterdam, said:

> My family, we are crazy (*somos unos perdidos*) .... In the south [of Rotterdam], we go to Caseron de Cacha, and we eat there at least once a week. At least. Before that it was called La Casa de Chicharron, and we were constantly going there.

Opinions about the food served in these restaurants were varied. For example, everybody agreed that the food at Picalonga was excellent and typically Dominican. An interesting phenomenon was Dominican food-serving restaurants set up by non-Dominicans, for example, by people born in Curaçao (sometimes with Dominican roots). As shown, Curaçaoans are familiar with Dominican people and culture due to centuries of migration between the islands. Of these restaurants, many said the food was good, but some mentioned that, although the food was good, it was not '100% Dominican' because the seasoning tasted different. One person I spoke to said: 'The food was very good, but there was something in the seasoning that was not Dominican. They add something different. There is nothing wrong with it, but that taste was different'.

Another manner of obtaining Dominican food was through women who cooked at home and then sold food to the public. The menus were shared through social media, for example, on Facebook pages posting the menu of the day.

The following subsections describe two food-related initiatives, how they were perceived by Dominicans and the functions they fulfilled for them.

5.4.2 El Malecon: Authentic Food in a Contested Space

On a Sunday night, I looked around and saw people doing all sort of things: men playing billiards and cards, a woman selling lottery tickets, people drinking beer or just sitting, keeping themselves busy with their telephones, other eating typical Dominican dishes, such as *pica pollo* and *moro de habichuela y pollo guisado*. Closing my eyes, I imagined myself in the Dominican Republic. I heard Dominican Spanish, loud talking and laughing, sounds of merengue, bachata and salsa. Its main function was unclear, but the entrance of this place gave the impression that food was the principal service. Welcome to restaurant-café El Malecon.

110   Post-Migration Experiences, Cultural Practices and Homemaking

I had been visiting restaurant-café El Malecon since 2008. Back then, it was run by a Pakistani family. The place had the ambiance of a typical Dutch *bruin café*, with wooden floors, a bar, a billiard table and a kitchen that made food to eat there or for take away. When the weather was good, tables were set up outside, and passers-by could hear bachata, merengue, salsa and talking in Spanish. In 2016, El Malecon was renovated and lost its cosy atmosphere, undergoing a transformation into a single open-plan space with lots of light.

El Malecon is known for good, authentic Dominican food that tastes authentically Dominican. Clientele consists mostly of Dominicans and also Curaçaoans who are familiar with Dominican food because of the large community living in Curaçao. There is a daily menu, which consists of typical Dominican dishes such as *chivo con moro* (goat with rice and beans), *chivo con arroz y habichuela* (goat with white rice and stewed beans), *carne de res con moro* (beef with rice and beans) and *picapollo* (fried chicken). *Carlos*, who lived alone, said he often eats there. He found it impossible to prepare a little bit of food – a cup of rice or piece of meat – so he barely cooked at home and went to El Malecon. The day before our interview, he went to eat there and said he would probably go the day of our interview. El Malecon seemed to help out a lot of Dominican men living alone.

El Malecon has additional functions. Firstly, it sold products. A night, El Malecon revealed a very creative way to cater to the Dominican community and at the same time make money. On one visit there after finishing my meal, an older woman – who would often be around and whom I saw earlier that day standing on a corner with a bright pink suitcase – came to clean my table. When she saw that I left some food, she offered to bring me a container to take the leftovers home. Helping me with the leftovers, she suddenly mentioned that she also sells food. She said that she seasons meat Dominican-style, makes up to-go packages and sells them for 10 euros. The only thing I would have to do at home is fry that meat – so easy! Then she told me that she also sells Dominican cheese and explained in a very detailed, step-by-step manner how I could prepare it: I could come home from a very long day at work, I could make a nice sandwich with this delicious cheese and go sit and enjoy it. She then asked if I wanted to see the merchandise. I told her that today I would not buy, but maybe next time. That was no problem. She gave me her telephone number and made sure I saved it in my phone under 'the old lady from El Malecon' (*la vieja del Malecon*). She said goodbye and emphasized that I should call her. The bright pink suitcase suddenly looked very different to me.

El Malecon's other function was providing a place for hanging out. During one of my visits, it stood out how this place transformed from one thing to another. One Sunday night, I went there for food. While eating, others were playing billiards and then bingo night commenced. Afterwards, around 9 p.m., the lights were turned off and the volume of the music got louder. I remember thinking: this place just went from community centre to disco. El Malecon is known for its 'Dominicanness', as *Laura* explained:

> I think that El Malecon is a meeting place of Dominicanness (un lugar de encuentro de la dominicanidad). I identify El Malecon as a piece of the Dominican Republic. There are a lot of serious, ambitious people in El Malecon. You can enjoy some music, there

Habichuela con Dulce *and* Noche Buena   *111*

is some good food. There is a disk jockey who gives you a welcome, who gives you a shout-out [For example, saying:] 'Greetings for Sabrina from Laura'. Listen, it is little piece of our country.

Laura's quote reveals El Malecon's different functions: a link to the Dominican Republic, a place to enjoy music and good food, but also a place where you are 'someone'. It provides a sort of recognition of your existence in a dark, solitary country where nobody knows you, *Laura* suggested. Her opinion about El Malecon echoes several other studies on immigrant public places showing how apart from being locations for public display of emigrants' identities, they are places for socializing and community-building (Miranda-Nieto & Boccagni 2020; Román-Vélasquez, 1999).

The different functions of El Malecon correspond to Ley's (2016) findings of immigrant churches not only having a religious function but also serving as a community centre, a social centre and a second home. Cancellieri (2015) also observes how communal spaces, such as mosques, can be a 'multifunctional territory' that lets people gather together to reconstruct an identity as well as exchange goods, information and services. The multiple functions of immigrant communal spaces have come to the fore in research beyond food. Wood (1997) mentions how a shopping centre with many Vietnamese shops lets Vietnamese immigrants feel like they are in Vietnam. Identifying these opportunities from within the community thus allows for an exploration of home outside the domestic space.

Due to its location in neighbourhood where there is a concentration of Dominicans living, El Malecon has, over time, become a place with many different functions. Being in the borough of the city where most Dominicans are concentrated, it is a convenient location to gather. Moreover, situated in a shopping centre, it is a place where different kinds of people pass by: women who do grocery-shopping, men who come and drink a beer with friends, non-Dominicans who like Dominican food, non-Dominicans who like the Dominican atmosphere of music and dance. Eventually, it also became a place to celebrate Dominican Mother's Day and Independence Day and to hold bingo nights. This is also what Collins (2008, p. 160) shows in a study about how Korean restaurants in Auckland are not a simple replication of restaurants in South Korean cities, but a 'smorgasbord of the Korean culinary and cultural landscape' that 'serve to unify objects …, practices … and bodies …. that while similar in some ways are not *a priori* connected to each other' (p. 160).

However, not everyone appreciated the multifunctionality of El Malecon. *Aurelia*, who owned a hair salon, described how one day after class at a beauty salon, she passed through the shopping centre and decided to enter the restaurant because she was really hungry. She lamented her choice of sitting there and said she would never to it again:

I know El Malecon. They told me that they renovated it, but the last time I was there, a couple of years ago, it had the atmosphere of a nightclub. Music, some men with a crate of beer, unbelievable, all the time drinking while playing billiards. It did not give me a good feeling …. El Malecon, for me now, is only for takeaway. But sit down there in this atmosphere of bachata and all these kinds of

112 Post-Migration Experiences, Cultural Practices and Homemaking

things? No. That does not goes well with food, with a restaurant. Even not in the Dominican Republic it is like that. Why is it necessary to have a fusion of nightclub, restaurant and bar all in one place? You do not know where you are. Am I in a bar, in a restaurant? You do not know what it is (*tú no sabes sabes qué relajo es*).

Aurelia experienced El Malecon as place without morals: a nightclub, men drinking lots of beer, playing billiards. She also criticized its multiple functions, which she found unusual for a restaurant in the Dominican Republic.

Interestingly, while the multiple functions of this one space were criticized, it is in fact not unusual in the Dominican Republic for one space to be used for other purposes. Fig. 6 shows how grocery stores and carwashes transform into dancing

---

The carwash

It is Sunday night. I'm driving on the Rooseveltweg, a major auto route in Willemstad, the capital city of Curaçao. In the distance, I can hear sounds of bachata. They seem to be coming from a carwash. I can see the possibility of music being played while washing cars, but this sounds like a party! I stop, park my car and when I enter the carwash, I can easily imagine being in the Dominican Republic. There's a band paying, newly washed cars, bachata music, Presidente beer, couples dancing: a typical Dominican scene.

Dominicans in Curaçao transplanted a typical Dominican way of inhabiting space to their post-migration context. In my trips to the Dominican Republic, I ended up at several carwashes that are a hybrid of actual carwash and bar. They are typical places to meet for dancing and drinking. While your car gets washed, there is music and partying into the night.

The *colmado*

It is Thursday at 7 p.m. in Bayahibe, a town on the south-eastern coast in the Dominican Republic. Bachata, merengue, salsa and dembow are blasting from the speakers at the highest volume. One of the grocery stores – a *colmado*, where people do their small-scale daily groceries – has just turned into a bar.

This *colmado* is open every day and brings Bayahibe residents, tourists and temporary workers in from 6 to 10 p.m. to listen to music, drink beer and meet up. When I enter, the owner welcomes me. I watch how the four young men who normally help customers with groceries have transformed into entertainers, pouring drinks like bartenders and moving to the sounds of salsa, merengue, bachata and dembow, which come via consecutive sets of four or five songs. A Dutch man whose business is in the tourism industry comes and warns me of Dominican men. He has seen me walking around in Bayahibe and lets me know if something were to happen, I can count on him. Thankful for his offered help and having been approached several times by curious Bayahibe local men, I never felt being in danger. This *colmado* shows how a place can have multiple functions and permit specific ways of inhabiting space with music, dancing and drinking.

Fig. 6. The Carwash and the *Colmado*.

Habichuela con Dulce *and* Noche Buena   ***113***

and *ambiente* spaces at night. These examples again show the centrality of these two elements in the lives of Dominicans.

El Malecon was also criticized by some respondents for the regular clients it attracted: people without morals, who talk loudly, buy pricey bottles of alcohol to show off. *Rafael* mentioned how he avoided it, unless he really wanted to eat something Dominican. He lamented the closing of another Dominican restaurant, which he found more neutral, more relaxed. *Arturo* also mentioned really loving the food, but avoiding the place because of the type of people inside:

> El Malecon is, like, we call it, a cave of thieves. People do business there. It doesn't matter what kind of business it is and the people there are depraved. There is a lot of opportunism. You can sit down, toast with these people – that does not cost anything – but they are people who are after getting something from another person. I have gone twice to eat because I really like the food. When I was working at a butcher he said to me: 'You are different from Dominicans who are there in El Malecon'. It is another type of Dominican, you see, they are people who are in business, who earn their money in one way or another. Dominicans who work are not like that. Dominican people are honest. We are decent. They have a lot of respect .... In each country, there are always people from the underworld, or however you want to call it, or people with other types of quality of life. So El Malecon is such a part .... And the people who are there are, they live for appearances. They don't even have food at home, but they are there, they buy a very expensive drink, to show the other people. The women are very .... they want expensive clothes, quality things. And also, they see who they can score to get a little bit. For people who want a quiet Dominican place, it is not a good place.

Arturo's quote reveals a totally negative perception of El Malecon's visitors. He did not approve of their lifestyle, feeling his values and lifestyle differ and lamenting the bad name Dominicans there give other Dominicans. This example clearly shows how a place that some might consider 'a piece of the Dominican Republic' is experienced totally differently by others. Also visible once again is the dynamic reflecting hierarchies of value (Scandone, 2018), where some of the community takes a contraposition towards a certain segment of the co-ethnic community.

This case reveals how, for some, El Malecon provided a space for Dominican ways of socializing and that it fostered feelings of home, such as a sense of community or the familiarity of authentic dishes. It also shows how, as in Cancellieri's (2015) research, practices of homemaking have no single, clear or fixed meaning shared by everyone. However, departing from Cancellieri, my research identified not gender but lifestyle as a major ground for difference. Wiles (2008) also shows differentiation in attitudes towards ethnic places in her study of New Zealanders' homes in London. For some, 'the pub' provides a home where they feel familiarity and belonging; meanwhile, others do not want to be associated with their

114   Post-Migration Experiences, Cultural Practices and Homemaking

community's behaviours at the pub because they do not recognize them as representative of 'being from New Zealand'.

5.4.3 La Tienda: Finding Products and Dominican Ways of Being Together

Unlike the Surinamese community, the Dominican community did not set up ethnic grocery stores as it increased in size (thus seeing a growth in people with similar food practices and product needs). A reason for this difference could be that Surinamese grocery stores and, later on, Turkish ones offered similar ingredients, so establishing separate stores was considered unnecessary. In 2014, however, one Dominican did set up a grocery store.

Entrepreneurship runs in the veins of the family behind it. In the Dominican Republic, the father of the owner had a *colmado*. At a certain point in time, after supplying Dominican products to 'tropical' stores (or: *toko*, a grocery store selling products from the Tropics in the Netherlands is often referred to as a '*toko*'), he decided to set up his own store, both online and at a market. After that, a physical store was set up, which grew into a large space with four sections: the shop, a dining area, the kitchen and a bingo/domino space in the basement.

La Tienda's main purpose was selling products, but it had additional functions and was valued for different reasons by members of the Dominican community. It sold typical Dominican products such as coffee (Amanda, Café Santo Domingo), condiments (Baldom, Goya), flour (Harina El Negrito), malt beverage (India, Goya) and coconut-based products (Jaha Crema de Coco). These products are bought via importers in the Netherlands or directly imported from the Dominican Republic. The latter were preferred by Dominican customers because they are considered fresh. The sister of La Tienda's owner regularly would go to the Dominican Republic and come back with products, for example, *oregano del mercado* (fresh oregano straight from the market). *Dulces* ('sweets') were also important for Dominicans and were brought back to the Netherlands in suitcases. During my research, I observed the store selling Dulce de Bonao and Dulce de Bani. It was cheaper to bring products via aeroplane, but salami, meat and cheese are not permitted in suitcases, so were imported by air freight. Something traditional that is part of this transnational circulation of commodities was *longaniza* (sausage). The owner's sister said it was difficult to find good *longaniza*, though she found someone in the Dominican Republic who would send it frozen in a container. The store sold it fried and frozen. The most sold products were salami, cheese and Presidente beer.

As part of its dining services, La Tienda had a daily menu, which could include not only *mangù*, *moro de habichuela/guandules* with meat but also sweets, snacks and drinks (coffee and pineapple juice). During one of my visits, I was called into the kitchen to learn how to peel a plantain, a skill every Dominican should possess. The peeled plantains were to be used to prepare *mangù* (Fig. 7).

La Tienda's products and food evoked different feelings in clients. I told *Mercedes* about the place and that they sold *mangù*, one of her favourite dishes. One day, we decided to go together. We entered, took a seat and ordered. At a table

Habichuela con Dulce *and* Noche Buena 115

Fig. 7. *Mangu Tres Golpes*.

near us sat a couple: a Dominican man and a Peruvian woman. The man started talking to us and I remember thinking: we just arrived a minute ago and are immediately immersed in the atmosphere. He even advised on what we should eat: a sandwich or a cheese empanada. *Mercedes* told me she never prepared *mangù* at home because it was so hard to find good-quality ripe plantains. Those she found in the past did not have the same taste as in the Dominican Republic and their texture was too watery. She no longer bothered to look for good plantains and thus made the dish less often than she wanted. But when on a holiday in the Dominican Republic, she made sure to eat it every day. At La Tienda, she looked around, recognizing typical Dominican condiments, coffee and sweets. She wanted to buy everything, but found all these things posed a real threat to her diet. Then she saw the lollypops she used to eat at secondary school and was brought back to her childhood. As the friendly couple was leaving, the man said: 'If I did not have to drive, I would drink a beer with you and dance'. It was 3 p.m. We ended our meal with typical Dominican cake and coffee. *Mercedes* was again transported back to the Dominican Republic. Just as we were about to pay and go, she spotted *longaniza*. We decided to stay a bit longer to taste it.

The afternoon with *Mercedes* revealed several things. It showed how she dealt with the absence of quality products: she stopped making dishes with plantains and enjoyed them when in the Dominican Republic or on our shared occasion. Furthermore, the store evoked feelings of nostalgia. Also, it became clear that a small place on a street in a Dutch city could offer Dominicans a space to recreate ways of socializing, with strangers sparking conversations, mingle in each other's business and thinking about dancing in the middle of the day.

I had been to La Tienda several times and found its atmosphere cosy, making me feel as though I were entering a living room. The owner explained that it was also his aim to create such a convivial atmosphere. The warmth was not only expressed though the place's décor but also in how the people who work there

116   Post-Migration Experiences, Cultural Practices and Homemaking

behaved. After having eaten there a couple of times, I started being welcomed as if I was a long-time visitor. After not having been there for a couple of months, one of the staff recognized me and greeted me warmly. She said it had been such a long time that she had seen me and asked where I had been all that time. She also asked about the friend who came with me twice.

Another typical Dominican way of socializing is playing bingo and dominoes. The cousin of La Tienda's owner came up with the idea of using their basement space to provide the Dominican community members a way to be together. It was also a way to increase more awareness about the store and attract regular customers.

Dominican customers would come to the store or order online from cities all over the country such as Haarlem, Lelystad, Tilburg, Leiden, Amersfoort and Zaandam. By focusing on a broader clientele, the store also created links with other immigrants communities. The target group comprised Dominicans and Colombians, which was also expressed by the Dominican and Colombian flags in the main window of the store. A young woman working at the store, who was the owner's niece, described the different kinds of customers as being mostly Dominicans, Colombians, Curaçaoans, Surinamese and Peruvians. She said that Dominicans and Colombians come to buy products and eat food; Curaçaoans and Surinamese eat food; and Peruvians buy Inca Cola and *aji aji* (chilli peppers). An interesting group of clients were Dominican beauty salons and their customers who ordered food.

This case of La Tienda revealed several points. Firstly, finding ingredients in a grocery store is not only a matter of shopping for products but also evokes nostalgia and memories. Secondly, it is a space for Dominican ways of socializing (Mankekar, 2002; Renne, 2007). Thirdly, the place creates links with other communities including immigrant groups. Fourthly, transnational space is important for recreating familiar practices.

5.5 Conclusion: Co-Ethnics, Cultural Practices and Feelings of Home

Knowledge about how the presence of co-ethnics affects practices – specifically *vis-à-vis* feelings of home – remains limited. Two points remain understudied: how material and social opportunities provided by co-ethnics are related to feelings of home and whether co-ethnics all have the same need and expectations from initiatives set up by other co-ethnics. This led to the guiding question of this chapter – *How do co-ethnics and the opportunities they provide affect cultural practices and feelings of home?* – which was approached by exploring other Dominicans' feelings of home and food opportunities in communal and domestic spaces.

Opinions about co-ethnics were varied. Some of the Dominicans' opinions about the presence of other Dominicans reflected great appreciation and the need to be together, which could evoke feelings of belonging to a community, human warmth and *ambiente*. Others, however, were reserved about whom and where they met. They perceived other Dominicans as untrustworthy people who do

Habichuela con Dulce *and* Noche Buena **117**

not want to progress and have low moral values. My respondents showed mostly Scandone's (2018) strategy of hanging on to hierarchies of value. Thus, perpetuating ethnic and class stereotypes and taking a contraposition towards a certain segment of the co-ethnic community. The other strategy, distancing oneself altogether from the co-ethnic community and adopting cultural features of the dominant society, was not applicable as no one really separated from the community as a whole. I observed a differentiation along lines of social class and lifestyle. What also became clear was that the division along class lines was recreated after migration.

In the domestic space, material practices, such as ingredient sharing, provided the possibility to recreate familiarity, experience the Dominican Republic and stay connected to the country. Social practices such as sharing food and celebrating traditions provided the possibility to recreate ways of socializing, creating a sense of community and human warmth. It seems that inside spaces became important for re-creating practices. While home in the Dominican Republic was experienced not only inside the domestic space but often outside with others, the results of my research indicate that inside spaces became important in the Netherlands for socializing and creating home in a Dominican way. This was simply because 'outside' was very different from what they were used to in the Dominican Republic in terms of weather and social environment.

With regard to the communal space, practices and feelings of home, the cases highlighted the multifunctionality of spaces. Different activities and cultural practices came together in one place: dancing, socializing, playing bingo and dominoes, eating, drinking and hanging out. This is similar to other studies about immigrant community spaces showing how a place with a certain initial function comes to have multiple functions (Cancellieri, 2015; Ley, 2008; Wood, 1997). The two cases also show the different meanings of home for members of the same co-ethnic community. Moreover, community spaces are not places where everyone feels at home. These community spaces provide feelings of familiarity, nostalgia, a sense of community, human warmth for only some people.

Chapter 6

Bread, Ugly Gravy and Boring Parties: Encounters With Dutch Food Practices

6.1 Introduction

> In my country, when you go to a birthday party, nobody is going to offer you coffee, *taart* [cake], een koekje ['a biscuit']. No. It is a party, so beer, Brugal with Coca-Cola, a cocktail. There could be a waiter serving you .... We went to the birthday party of a friend. And the cake arrives at the table, there were three or four types of cake, *vlaai, noem maar wat* ['custard/rice/fruit pie, you name it']. Cake and coffee. I do not drink coffee at that time of the day and I do not like tea. So I said: 'I want a beer'. And I asked my husband whether I said something strange. In my country they also offer you dinner, and at the end of the night we will sing with the cake. Here they eat the cake first. And these are things that surprise you, and you say: 'This is so different'. Or they invite you to a birthday dinner and then that same cake, *een hapje* [a snack], soup and then it ends. In my country we eat. We have a culture of eating, eating a lot. And while you are eating they always offer you more.

This quote shows how customs in Dutch society can clash with customs from the Dominican Republic. *Mariasela* described how after overcoming several cultural shocks, she found her way in the Netherlands and learned to deal with what she perceived as Dutch culture. Something that, as she put it, shocked her was Dutch birthday parties, specifically the kind of food that is served, the sequence in which it is served and the quantities. There are more stories, like *Mariasela*'s, of immigrants' encounters with different food practices post-migration about how these differences compel negotiation and even changes in practices.

This chapter explores the relationship between the receiving society and immigrant homemaking. It examines which unfamiliar practices and customs immigrants had to deal with in trying to recreate home and the negotiations they made

---

Post-Migration Experiences, Cultural Practices and Homemaking:
An Ethnography of Dominican Migration to Europe, 119–136
Copyright © 2023 by Sabrina Dinmohamed
Published under exclusive licence by Emerald Publishing Limited
doi:10.1108/978-1-83753-204-920231006

120 Post-Migration Experiences, Cultural Practices and Homemaking

due to these encounters. It also shows how the encounter with these unfamiliar practices and customs could lead to changes. By 'the receiving society', I mean the Netherlands' dominant cultural group as well as other immigrant communities. In my research, this constitutes Dutch natives and the Surinamese, Dutch Caribbean, Moroccan and Turkish immigrant communities, who have been residing in the Netherlands for approximately three generations. The term 'unfamiliar practices' refers to material, social and cultural practices of the native Dutch and the large immigrant communities that could influence Dominicans' practices.

In immigrant homemaking studies, there have been some attempts to show how certain characteristics of the receiving society affect immigrants' ways of creating home. Limitations are found in the physical and material sphere: factors such as spatiality, regulations, construction norms and availability of objects to purchase in the receiving society affect or suppress immigrants' attempts to transform the spaces in which they live into meaningful places they can relate to (Gram-Hanssen & Bech-Danielsen, 2011; Hadjiyanni, 2009). Limitations are also found in the social and cultural sphere (Boccagni, 2013; Meijering & Lager, 2014). How material and socio-cultural conditions lead to negotiations in practices and feelings of home remains unclear, as does whether these negotiations lead to changes in practices. This leads to the principal question guiding this chapter: *How do receiving society characteristics affect cultural practices and feelings of home?* The argument is that the receiving society not only stands in the way of recreating practices but also provides opportunities to get acquainted with new practices, as migration may open up new ways of living. As such, it provides new ways of creating home.

To demonstrate this, I explore, firstly, Dominicans' encounters with the receiving society. Based on what several studies show about how receiving society characteristics affect immigrant food practices, I decided to follow Parasecoli (2014), Giovine (2014) and Wandel et al. (2008) in dividing characteristics into material and social. Material characteristics include dishes, availability of products and ways of food preparation. Social characteristics refer to different household composition, organization of consumption and celebrations. Secondly, to get a picture of how they experience these encounters, I examine how they deal with the encounters. Burke (2009) provides a starting point to understand how immigrants have various ways of reacting to the encounter. These include (1) acceptance, which the author calls 'the fashion for the foreign' (p. 79); (2) resistance, which aims to defend a culture by closing it off or isolating it; (3) segregation, which aims to maintain part of a culture, free from foreign contamination; and (4) adaptation, 'a double movement of de-contextualization and re-contextualization that lifts an item from its original setting and modifies it to fit its new environment' (pp. 93–94). Lastly, I analyze the different outcomes. Migration can cause cultural change and processes of hybridization, but what do changed practices look like and which 'flavours' can be distinguished? Mehta and Belk (1991) show how practices become hybrid; in their study, immigrants recreate India by using cultural material objects, but these original objects are also mixed with elements of the host society's culture, showing both preservation and adaptation of their culture in daily life. Diner (2001) mentions 'culinary inventions' referring to fusions of old (tradition) and new (invention) in foods and food practices.

Bread, Ugly Gravy and Boring Parties **121**

I elaborate on how contextual characteristics affect practices in three subsections. The first describes the encounter with typical Dutch food, products and ways of preparation. The second elaborates on how other immigrant communities' food infrastructures provide Dominicans with opportunities. The third subsection focuses on social characteristics of the receiving context and describes unfamiliar food customs Dominicans reported encountering. The last section reflects upon the relationship between receiving society characteristics, practices and homemaking.

6.2 Encounters with Dutch Food: Challenges and Opportunities

This section describes Dominicans' encounters with Dutch food practices and the reactions to them. But first, what exactly is Dutch food?

6.2.1 Dutch Food

When I Googled 'What is typical Dutch food?' many different dishes came up. Most commonly were dishes consisting of potatoes, meat and vegetables; *erwtensoep* (pea soup); *hutspot* (potato, carrot and onion mash often eaten in winter, usually with meat on the side); *stamppot* (potato mash with ingredients such as kale, endive, cabbage or sauerkraut, often served with smoked sausage and gravy); *hachee* (meat, fish or poultry and vegetables, stewed into a thick gravy with vinegar, cloves and laurel leaves); *pannekoeken* (larges pancakes, usually eaten for dinner, with various toppings and fillings, including syrup, powdered sugar, apples, cheese, spinach and bacon). Apart from dishes, fast-food came up, such as *patat met mayonaise* (French fries and mayonnaise), *kroket* and *bitterballen* as did some sweets, such as *stroopwafels* and *drop* (licorice). Other results were *haring* (herring), *hagelslag* (chocolate sprinkles), *poffertjes* (small pancakes) and *oliebollen* (kind of dougnuts). To what extent this food referred to as typical Dutch is actually consumed by the native Dutch is another topic of research. Also, within the Netherlands there is internal culinary variation. The southern province of Limburg, for example, has its typical *zoervleisj* (a kind of stewed meat) and the northern province of Friesland has its typical *nagelkaas* (cheese with cumin and cloves).

Interestingly, some websites also consider Indonesian and Surinamese dishes as typical Dutch food. Due to colonial ties, the Netherlands has large Indonesian and Surinamese populations, with restaurants everywhere, particularly in the big cities. Especially in those with a major immigrant presence, the Dutch have access to food from many cuisines and traditions.

According to Dominicans in my research, typical Dutch dishes were *stamppot met rookworst*, potatoes, vegetable and meat and *erwtensoep*. The typical Dutch products they cited were potatoes, vegetables (spinach, cauliflower, broccoli, sauerkraut, chicory, Brussels sprouts), *appelmoes* (apple sauce) and *biefstuk* (steak, raw), *kroket* (croquette), *karbonade* (pork chop) and *rookworst* (smoked sausage).

122 Post-Migration Experiences, Cultural Practices and Homemaking

6.2.2 Dealing With the Encounters: Four Scenarios

There are four different scenarios which describe Dominican immigrants' encounters with food differences in the Dutch context. Firstly, Dutch food caused feelings of horror and surprise. Many Dominicans I have spoken did not like Dutch food. *Petronila*, who came to the Netherlands in 1991 with her half-Dutch husband described her early encounter with a typical Dutch ingredient:

> Potatoes with vegetables and meat, that is Dutch food. That was the first thing I ate when I arrived in the Netherlands. They put in front of me *boerenkool* [kale] with that sausage and I was like: how nice. First, because I did not eat potatoes. For me, potatoes is what they give you in the hospitals in the Dominican Republic. So, those herbs mixed with all those potatoes was horrible for me .... No, I do not eat potatoes. They remind me of hospitals, that is what they give you. A little boiled potato.

Aurelia also associated potatoes with illness. She said she liked some Dutch dishes, but did not make them:

> No, no, I do not prepare *esa vaina* ['that stuff']. To begin with, a Dominican only eats potato mash when he is sick. When you cannot chew, they give you potato mash. I enjoy good health, and me and my kids do not eat potato mash. They do not like it. If they would like it, maybe I would prepare it, but no. The sausages they do like, but I give it to them with rice .... *Erwtensoep* I like, but I never prepared it in my house, nor am I interested in learning it. I buy a can. Or when somebody prepares it, I eat it because it is really nice. No, the day my husband finds me preparing *erwtensoep*, he is going to faint.

Aurelia's story shows how Dutch food was really strange for her and, using the phrase *esa vaina* ('that stuff'), she expressed something akin to 'who would ever prepare that?' Saying that she liked *erwtensoep* (pea soup) but would never prepare it conveyed a self-distancing in a *esa vaina*-kind of way. Respondents also encountered unfamiliarity in products, such as bread and gravy. The constant consumption of bread was also something that struck Dominicans as odd: bread at breakfast, bread at lunch and bread with a hot evening meal. *Valentina* described her intention to adjust to Dutch ways, but struggled with bread. Her story shows how she tried, though it was difficult, and found a balance in bread consumption. Still, she maintained her familiar warm midday meal because that is familiar to her and makes her feel at home:

> So I thought: I will adjust. It was difficult in the beginning because in the morning, afternoon, evening it is: bread, bread, bread,

bread. I find that strange. Now I am eating bread, for example, but that is because I do not have another options. But when he [her son] comes from school, I always try to give him something warm and not only bread.

Something else that caused strong feelings was Dutch gravy and Dominicans mention its unattractiveness. *Sandra* expressed liking some Dutch dishes and vegetables (*groenten*), but found the gravy horrible:

The potatoes and the meatballs. I see it in [Dutch variety store] HEMA and every time I see it, I think: I cannot eat that. For example, potatoes with spinach I like and *groenten* in general. I like it, but this strange thing with the sauce, I think: oh my God, how can a sauce turn out that ugly.

These stories do not only show rejection but also ideas about what was 'normal' food. This dynamic emerges in other research about immigrants' encountering new foods in the receiving society (Brown, Edwards, & Hartwell, 2010; Petridou, 2001; Rabikowska, 2010). Immigrants may have fixed ideas about taste, appearance and structure of food and what would be 'normal'.

Secondly, a different scenario is Dominicans appreciating the encounter with Dutch food. *Sergio* came to the Netherlands when he was 13. His mother was married to a Dutch man, which led to his bicultural approach of eating at home. His first encounters with Dutch food were positive, except for the Brussels sprouts. He said there would be a combination of Dominican and Dutch dishes at home, and mentioned liking *poffertjes*, pancakes and peanut butter. For him, Dominican food did not necessarily evoke feelings of home and he considered the different choices in the Netherlands as an opportunity. *Virginia*, aged 55 at the time of our interview, was born and raised in La Vega, in the centre of the Dominican Republic. She appreciated the food varieties she came to know post-migration. She was 38 when she arrived in the Netherlands, after a short period in Belgium. She was widowed now, but was married to a Dutch man with whom she has a daughter. In her home, she kept a combination of Dominican and Dutch food. She said she liked Dutch food and mentioned how she incorporated *groenten* (vegetables) into her diet. *Virginia* added that though she made rice several times a week, she also made potatoes, which is typical Dutch food according to her. She also mentioned something other Dominicans mentioned: in the Netherlands people eat more vegetables and greens. They would incorporate the Dutch word 'groenten' in a Spanish sentence.

Thirdly, Dominicans also get acquainted to food from other countries and immigrant communities. These stories showed how encounters with non-Dominican foods in the receiving country were taken as an opportunity to get acquainted with new dishes and products and thus broaden one's horizons (Bonhomme, 2013; Philipp & Ho, 2010). Like *Virginia*, other respondents said they appreciated the variety of food they came to know after migration and sometimes specifically

124 *Post-Migration Experiences, Cultural Practices and Homemaking*

mentioned liking the food of other immigrant communities in the Netherlands, for example, Italian, Surinamese, Mexican and Thai. *Bryan*, a personal fitness trainer living in Rotterdam, said he was conscious about consumption choices. He also had a very broad interest in other cuisines and really loved Surinamese food (roti). His mother, who lived near him, often cooked for him. When asked whether his mother, living for over 20 years in the Netherlands, prepared Dominican food regularly, he replied:

> No, she does not either. She has already adjusted to Dutch society. She eats roti often, and my favourite food is chilli con carne. She prepares it when I visit her, most recently being yesterday. She knows what I like. Spaghetti also.

Bryan's story reveals several things about his and his mother's food consumption. Eating dishes other than Dominican ones is equated by him with being adjusted well, which for some Dominicans meant progress after migration, making use of what the receiving society has to offer. Furthermore, *Bryan* has broad culinary interests, including Surinamese and Italian food in his culinary repertoire. Some stressed the importance of broadening their horizons and that migration provided that opportunity. They had been eating Dominican food all their lives and that being in the Netherlands provided the chance to try other cuisines. This resonates with one of Hage's (1997) element of home, namely opportunities.

Fourthly, not liking Dutch food does not mean they discard everything that is Dutch. Some incorporate certain ingredients or adapt to their own taste. In Chapter 4 *Casandra* explained the importance of Dominican food in her daily life: it is what she likes and what makes her feel good. For *Casandra* consuming and preparing Dominican food connected to human warmth and sense of community, something she finds important in feeling at home in the Netherlands. However, she does not discard Dutch food. Like others she characterized Dutch food as boring, without much taste and not very varied (a distinct fact from Dominicans' observation that the Netherlands has a lot of variety in cuisines). She mentions that when she prepares Dutch food, she uses additional seasoning, not just salt and pepper:

> It is not that I do not like Dutch food, but I think that Dutch food is dry, cold, without colour, without variation, without taste. The only thing is salt and pepper .... Also, for a potato mash, they do not add butter or milk. They do something else here. We add a little bit of salt, some garlic, our *sazón completa*, so it has a taste other than only salty.

Aurelia, who said she would never prepare Dutch dishes in her home, did mention incorporating Dutch *spekjes* (bacon) in her *moro de guandules*. *Aurelia's* quote comes close to what Phillip and Ho (2010) call a 'creolised taste of home', as a consequence of migration opening up a whole new market of products to use.

Bread, Ugly Gravy and Boring Parties **125**

Another applicable description is Fontefrancesco et al. (2019) 'gastronomic syncretism', referring to the combining of host and home food ingredients:

> Normally, there [Dominican Republic] they prepare everything in one pot. They cook the pigeon peas, after that they fry the seasoning, you mix it and then add water. After that you add the water, and everything cooks together. But I prepare my white rice separately, then fry everything and add the washed pigeon peas which then absorb the taste of the seasoning. Then I add Chinese sauce and after that, I sometimes add *spekjes*, so that it tastes even better.

Having shown how the characteristics of the receiving context affected Dominicans' food practices, I turn to another trait of the context: other immigrant communities' food infrastructures and their way of providing Dominicans with opportunities.

6.3 Finding Ingredients: The Importance of Other Caribbean Communities

As an extensive Dominican food infrastructure does not exist in the Netherlands – the way it does, for example, in New York (see Marte, 2011) – and many products still have only limited availability in mainstream grocery stores, Dominicans rely on other immigrant communities with similar product needs who set up grocery stores and facilitated the recreation of Dominican food practices. Describing product finding and its relationship with the receiving society brings to mind two scenarios: the Dominicans who settled in large cities alongside other immigrant communities and the Dominicans who settled in municipalities with no or low percentages of immigrants.

The first wave of Dominican immigrants arrived in the Netherlands in the 1980s, after the arrival of many immigrants from Suriname, a colony of the Netherlands until becoming an independent state in 1975. Around that year, many Surinamese decided to come to the Netherlands. With their arrival, a new infrastructure of food ingredients was set up in the Netherlands' big cities. Products previously unavailable became available in Amsterdam, The Hague and Rotterdam, cities with Surinamese concentrations. Yucca, plantains, salted codfish, okra, bitter melon, eggplant and different kinds of leafy vegetables found their way to the Dutch food market.

Dominicans who settled in the big cities also got acquainted with this Caribbean community with similar product needs. They mention how ingredients have always been easy to find in Amsterdam and how they always had had access to Dominican products. *Carlos*, who arrived to the Netherlands in 1986, noted how ingredients have always been easy to find in Amsterdam, thanks to the Surinamese community:

> We have had access to Dominican products. Yucca, for example. The Surinamese .... luckily for us, the Antillean and Surinamese immigrants, who came before us, also brought their culture, which

126 Post-Migration Experiences, Cultural Practices and Homemaking

is very similar to ours and thus also their ingredients, which are fundamental for our dishes.

Sandra and *Valentina* both lived in municipalities where ingredients were difficult to obtain and later on moved to, respectively, Amsterdam and Rotterdam, so they could compare their present and previous situations. *Sandra* mentioned that Dominican food has an important place of her life. When she first moved to the Netherlands, she lived in Enschede, where it was difficult to find ingredients for Dominican dishes. Every weekend she would make the two and a half-hour trip to Rotterdam to buy plantains, rice and meat. Now in Rotterdam, however, with so many other Caribbean immigrant communities, it was much easier to find ingredients. *Valentina* said she chose her neighbourhood in Amsterdam specifically to have easier access to the ingredients:

> When I was living in Amstelveen, I thought: I have to go all the way to Bijlmer, to Ganzenhoef. Every Saturday I went from Amstelveen to Ganzenhoef and then fully packed back to Amstelveen .... Back then in Ganzenhoef, I do not know whether this is still the case, there was an Antillean-Chinese boy and he had a *toko*, where I bought my things .... And that was also one of the reasons which made me think: I am not going to live forever in Amstelveen, I need to go in the direction of Amsterdam. That is how I came to live in Amsterdam West after my studies .... I was mentally tired, every time that I wanted to cook something, I needed to go to Bijlmer. And I started searching, and now I live near the Kinkerstraat, where there is a Surinamese *toko*.

Sandra's and *Valentina's* stories show the importance of large cities for finding ingredients at *toko*'s, the effort they made in the past and appreciation for the ease with which they came to obtain their ingredients. Their experiences underscore what Law (2001, p. 277) finds, that 'the absence of a familiar material culture and its subtle evocations of home is surely one of the most profound dislocations of transnational migration'. Several studies show that ingredients from the country of origin evoke feelings of nostalgia and familiarity (Brown & Paszkiewicz, 2017; Komarinsky, 2009).

In the other scenario, consisting of Dominicans who have settled in municipalities with a lower percentage of immigrants with similar product needs, the solution is travelling to other cities. This requires some planning; they buy enough to get them through a week or a month and/or coordinate getting specific ingredients with when they made a dish. *Olivia*, who lived in De Meern, a municipality of approximately 20,000 inhabitants near the city Utrecht, told me about her experiences of product finding. The supermarket near her house, called Plus, sometimes would sell plantains, tamarind and coconut, but she chose to go to Utrecht, where she could always find what she needed at the Hindustani store. Hindustanis comprise a cultural community within the Surinamese community.

Olivia said that everything imaginable could be found there. She deemed it useless to bring a whole suitcase full of products back from the Dominican Republic, which Dominicans often did. She emphasized how sometimes you have to make more effort, but everything can be found in the Netherlands. She then told me how she went about buying products and continued on how she could find everything she needed:

> I go on Saturdays. I tell my partner: 'Come, let's get the car, we are going to the toko'. Then he already knows. Then we go buy everything I need, for the entire week. I cook three times a week Dominican and I get everything there. And the rest of the week I prepare potatoes, what he likes.

Casandra said it was hard to find ingredients in Zoetermeer, so she went to another city:

> No, it is not easy. You have to go to the Surinamese [stores] and here you do not have them. Turkish yes, but Surinamese not, for buying the vegetables I need. I always have to go to the market in The Hague. There you can find plantains and things like that, pumpkin, which is delicious in *sancocho* or with beans. They also sell the sweet potatoes. Almost all vegetables you can find at the market, but it also depends on the season.

Asked whether all the effort demotivated her from making a Dominican meal in the Netherlands, she said:

> Of course not. For *habichuela con dulce* and *arroz con leche* you need condensed milk. Now, they sell it in [Dutch supermarket chain] Albert Heijn, but in the past not. The same with evaporated milk, Carnation, that they do not sell in the supermarkets. They sell it somewhere in The Hague. But when we want to make something, we are going to look for it. Why should we leave it?

The stories of others also show not only the planning dimension to product finding but also the efforts they were willing to take. This contradicts Vu and Voeks' (2012) findings about changing foodways of Vietnamese immigrants in California, where geographical distance to Vietnamese food products caused a decline in making dishes from the country of origin. My results were in line with Mehta and Belk's (1991) study showing that Indians who have difficulty finding spices for their Indian dishes keep large pantries of spices, which they collect from travels to areas with larger Indian communities.

Dominicans living outside Amsterdam, The Hague, Rotterdam and Utrecht, however, have witnessed shifts in the availability of products. It was no longer only the Surinamese who sold products Dominicans needed for their dishes.

128   Post-Migration Experiences, Cultural Practices and Homemaking

Many of my respondents also mentioned Turkish and Chinese stores, where they found oregano, cilantro, parsley, plantains and yucca. Even giant grocery chain Albert Heijn began offering products from the Tropics. *Petronila* lived in Nieuwe Vennep, a city 45 kilometres south of Amsterdam with approximately 30,000 inhabitants. In the past, she would travel to the Dominican Republic with one extra suitcase specifically for condiments and products, or she would get her products from the Haagse Markt, a big open market in the city of The Hague:

> Well, [I would go] to the market of Amsterdam, Albert Cuyp, or Rotterdam or The Hague also. My husband was always going because he was working nearby. So he would ask me what I needed, and I would say to him: 'Okra, bring me everything that you see'.

She also described how things have changed over the years in Nieuw Vennep:

> Yes, now in the Netherlands they [products] are very easy to find. When I arrived here, Ave Maria, when I found a plantain some-where, glory. But now it is [easy]. In the Turkish *toko's*, there they have everything, yucca, plantains, pumpkin. There is everything if you want to prepare something here [the Netherlands]. I do not have carry my luggage full of condiments anymore. That is what I did.

Petronila's story shows, firstly, how product limitations in the Netherlands led to transnational practices, namely, bringing products from the Dominican Republic. All Dominicans, including those who lived near the Surinamese stores, brought products back from their holidays in the Dominican Republic. It was custom-ary and originated in the idea that products from the Dominican Republic are fresher and tastier. For these Dominicans living farther away from the ingredient infrastructure, bringing products back from holidays was even more important. Secondly, other migrant communities also offered products, creating new connec-tions through shared food-related needs. It was no longer only the Surinamese (*los Hindustanos*) who sold products Dominicans needed for their dishes. Many of my respondents also mentioned Turkish and Chinese stores, where they found oregano, cilantro, parsley, plantains and yucca. Even giant grocery chain Albert Heijn began offering products from the Tropics.

These experiences show the important role of other immigrant communities in re-creating familiarity. Their shops facilitated the creation of a new life and even home after migration due to easier access to products, similar as to what Brown and Paszkiewizc (2017) show when describing how shops selling Polish products let Polish immigrants recreate home in the United Kingdom with products from their own country.

Access to ingredients was not the only factor leading to negotiation; costli-ness also was a factor and price is a determinant in what is bought, prepared and consumed. *Aurelia* mentioned the economics of eating Dominican food and her

Bread, Ugly Gravy and Boring Parties **129**

preference for variety. Preparing Dominican food was considered expensive and thus impossible to eat daily. She limited the consumption of it:

> I do not prepare Dominican food every day. It would be too expensive. But at least three times a week, you see rice on this table, yucca, plantains and all the basics of there. But consuming plantains here in the Netherlands would not be really practical because it is really expensive .... And I also like to vary. One day rice, the next day pasta with salad and bread, more Italian. I like Indian food a lot, chicken madras.

Another way of dealing with thee costliness was substitution of Dominican ingredients with products found in the Netherlands. One day I was walking in the city centre of Amsterdam. I entered Douglas, a perfume and make-up store, and one of the employees approached, asking whether I needed some advice. We started talking and I noticed a Dominican-Spanish accent in her Dutch pronunciation. I asked her whether she was Dominican and she confirmed she was. She mentioned how she migrated from the Dominican Republic to Spain and then the Netherlands. I told her about my research, and we started talking about food. I mentioned how I like *pastelon de platano maduro* and she told me how that was also one of her favourites. However, because of the quality of the plantains (they need to be brown), and even more so, because of their price in the Netherlands, she used pumpkins in the dish instead.

As mentioned in Chapter 5: regardless of the increased possibilities to get ingredients, Dominicans still brought ingredients from the Dominican Republic because of their higher quality, taste and price. What people can bring, however, is limited due to suitcase restrictions. *Analisa*'s story shows what Komarnisky (2009) highlights, namely the fact that people are controlled by regulations when it comes to obtaining seeds, roots, fresh fruits and vegetables. *Analisa* lived in IJsselstein, where ingredients were not easily found or really expensive. She continued to tell me that once she finished her current salami supply, she would leave it at that. It should be Dominican salami or no salami at all; hers was a Dominican home. And she mentioned that she was not going to buy 'the expensive Dominican salami sold in the Netherlands'. She brought back whatever she could from the Dominican Republic in her suitcase:

> I bring *Baldóm sazón completo* and *Baldom sazón criollo*, they are almost the same. And of course oregano. Normally, oregano from there is always here, but also salami. Look, salami .... now I risk it. Once he [her husband] returned alone to the Netherlands from his first time he was Santo Domingo. I sent a lot of salami with him. But he had a lot of trouble in Spain, because he travelled via Spain. They took away all the salami, they took away everything. After that I was scared and didn't bring anymore, but now I'm going to do it. My friend says: 'Why don't you dare bring salami?' I say: 'Alright, yes, I will. I now take the risk and bring my salami'.

130   Post-Migration Experiences, Cultural Practices and Homemaking

6.4 Food Customs in the Netherlands: Adaptation and Rejection

Migration to the Netherlands not only led to encounters with unfamiliar dishes, preparation styles and ingredients (or lack thereof) but also different food-related customs influenced by different consumption schedules, social organization and celebrations.

6.4.1 No Warm Meals at Noon

The stories about encounters with a different consumption schedule reflect similarities with descriptions by Parasecoli (2014) and Wandel et al. (2008). Their studies show how food practices undergo various degrees of transformation to adapt to a dissimilar way of life and how work schedules cause changes in migrants' consumption patterns. Dominicans are generally accustomed to consuming a warm meal at midday. In the Dominican Republic the main warm meal is consumed around noon. This difference shows two types of reaction of respondents. Some maintained the custom of eating a warm midday meal, which *Mercedes* emphasized the importance of:

> I eat a warm lunch. I can have a sandwich, I can have a *broodje* [sandwich] sometimes. I have that feeling that if it is not warm, like a warm meal, I feel like I have not eaten. I have that, that's in my DNA, for sure. I need to eat proper food …. Well, if I have to eat a sandwich, then I will go for a warm one, a panini or something like that. Yes, I need something warm in my stomach for lunch and dinner.

Petronila's experience showed that the difference in customs created conflicts for her and her children. When her children were in primary school, which would finish at 2 p.m., she would always give them a warm meal when they got home. Her two sons would very often bring other children home to play. For her, it was perfectly normal to offer them a warm meal as well. The mothers of these children, however, asked her not to do that, which was almost impossible for her. How could she only give food to her own children and not to the others who were playing at her home. As a consequence, the playdates at her home stopped and she let her children play at the Dutch children's houses. This led her children to be shocked to find they had to leave when their friends and parents would eat. She had difficulties understanding why Dutch people practically excluded others who do not belong to the household with regard to food, though over time, she and her children got accustomed to it. Her children are in their 20s now and have their own consumption schedule due to work and studies, though *Petronila* has maintained the custom of a warm midday meal.

Petronila's experiences reflect not only a difference in consumption schedules but also how for Dominicans, offering food is an expression of hospitality and taking care of another. *Petronila*'s sense of conflict may be rooted in differences

Bread, Ugly Gravy and Boring Parties **131**

in social organization: a shift from a community-based lifestyle to a more individualistic one (Giovine, 2014) or, more specifically, from a culture where food expresses hospitability, human warmth and care to one where it does not necessarily do so.

However, the majority adapted to the Dutch custom of eating bread or something light for lunch. *Idelisa*, for example, had a practical attitude. She spoke about the importance of a warm meal, but said she was willing to adapt. She arrived in the Netherlands in 2014, after having lived in Italy for a couple of years, and very consciously maintained this custom. She was learning Dutch to find a job, and while she has continued eating a warm midday meal, she already anticipates a future when this will not be possible and eating a sandwich will be more practical:

> I did not leave my custom behind. Here the Dutch eat a lot of bread, in the morning, in the afternoon, in the evening dinner. But I do not at that time. I always have my meal at 12, my rice .... Yes, when I find a job, I would have to adapt to the job. What I do now is [have a warm midday meal] because I am at home, but when I work things will change.

Marte (2008, p. 392) also describes something similar in the case of Dominicans in New York City, stating that the

> the *desayuno, comida, y cena* ['breakfast, lunch and dinner'] which in the Dominican Republic have set times, is more flexible in NYC and it has come to depend on who earns income and cooks the foods in each household.

6.4.2 Changed Household Composition and Living Alone

Another encounter Dominicans had in the Netherlands relates to differences in social organization from being surrounded by an extended family with lot of relatives in one home to just having a nuclear family or even living alone. This shift affected both men and women.

Men who migrated alone, for example, were confronted with the fact that presence of Dominican dishes could not be taken for granted; they had to learn to cook or find other solutions. *Pedro* was living with his wife and child in Santo Domingo before he came to the Netherlands at age 24. After our first interview, *Pedro* invited me over to his house several times. I would help him with translating some Dutch letters and he would thank me by cooking for me. I would request what I was craving for, like a good a*rroz moro* (Fig. 8). To give it an extra touch he would make something like *morir soñando*, a very tasty combination of milk and orange juice. Another day *Pedro* cooked for me; the menu was *platano frito* with salami. While boiling the plantain, cutting it into pieces and frying it, he explained how after migrating he was forced to learn to cook because in the Dominican Republic his

132 Post-Migration Experiences, Cultural Practices and Homemaking

Fig. 8. Pedro's *Arroz Moro*.

mother or his wife would cook. Additionally, in the Netherlands, living alone and working fulltime did not allow him to cook his Dominican dishes and forced him to buy food. Still, he said that Dominican food always remained important:

> I can cook three times a week, because I work. I do not have the time every day. Sometimes I buy Surinamese or Chinese food when I am busy. But Dominican food remains important. It is always there.

Pedro's story shows how he adapted to his situation of migrating alone, living alone and working fulltime: he learned to cook, but also sought compromises.
   The change in social organization also affected women, who in the Dominican Republic were generally responsible for food preparation and who in the Netherlands could no longer rely on extended family to prepare meals when they were out working. *Mariasela*'s story shows how she juggled work and cooking, as part of taking care of her family: eating Dominican dishes sometimes and preparing them when she had the time for it. As *Mariasela* explained, Dominican dishes in general required a lot of preparation time:

> It is a time-consuming cuisine. It is not like preparing potatoes with meat. You have to cook a lot, and this takes time, time which I do not always have. But a Friday, Saturday or Sunday, I take the time to be a couple of hours in the kitchen and preparing Dominican food.

Marte's (2008) work about the food practices of Dominican immigrants in New York City takes the example of *sancocho* to comment on the relevance of a specific

Fig. 9. Pasta Dominican Style With a Slice of Plantain on the Side.

context. Marte (2008) mentions how a change in social organization influences the preparation of a dish, making this the least frequently cooked Dominican dish:

> Sancocho is the most place-specific Dominican staple dish. It is a festival food prepared on Sundays, in an outdoor environment filled with music, drinking and close socializing with family, neighbours and passers-by, attracted to the smells and the music. This traditional context makes the presence of sancocho in NYC particularly problematic. It is difficult to gather many of the family and friend at the same time, due to the scattered locations where they live, due to different jobs schedules and responsibilities during the week. (p. 227)

With regard to dealing with the differences, I observed adaptation to the current situation. A different social organization can lead to various solutions: replacing immigrant culture food with quicker options available in the host culture; buying food from the immigrant culture; cooking traditional dishes on weekends and preparing quick, simple dishes during the week (Giovine, 2014; Srinivas, 2006). *Pedro* and *Mariasela*, but also others mentioned how they would prepare quick meals during the week and Dominican food over the weekend. These quicker options could be dishes made from what they considered typical Dutch products such as

134 Post-Migration Experiences, Cultural Practices and Homemaking

potatoes, vegetables (spinach, cauliflower, broccoli) and a piece of meat that is simply fried on each side without any seasoning except salt and pepper. *Isabel*, who lived with her husband and three children, explained how having less time implied not cooking time-consuming Dominican foods. On the day of our interview, she arrived home at 6 p.m. and afterwards had a Zumba class. There was no time to cook a Dominican dinner and thus she prepared mashed potatoes with broccoli and salami. While she herself did not consider this a Dominican meal, consuming salami for dinner is very Dominican, so I saw it as a fusion of typical Dutch and typical Dominican foods. Some who prepared what they considered a quick foreign dish used Dominican seasoning. Once I was invited for a quick meal. When I entered and saw the spaghetti, I said: 'Oh, we are eating Italian today'. The answer then was: 'No, we are eating pasta Dominican-style' (Fig. 9).

6.4.3 Maintaining Dominican Ways of Celebrating

> Oh this Christmas
> I feel very sad
> Oh I do not have family here
> And I am not near
>
> Oh my mother
> I am so far
> Merry Christmas and a happy new year
> Oh my mother
> I know you miss me
> That I won't celebrate with you
> Christmas and Easter
>
> (Translated by the author)

In his song 'Navidad sin mi madre' El General Larguito tells the story about having to celebrate Christmas elsewhere, outside the Dominican Republic, without family. In this Christmas merengue (*merengue navideño*) the difficulties of many Dominican migrants are expressed.

Apart from encounters with different consumption schedules and social organization another encounter with different food practices was experienced in celebrations. Characteristic of Dominican foodways were certain food customs related to specific holidays. Two holidays are especially important. In the week before Easter, during the festivities of *Semana Santa* (Holy Week), food is central. Special food is prepared for *Semana Santa*, usually in large quantities for extended family and visitors. Part of celebrating Easter in the Dominican Republic was the sharing of *habichuela con dulce* (sweet bean dessert) which is an unknown practice in the Netherlands. Christmas is another important food festivity, celebrated on 24 December (Noche Buena). Dinner on the 24th is meant for sharing, and eating with a group of people is important. While the Netherlands and the Dominican Republic share the same Christian background the role of food differed.

Bread, Ugly Gravy and Boring Parties **135**

Furthermore, in celebrating birthdays or other events not only food took a central role but music and dance as well. Asked what she still missed about the Dominican Republic, *Margarita* said many things, but added that whether you want to or not, you adjust, sometimes without even noticing. There was one thing, however, to which she could not adjust: the Dutch birthday gathering:

> One thing that shocked me here were birthdays. Sister, look, in my family, when my birthday was approaching, my mother would start to search for a pot to prepare sancohco. At this party you would stay up until dawn, whether you would like it or not. It was a party with sancocho and we would go on .... That is how it was. I come here to the Netherlands and you have group of Dutch people sitting in a circle. Do you know that circle when somebody dies, in church? Well, that one. And then the coffee, the cake, the biscuit with cheese on it, the piece of *wurst* ['sausage'] and every-body talking about personal stuff. And I said to myself: this is not the birthday party I am going to have .... When we talk about a party, I talk about a party with dancing until you sweat and have to put on some new clothes because those clothes are not going to dry until tomorrow morning.

Margarita's quote highlights differences in food preparation, the food offered and other aspects, such as music and dancing.

This section showed that with regard to changes in the social aspects of food practices, Dominicans are open to being practical and incorporating into their own routine receiving context practices, such as the time a warm meal was eaten. However, Dominican ways of celebration remained important, were maintained, and there was resistance towards adopting Dutch ways of celebrating special days because they stand in the way of home feelings like sense of community, *ambiente* and human warmth. Especially *ambiente*, a cheerful atmosphere, is at the heart of 'Dominicanness' and a need for it seems to run through Dominicans' veins.

6.5 Conclusion: Receiving Society Characteristics, Practices and Homemaking

The aim of this chapter was to examine how characteristics of the receiving society affect practices and feelings of home. The principal question guiding this chapter was: *How do receiving society characteristics affect cultural practices and feelings of home?* I explored Dominicans' experiences with food practices in the Netherlands, their attitude towards these new encounters and possible changes in practices. I examined this by distinguishing between material and social characteristics.

As for material characteristics, Dominicans encountered native Dutch dishes as well as dishes from other immigrant communities such as the Surinamese and the Chinese. They also encountered new products, which got rejected (gravy) or partially incorporated (bread, cheese, vegetables). The encounters with different dishes, ingredients and preparation styles evoked different attitudes; they were

136   *Post-Migration Experiences, Cultural Practices and Homemaking*

mostly acceptance and rejection, to use Burke's categorization. The ways Dominicans dealt with the encounters show that (1) food from the receiving country was considered as something providing opportunities to get acquainted with new dishes and products and thus the broaden horizons; (2) food from the receiving country was rejected due to taste and ways of preparation; and (3) there was no total adoption of Dutch dishes, but rather of certain products. Exploring this material characteristic showed the importance of other immigrant communities and the opportunities they provided.

As for social characteristics, Dominicans got to know other ways of social organization that affected what they consumed, when and with whom. Some of these encounters were specific to the Dutch context (consumption schedule, frequency of warm meals) and some were more migration-related (migrating alone and thus living alone). The exploration about encounter with Dutch context characteristics showed that (1) Dominicans were open to being practical about consumption schedules and quicker meals, and they adapted; (2) Dominicans stayed attached to the ways festivities were celebrated while there was resistance to Dutch ways of celebrating birthdays, for example; and (3) the receiving context characteristics could stand in the way of re-creating social food practices and thus impede feelings of home, such as human warmth and *ambiente*.

With regard to changes in the material aspects of food practices, no dish was created that had not previously been consumed in the Dominican Republic. Nor was there fusion between authentic Dutch and Dominican dishes, for example, *stamppot* with *pollo guisado*. However, while Dominican immigrants have not yet invented new dishes – as, for example, has been recorded in the United States among Italian immigrants (Diner, 2001) and Cubans (Darias Alfonso, 2014) – Dominicans adopted some of the elements they encountered. Burke's (2009) 'adaptation' comes to the fore in what Fontefrancesco et al. (2019) refer to as 'gastronomic syncretism', the combining of host and home food ingredients. This adaptation also manifested in a hybridization of the weekly menu, which showed Dominicans incorporating dishes from other cultures as well as becoming part-time consumers of Dominican dishes. This was the result of appreciating new dishes and of time constraints.

With regard to changes in the social aspects of food practices, Dominicans in my research were open to being practical and incorporating into their own routine receiving context practices such as the time a warm meal was eaten. However, Dominican ways of celebration remained important, were maintained, and there was resistance towards adopting Dutch ways of celebrating special days. This resistance, however, was not the way Burke (2009) describes it; it was not about defending Dominican ways, but more that those ways were considered 'normal'.

The relationship between context, food and home also revealed that, firstly, receiving contexts are not homogenous; some parts of the country provide easier ways to make home than others. Secondly, limitations in the receiving context demand a form of transnational homemaking wherein migrants keep orientating themselves to their country of origin to be able to recreate practices that give them a feeling of home.

Chapter 7

Conclusions

The stories of Dominican immigrants in the Netherlands exposed several things about the nature of immigrant homemaking, immigrant settlement experiences and Dominican migration to Europe.

7.1 The Nature of Immigrant Homemaking

In my treatment of Dominican migration to the Netherlands, I explored immigrant homemaking by focusing on the meaning of cultural practices and its embeddedness in a context. Many insightful studies investigate immigrants' homemaking, and I sought to add to these by exploring the nuances. In particular, I followed Boccagni (2017), who calls attention to home as a process wherein people attach a sense of home to their life circumstances, depending on their assets and the external structure of opportunities. The stories of Dominicans presented in this book brought out several points with respect to the feelings of home, location of home and homemaking.

Regarding home feelings, I made the deliberate choice to separate feelings from practices, to explore whether a practice indeed evoked feelings of home, without assuming or suggesting that ' "feeling at home" meant and was experienced by everybody as the same thing' (Duyvendak, 2011, p. 42). There seems to be differentiation in what feelings of home are, which go beyond the feeling of familiarity and even include the appreciation of unfamiliarity, which some immigrants happily deal with as opportunities to broaden one's horizon, confirming the importance of Hage's (1997) home element of opportunities. This separation of feelings from practices also let emerge some additional elements of home such as the aforementioned human warmth and the importance of a certain atmosphere. These elements were created with others, inside the home but also outside it. This points to the fluidity of the private–public divide – where home begins and ends – which is not rigid (Boccagni & Brighenti, 2015). My research suggests that what home is (thus the feelings by which home is characterized) differs along national and cultural lines. We therefore must take care not to categorize feelings of home or homemaking only according to western European organization of

---

Post-Migration Experiences, Cultural Practices and Homemaking:
An Ethnography of Dominican Migration to Europe, 137–144
Copyright © 2023 by Sabrina Dinmohamed
Published under exclusive licence by Emerald Publishing Limited
doi:10.1108/978-1-83753-204-920231007

138   Post-Migration Experiences, Cultural Practices and Homemaking

life and make sure to let immigrants themselves tell what they exactly mean when mentioning that something feels like home.

With regard to the location of home differentiation is seen. It became clear that feelings of home are not always or only related to the country of origin or receiving society, but that they can also be related to other countries in a migration trajectory. Those places, too, may provide migrants with a new location of home or acquaint them with new elements of home. Indeed, migrants may not go directly from country A to country B, but have a trajectory which consists of different countries. My findings indicate that a migration trajectory spanning several countries affects the location of home and feelings towards the country of origin. For example, some Dominican immigrants reached the Netherlands via migration to the Dutch Caribbean islands, which for some eventually became home. This raises questions about how homemaking takes place in a stepwise migration trajectory. For example, are homemaking processes different when a migrant knows they are not going to stay in a particular place?

This book began with a part of *Bryan*'s story. He was proud of his Dominican heritage and strongly identified as Dominican (*mil por mil*, as Dominicans often say). However, Dominican food was not important to him. I struggled to make sense of this juxtaposition in relation to Dominican cultural practices and making a home in the Netherlands. Do immigrants then not always strive to recreate familiar practices from the country of origin? In fact, I found a continuum, from practices of the country of origin being important for homemaking to them being unimportant, with different flavours in between. My research indicates that practices from the country of origin can play an important role in immigrants' putting down roots and creating attachments in the receiving society. They can evoke feelings of connection to the country of origin as well as a sense of human warmth and community. Yet, practices from the origin country serve not only to keep connections with it alive but also as a bridge to life in the new society, helping to create home there. Furthermore, homemaking is not only about recreating the familiar. It can also be focused on incorporating unfamiliar elements encountered in the receiving society. I found that a receiving society not only obstructs but also provides opportunities. Here I would emphasize that immigrants who chose to make home through practices brought from their country of origin were also positive about practices they encountered in the receiving society. Thus, giving importance to practices from the country of origin can coexist with an openness to new practices. An individual's preference for maintaining practices from the country of origin can therefore meld with receptivity to opportunities encountered in the receiving context.

I argued for taking into account the contextual embeddedness of immigrants' homemaking. *Sandra*'s story illustrated the importance of other Dominicans, as part of the receiving context, with regard to food-related opportunities. But did such opportunities evoke feelings of home? Various studies identify co-ethnics as a part of the receiving context that helps to foster immigrant homemaking. My study confirmed this, but for Dominicans in the Netherlands, the function of co-ethnics was not straightforward. While co-ethnics are important, my findings

Conclusions **139**

highlight the fact that people seemingly from the same category or group did not all have the same homemaking needs or opportunities. Immigrants might encounter co-ethnics with whom they in their country of origin would never have spent time or shared practices. When studying homemaking practices of immigrants, it is therefore crucial to steer clear of employing groupist ways of thinking.

Valentina's story about ingredient finding and her choice to move to a more multicultural neighbourhood in Amsterdam raised questions about the characteristics of the receiving society. What, besides limited availability in the Netherlands of products for making Dominican food, posed challenges for her food practices? How did she deal with those conditions, and did they affect her feelings of home? Theoretically, I approached the wider receiving society by separating its social and material characteristics. Furthermore, I made the methodological choice to interview Dominicans in different geographical areas within the Netherlands. My results underscore that the receiving society is not a homogeneous entity. It is misleading to speak of 'the' receiving society when studying immigrants' settlement processes. Receiving societies can be very different. Cities with large immigrant populations, for example, offer more opportunities both to recreate practices (due to different people sharing similar practices) and to encounter variation in practices. In this research, Dominicans' connections with other Caribbean communities was clearly evident in the food ingredients they have in common. For immigrants, there is no doubt that the receiving society is experienced as very different, depending on where they ended up: in a culturally diverse environment, in an urban setting or in a small village.

With this in mind and being a proponent of comparative approaches, I would advocate the use of comparative techniques for further study of how contextual characteristics influence homemaking. A comparative approach offers the possibility to explore, in a nuanced way, how contexts with different characteristics influence homemaking practices, similar, for example, to the way immigrant integration researchers have studied the relation between the integration policies of different European countries and the actual integration of immigrants there. The comparison could be not only between countries but also between local contexts, for example, culturally diverse versus less diverse cities or urban versus rural settings within one country, such as the Netherlands. Another valuable dimension for further study is how immigrants and their own needs affect receiving contexts. I expect not only that receiving contexts influence how immigrants make home but also that immigrants affect the receiving context through their needs and what they have to offer.

As a last note on contextual characteristics and homemaking, I approached the receiving context in my study as consisting of two aspects: a possible co-ethnic community and the larger receiving society. Yet, my results point to an additional context wherein negotiations take place as a result of migration: the domestic context. For example, even in stories showing strong orientation towards the country of origin, immigrants could not always make home the way they wanted or preferred. This may occur due to embeddedness in a certain household structure, having a non-Dominican partner or living alone.

140 Post-Migration Experiences, Cultural Practices and Homemaking

So far, I have argued for a differentiation in meanings of home and home-making practices and for consideration of the interaction between individual and contextual characteristics. What should also be kept in mind is the very dynamic nature of immigrant homemaking, which is expressed in its temporality as well as its openness. Over time in the post-migration years, immigrants might become less focused on their country of origin due to life changes. Or, conversely, immigrants might become more orientated to practices from their country of origin due to renewed appreciation for these. With regard to openness, my study revealed that new aspects of the country of origin can intrude into existing practices. This points to several conclusions on the nature of homemaking:

- It finds its origins in an arena of different feelings of home.
- It comes about at the intersection of individual characteristics/preferences and contextual opportunities and constraints.
- It occurs not only in relation to co-ethnics but also in relation to other (immigrant) communities in the receiving society.
- It is dynamic due to its temporal and open nature.
- It takes place in different spaces (e.g. domestic, communal, receiving society and transnational).

7.2 Immigrants' Cultural Practices and Post-Migration Experiences

This research moved away from understanding the lives of immigrants through the lens of integration or assimilation towards a perspective that acknowledges the importance of lived experiences of migration, cultural practices and the meaning of home (Hondagneu-Sotelo, 2017; Sørensen, 1994). I hoped to bring a nuanced picture of immigrant settlement. I found that attention to feelings of home and cultural practices could provide an entry point to knowledge about immigrants' attachments to both the country of origin and the receiving society and their settlement experiences. In this regard, three points merit emphasis. Firstly, yes, it is important to urge immigrants to participate in the receiving society: to find a job, get to know the receiving societies' customs and learn the language. However, immigrants' engagement in practices from the country of origin is not necessarily negative or a sign of separation from the receiving society. Such engagement may actually serve as a bridge to life in the new society, enabling an immigrant to put down roots and feel at home. This feeling of home should also be taken into account when measuring integration and labelling it as successful or unsuccessful.

Secondly, there is internal diversity within groups of people from the same country with regard to the location of home, feelings of home and homemaking practices. Immigrants from the same country may be very differently attached to practices from their country of origin and/or the receiving society. Finding a way into and being part of a new society appears to be a highly differentiated affair and there is diversity within groups of people from the same country with regard

Conclusions **141**

to how they root post-migration. This underscores Brubaker's (2002) idea about ethnic communities' heterogeneity.

Thirdly, rooting in and attachment to the receiving society have a greater chance of success when there is consciousness that immigrants' well-being in the receiving society is a two-way street. Scholars investigating the position of immigrants and role of the receiving context in their positioning (economic, social and cultural) have argued that the ways immigrants relate to the receiving country depend not only on individual characteristics but also on structural conditions (Castañeda, 2020; Ghorashi, 2003; Portes & Rumbaut, 1990; Reitz, 2002; Da Graça, 2010). Indeed, the building of a new life occurs at the intersection of the opportunities in the receiving society and immigrants' own efforts. The stories about home recounted in this book indicate that in order to feel attached to the receiving society immigrants need to feel included. Moreover, they tell us that forms of exclusion, like racism and discrimination, hinder attachments, belonging and feeling at home, even when the immigrant seems to be participating 'successfully' in the primary domains of integration. Chapter 2 presented the story of *Victor*, whose mother came to the Netherlands in the belief that she would be better able to provide her children with basic needs like food and shelter. *Victor* served in the Dutch army and eventually finished law school, after which he became a successful entrepreneur offering legal services. I met him during my last trip to the Dominican Republic in 2022. He told me of his reasons for returning to the Dominican Republic:

> I have done everything to be a good citizen in the Netherlands, but still I am always treated as a second-class citizen. I do not want my daughter to grow up in a racist society, a society where she will never be enough. That is why I returned to the Dominican Republic, a place where I and my qualities are appreciated, where I belong.

Victor's story is not an isolated one. Aranda (2009), too, found, in her study about Puerto Rican migration and settlement in South Florida, that these migrants left places like Washington DC, and Texas due to racism and discrimination and chose other destinations within the United States, like Miami, where they felt welcome.

7.3 Dominican Migration: An Agenda for Future Research

In the stories of Dominicans in the Netherlands several points emerge with regard to the study of Dominican migration in general. Firstly, the importance of studying stepwise migration processes comes to the fore. My research reveals that in recent years many Dominicans who first migrated to Spain, migrated a second time to the Netherlands. A different stepwise trajectory which has existed for a longer time is that from the Dominican Republic to the Dutch Caribbean islands to the Netherlands. This confirms that, due to history and current ties,

142 Post-Migration Experiences, Cultural Practices and Homemaking

intra-regional migration to the Dutch Caribbean islands will always be linked to migration to the Netherlands in Europe. Future research could explore decision-making processes involved in that trajectory and answer questions like does the position of these islands as part of the Dutch kingdom influences regional migrants' choice for the islands? When do immigrants from the Dominican Republic get the idea to go to the Netherlands during their migration? Are most Dominicans on the Dutch Caribbean islands in fact planning to migrate to the Netherlands? If so, did they have that plan upon arrival, but for some reason have not yet taken the step? With regard to the Dominicans who come from the islands – of whom many have Dutch citizenship upon arrival in the Netherlands – their stories demonstrate that having citizenship does not necessarily make insertion in Dutch society easy. Milia-Marie-Luce (2009, p. 98), in her study about Puerto Rican migration to mainland United States and French West Indians to France, confirms that 'the possession of citizenship does not constitute a guarantee of acceptance or inclusion for migrants'.

Secondly, the migration of Dominicans to the Dutch Caribbean islands constitutes a special kind of South-South migration flow. Its study would shed light on a case in which predominantly unskilled, poor immigrants settle and create a home in a place without immigrant incorporation programmes and with limited social security services (the Dutch Caribbean islands), but which is connected to a country belonging to the 'North' (the Netherlands). Some efforts have been made to delve into Dominican migration to the islands (De Boer, 2016; Dinmohamed 2012, 2017, 2021; SOAW, 2014), but there remains a whole arena still to explore. My own perception of a vast terrain yet to be grasped always intensifies when I am in Curaçao, observing the many different migrant communities there. A more profound study of Dominicans migrating to, for example, Curaçao would add valuable knowledge on the much-understudied South–South migration flows (Dinmohamed, 2017). Exploring homemaking practices of Dominican immigrants on the islands can provide a different view on settlement processes of immigrants in societies other than the much studied western European and North American ones. Much of the existing immigrant homemaking literature is overly focused on these types of receiving societies and South-North migration. It cannot be assumed that the process of homemaking of immigrants in other parts of the world follows along the same lines and is similar.

It is important, however, not to approach these islands as homogenous, as the Leeward and Windward islands differ from each other linguistically, culturally, climatologically and possibly socially. This point also came to the fore in the stories of Dominicans who had lived on the different islands. Those who had lived on Sint Maarten before migrating to the Netherlands said they felt at home there, in contrast to those who had lived in Curaçao or Aruba. It would be worthwhile to further explore whether certain characteristics of the receiving context are more conducive to immigrants' feelings of home.

Thirdly, there is value in studying Dominicans' relations with other (Caribbean) communities. Chapter 5 examined the role of the Surinamese food infrastructure in helping Dominicans create home in the Netherlands. It would be valuable to further explore how Caribbean communities facilitate one another in

Conclusions **143**

multiple areas. Noteworthy in this regard is, for example, the 'pleasure circuit' – a term used by Sansone (2009) referring to the party and leisure scene – in which Curaçaoans adopt a cultural element of Dominicans, namely bachata music, to organize their parties around. It would be interesting to get insight into Dominicans' ideas about whether those parties provide them an opportunity to find and feel a Dominican atmosphere.

Fourthly, there is still much to learn about the Dominican immigrants in the Netherlands, the development of a social and cultural infrastructure and the development of the second generation. Do Dominicans in the Netherlands differ in key respects from those elsewhere in the world such as New York and Madrid? Can similarities be found across European countries? Or do the lives of the migrants in the Netherlands show entirely different patterns?

Another question is whether migration to the Netherlands brings about the results that Dominican migrants envisioned. Frank Reyes sang about the economic goals that had to be attained before the migrant could return to the Dominican Republic. Is this the only measure of a successful migration? How can we assess the success of migration? Some Dominicans in my research criticized co-ethnics who were insufficiently focused on personal betterment – often equating a lack of ambition with too much focus on Dominican culture and social contacts with other Dominicans (instead having a mixed social group and being more open to other communities). This attitude unknowingly reproduces ideas from the immigrant integration debate in the Netherlands. The stories in this book indicate that what is considered 'success' is differentiated. It is indeed related not only to participation in the primary domains of integration and to social mobility but also to being able to provide food and shelter, and to having opportunities for broadening one's horizons. Many first-generation Dominicans have, by now, resided in the Netherlands for many years. They might be able to provide valuable reflections on these questions.

The character in Frank Reyes' song laments that he cannot yet return. The Dominicans in my research were divided about return. In this regard, I would advance the idea that return is not always or only related to material achievements; thus, that a migrant may only return after having attained economic goals. The picture is more nuanced, and cultural and social reasons may play a role in the decision (Baerga & Thompson, 1990; Brennan, 2004). Some Dominicans do go to Europe with the idea of returning. This came to the fore in the story of a lady I met at Casa Migrante while doing my volunteer work. She said that as soon as her daughter finished her studies she would return to the Dominican Republic, where she had already built a house. However, others think of returning only after they come to realize that life in Europe is not what they thought it would be. Economic advancement is important, but social and cultural customs may ultimately play a larger role than many realized before migrating. *Pedro*, whose story has so often been mentioned in this book, told me at one of our many get-togethers that he wanted to buy a house in Paraiso, his hometown in south-eastern Dominican Republic. If he had an income of 1,000 euros a month, he said, he would return without thinking twice. When he mentions the house he sees himself living in, with its two stories and a little roof terrace, I am reminded of a picture he had

144 Post-Migration Experiences, Cultural Practices and Homemaking

cut out and hung at his desk. Such is the power of visualization. He continued, 'Then when I die, it wouldn't matter, because it would happen on the nicest place on earth'. His words rang like poetry, and I realized that we should cherish the stories of migrants, like we cherish poetry.

Appendix

List of Food Names

This is a list of food Dominicans in this research mentioned: the typical Dominican food and foods encountered in the Netherlands.

Dominican

Arepa	Cornmeal and coconut cake
Arroz con leche	Rice with milk
Arroz con coco/con fideo	Rice with coconut/noodles
Asopao	Rice soup
Bija	Annatto, orange-red seeds of the achiote tree used for food colouring and substitution for tomato paste
Chaca	Cracked corn pudding, consisting of milk, corn, vanilla, cinnamon and cloves
Chenchen con chivo	Cracked corn pilaf dish, originating in San Juan De La Maguana
Chimichurris	Street burgers that are topped with cabbage and a sweet sauce made with ketchup and mayonnaise
Cilantro ancho	Culantro
Concón	Crust of crispy rice formed at the bottom of the pot when rice is cooked
Ensalada Rusa	Potato salad made with carrots, eggs, beetroot, Christmas food
Flan	Custard dessert
Habichuela con dulce	Sweet bean dessert. Cooked beans, sweet potato, coconut and sugar
Kipe	Deep fried bulgur rolls, usually eaten as finger food, originating in the Middle East
La Bandera	Dominican flag: rice with beans and stewed meat
Locrio	Rice dish, consists of seasoned rice with some kind of meat, such as chicken, Dominican salami or pork
Mamajuana	Alcoholic beverage made with rum, red wine, tree bark, spices and herbs
Mondongo	Stew made with beef tripe, onion, garlic, peppers, carrots, potatoes, tomato sauce and cilantro

146   Appendix

Moro de habichuelas/ guandules	Rice cooked with beans or pigeon peas.
Majarete	Pudding made with freshly grated corn off the cob
Mangù	Plantain mash, breakfast
Mofongo	Deep-fried green plantains mashed together with other ingredients such as pork or seafood
Morir soñando	Milk and orange juice
Pescado con coco	Fish in coconut sauce
Pastel en hoja	Plantain and root vegetables dough filled with meat and made into a pocket using plantain leaves
Sancocho de siete carne	Meat stew
Pastelón	Sweet plantain casserole, mashed sweet plantains layered with savoury ground beef and topped with melted cheese
Pica pollo	Deep fried chicken seasoned with lemon, garlic and Dominican oregano.
Pimiento	Pepper
Salsa Ranchera	Sauce based on tomatoes, vinegar, salt, onions, corn and sugar.
Sopita	(chicken) cube bouillon
Tostones/frito verde	Fried plantains, side dish
Tres leches	Sponge cake, soaked in three kinds of milk and topped with whipped cream
Yaniqueque	Fried bread with a crispy and crunchy texture, made with flour, salt, melted butter and baking powder

Encountered in the Netherlands

Appelmoes	Apple sauce
Biefstuk	Steak, raw
Chicken madras	Indian, a madras curry is a fairly hot curry with a dark red thick sauce
Erwtensoep	Pea soup
Groenten	Vegetables, greens
Frikandel	Dutch snack, a long and skinless fried sausage mostly comprised beef, pork and chicken
Hello Fresh Box	A meal delivery service that ships weekly ingredients, with the goal of healthy meals preparation
Karbonade	Cutlet

Appendix **147**

Kroket	Dutch snack filled with a meat ragout with a crispy and crunchy outside
Pannekoeken	Large pancakes, usually eaten for dinner, with various fillings, ranging from syrup, powdered sugar and apple to cheese, spinach and bacon
Patat met mayonaise	French fries and mayonnaise
Rookworst	Smoked sausage, smoked sausage made of ground meat, spices and salt
Roti	Indian-Surinamese dish, flat bread served with meat and vegetables
Stamppot	Potato mash with ingredients like kale, endive, cabbage or sauerkraut, often served with smoked sausage and gravy
Saté ku batata	Curaçaoan street food, meat, potatoes and peanut sauce

Bibliography

Abbots, J. (2016). Approaches to food and migration: Rootedness, being and belonging. In J. Klein & J. Watson (Eds.), *The handbook of food and anthropology* (pp. 115–132). London: Bloomsbury.

Abaunza, C. (2017). 500 años de historia entre el Reino de los Países Bajos y la República Dominicana. Santo Domingo: Embajada del Reino de los Paises Bajos ante la Repiblica Dominicana y Haiti.

Al-Ali, N., & Koser, K. (2002). *New approaches to migration? Transnational communities and the transformation of home.* London: Routledge.

Allen, R. (2003). Acceptatie of uitsluiting. Enkele belangrijke invalshoeken voor de discussie over beeldvorming over immigranten uit de regio en over de Curaçaoënaars. In R. Allen, C. Heijes, & M. Marcha (Eds.), *Emancipatie en acceptatie. Curaçao en Curaçaoënaars. Beeldvorming en identiteit honderd veertig jaar na de slavernij.* (pp. 72–90) Amsterdam: SWP.

Allen, R. (2006). Regionalization of identity in Curaçao: Migration and diaspora. In R. Gowricharn (Ed.), *Caribbean transnationalism: Migration, pluralism and social cohesion* (pp. 79–98). Lanham: Lexington Books.

Aranda, E. (2009). Puerto Rican migration and settlement in South Florida: Ethnic identities and transnational spaces. In M. Cervantes-Rodriguez, R. Grosfoguel, & E. Mielants (Eds.), *Caribbean migration to Western Europe and the United States. Essays on incorporation, identity and citizenship* (pp. 111–130). Philadelpha, PA: Temple University Press.

Baerga, M., & Thompson, L. (1990). Migration in a small semiperiphery: The movement of Puerto Ricans and Dominicans. *International Migration Review, 24*(4), 656–683.

Barajas Sandoval, L. (2008). *Integration and development trajectories: Latin American populations.* Working Paper No. 461. Institute of Social Studies.

Bhatti, M., & Church, A. (2000). 'I never promised you a rose garden': Gender, leisure and home-making. *Leisure Studies, 19*, 183–197.

Blunt, A. (2005). Cultural geography: Cultural geographies of home. *Progress in Human Geography, 29*(4), 505–515.

Blunt, A., & Varley, A. (2004). Introduction: Geographies of home. *Cultural Geographies, 11*, 3–6.

Boccagni, P. (2013). What's in a (migrant) house? Changing domestic places, the negotiation of belonging and home-making in Ecuadorian migration. *Housing, Theory and Society, 31*(3), 277–293.

Boccagni, P. (2017). *Migration and the search for home.* New York, NY: Palgrave Macmillan.

Boccagni, P., & Brighenti, A. (2015). Immigrants and home in the making: Thresholds of domesticity, commonality and publicness. *Journal of Housing and the Built Environment, 32*, 1–11.

Bonhomme, M. (2013). Cultura material y migrantes peruanos en Chile: Un proceso de integracion desde el hogar. *POLIS Revista Latinoamericana, 12*(35), 1–15.

Brennan, D. (2004). *What's love got to do with it. Transnational desires and sex tourism in the Dominican Republic.* Durham, NJ: Duke University Press.

Brown, L., Edwards, J., & Hartwell, H. (2010). A taste of the unfamiliar: Understanding the meanings attached to food by international. *Appetite, 54*, 202–207.

150 Bibliography

Brown, L., & Paszkiewicz, I. (2017). The role of food in the Polish migrant adjustment journey. *Appetite, 109*(February), 57–65.

Brubaker, R. (2002). Ethnicity without groups. *European Journal of Sociology, 43*(2), 163–189.

Bucerius, S. (2013). Becoming a 'trusted outsider': Gender, ethnicity, and inequality in ethnographic research. *Journal of Contemporary Ethnography, 46*(2), 690–721.

Burke, P. (2009). *Cultural hybridity*. Cambridge: Polity Press.

Burns, C. (2004). Effect of migration on food habits of Somali women living as refugees in Australia. *Ecology of Food and Nutrition, 43*(3), 213–229.

Cancellieri, A. (2015). Towards a progressive home-making: The ambivalence of migrants' experience in a multicultural condominium. *Journal of Housing and the Built Environment, 32*, 49–61.

Castañeda, E. (2000). Urban contexts and immigrant organizations: Differences in New York, El Paso, Paris, and Barcelona. *The Annals of the American Academy of Political and Social Science, 690*(1), 117–135.

CBS. (2016). Afbakening generaties met migratieachtergrond. Retrieved from https://www.cbs.nl/nl-nl/achtergrond/2016/47/afbakening-generaties-met-migratieachtergrond. Accessed on July 26, 2020.

CBS Aruba. (2004). *Double or quits. A study on recent migration to Aruba 1993–2003*. Oranjestad: Central Bureau of Statistics Aruba.

Christou, A., & Janta, H. (2019). The significance of things: Objects, emotions and cultural production in migrant women's return visits home. *The Sociological Review, 67*(3), 654–671.

Collins, F. (2008). Of kimchi and coffee: Globalisation, transnationalism and familiarity in culinary consumption. *Social & Cultural Geography, 9*, 151–169.

Da Graça, A. A. (2010). Etnische zelforganisaties in het integratieproces: Een case study in de Kaapverdische gemeenschap in Rotterdam. Ph.D. thesis, University of Tilburg, Tilburg.

Darias Alfonso, I. (2012). We are what we now eat: Food and identity in the Cuban diaspora. *Canadian Journal of Latin American and Caribbean Studies, 37*(74), 173–206.

Dayaratne, R., & Kellet, P. (2008). Housing and homemaking in low-income urban settlements: Sri Lanka and Colombia. *Journal of Housing and the Built Environment, 23*(1), 53–70.

De Boer, E. (2016). *500 Years of migration flows between the Dominican Republic and the Caribbean part of the Kingdom of the Netherlands*. Embassy of the Kingdom of the Netherlands for the Dominican Republic and Haiti.

Després, C. (1991), The meaning of home: literature review and directions for future research and theoretical development, *The Journal of Architectural and Planning Research, 8*, 96–115.

Diner, H. (2001). *Hungering for America: Italian, Irish, and Jewish foodways in the age of migration*. Cambridge: Harvard University Press.

Dinmohamed, S. (2007). Migranten in de Nederlandse Antillen (1). *Modus, 7*(4), 5–9.

Dinmohamed, S. (2008). Migranten in de Nederlandse Antillen (2). *Modus, 8*(1), 5–11.

Dinmohamed, S. (2012). Visa para un sueno: Dominicaanse migranten in het Koninkrijk der Nederlanden. *Amigoe*, September 8.

Dinmohamed, S. (2017). Sabor Quisqueyano. Homemaking of Dominican immigrants in Curacao. In C. Felbeck & A. Klump (Eds.), *Dominicanidad/Dominicanity: Perspectivas de unconcepto (trans-)nacional/perspectives on a(trans-)national concept* (pp. 145–158). Frankfurt am Main: Peter Lang.

Dinmohamed, S. (2021). *Dominican flavours in a new context:. Homemaking and food practices of Dominican immigrants*. Ph.D. thesis, University of Amsterdam, Amsterdam.

Bibliography   151

Dinmohamed, S. (2023). Exploring immigrants' experiences through cultural practices and homemaking: the case of Dominican immigrants' food practices. *Journal of Ethnic and Racial Studies*. doi:10.1080/01419870.2023.2165416

Duany, J. (2005). Dominican migration to Puerto rico: A transnational perspective. *Centro Journal, City University of New York, 17*(1), 242–269.

Duany, J. (2008). *Quisqueya on the Hudson: The transnational identity of Dominicans in Washington Heights.* New York, NY: Dominican Studies Institute, City University of New York.

Duyvendak, J. (2011). *Politics of home: Belonging and nostalgia in Western Euorpe and the United States.* Basingstoke: Palgrave Macmillan.

Fontefrancesco, M., Barstow, C., Grazioli, F., Lyons, H., Mattalia, G., Marino, M., ... Pieroni, A. (2019). Keeping or changing? Two different cultural adaptation strategies in the domestic use of home country food, plant and herbal ingredients among Albanian and Moroccan migrants in Northwestern Italy. *Journal of Ethnobiology and Ethnomedicine, 15*(11), 1–18.

Friedman, J. (1997). Global crises, the struggle for cultural identity and intellectual porkbarrelling: Cosmopolitans vs. locals, ethnics and nationals in an era of dehomogenisation. In P. Werbner & T. Modood (Eds.), *Debating cultural hybridity: Multi-cultural identities and the politics of anti-racism* (pp. 70–89). London: Zed.

Ghorashi, H. (2003). *Ways to survive, battles to win. Iranian Women exiles in the Netherlands & United States.* Hauppauge, NY: Nova Science Publishers.

Gill, H. (2012). *Querido emigrante: Musical perspectives of Dominican migration.* Working paper.

Gill, H. (2002). Querido emigrante: Musical Perspectives of Dominican Migration. University of Oxford Institute of Social and Cultural Anthropology. Transnational Community Programme Working Paper #WPTC-02-12.

Giovine, R. (2014). The shifting border of food perceptions and cultural identity in Maghrebi Muslim migrants. *Communication, 8*(1), 25–40.

Gram-Hanssen, K., & Bech-Danielsen, C. (2011). Creating a new home. Somali, Iraqi and Turkish immigrants and their homes in Danish housing. *Housing and the Built Environment, 27,* 89–103.

Grasmuck, S., & Pessar, P. (1991). *Between two islands. Dominican international migration.* Berkeley, CA: University of California Press.

Graziano, F. (2013). *Undocumented Dominican migration.* Austin, TX: University of Texas Press.

Guilamo, S., Flores, A., Reyes, A., & Perez, M. (2023). *Movimientos migratorios en República Dominicana: Su impacto en los jóvenes.* Santo Domingo: Pontificia Universidad Católica Madre y Maestra.

Gutierrez, M. (2006). *Motherhood & social networks. Female Dominican transnational migration to the Netherlands.* Master thesis, University of Amsterdam, Amsterdam.

Hadjiyanni, T. (2009). Aesthetics in displacement-Hmong, Somali and Mexican homemaking practices in Minnesota. *International Journal of Consumer Studies, 33,* 541–549.

Hage, G. (1997). At home in the entrails of the west: Multiculturalism, ethnic food and migrant home-building. In H. E. Grace (Ed.), *Home/world: Space, community and marginality in Syndey's west* (pp. 99–153). Annandale: Pluto Press.

Hernández, R. (2002). *The mobility of workers under advanced capitalism.* New York, NY: Columbia University Press.

Hirschman A. (1996). Melding the public and private spheres: Taking commmensality seriously. *Critical Review, 10*(4), 533–550.

Hoffman, E. (1989). Lost in Translation: A Life in a New Language. London: Minerva.

Hondagneu-Sotelo, P. (2017). At home in inner-city immigrant community gardens. *Journal of Housing and the Built Environment, 32,* 13–28.

152   Bibliography

International Organization for Migration. (2017). *Perfil migratorio República Dominicana.* Santo Domingo: International Organzation for Migration.

Janssen, M. (2007). *Reizende sexwerkers. Latijns-Amerikaanse vrouwen in de Europese prostitutie.* Apeldoorn/Antwerpen: Het Spinhuis.

Kempny, M. (2012). Rethinking native anthropology: Migration and auto-ethnography in the post-accession Europe. *International Review of social Research, 2*(2), 39–52.

Kershen, A. (2002). *Food in the migrant experience.* Burlington: Ashgate Publishing Company.

Komarnisky, S. (2009). Suitcases full of mole: Travelling food and the connections between Mexico and Alaska. *Alaska Journal of Anthropology, 7*(1), 41–56.

Kothari, U. (2008). Global peddlers and local networks: Migrant cosmopolitanisms. *Environment and Planning D: Society and Space, 26*(3), 500–516.

Lam, T., & Yeoh, B. (2004). Negotiating 'home' and 'national identity': Chinese-Malaysian transmigrants in Singapore. *Asia Pacific Viewpoint, 45*, 141–164.

Lamont, M., & Aksartova, S. (2002). Ordinary cosmopolitanisms: Strategies for bridging racial boundaries among working-class men. *Theory, Culture & Society, 19*(4), 1–25.

Law, L. (2001). Home cooking: Filipino women and geographies of the senses in Hong Kong. *Cultural Geographies, 8*(3), 264–283.

Levitt, P. (2001). *The transnational villagers.* Berkely, CA: University of California Press.

Ley, D. (2008). The immigrant church as an urban service hub. *Urban Studies, 45,* 2057–2074.

Lilón, D., & Lantigua, J. (2004). Dominican transmigrants in Spain. In E. Sagas & S. Molina (Eds.), *Dominican migration: Transnational perspectives* (pp. 135–153). Gainesville, FL: University Press of Florida.

Liukku, A. (2020). *Zorgen om Dominicaanse Rotterdammers. Gemeente start onderzoek.* Retrieved from https://www.ad.nl/rotterdam/zorgen-om-dominicaanse-rotterdammers-gemeente-start-onderzoek~a31f3ea2/

Longhurst, R., Johnston, L., & Ho, E. (2009). A visceral approach: Cooking 'at home' with migrant women in Hamilton, New Zealand. *Transactions of the Institute of British Geographers, 34,* 333–345.

Mallett, S. (2004). Understanding home: a critical review of the literature .*The Sociological Review, 52*(1), 62–89.

Mankekar, P. (2002). 'India Shopping': Indian gorcery stores and transnational configurations of belonging. *Ethnos, 67*(1), 75–97.

Marte, L. (2008). *Migrant seasonings: Food practices, cultural memory and narratives of 'home' among Dominican communities in New York City.* Ph.D. thesis, University of Texas at Austin, Austin, TX.

Marte, L. (2011). Afro-Diasporic seasonings. Food routes and Dominican place-making in New York City. *Food, Culture & Society, 14*(2), 181–204.

Mehta, R., & Belk, R. (1991). Artifacts, identity and transition: Favorite posessions of Indians and Indian immigrants to the U.S. *Journal of Consumer Research, 17*(March), 398–411.

Meijering, L., & Lager, D. (2014). Home-making of older Antillean migrants in the Netherlands. *Ageing & Society, 34,* 859–875.

Milia-Marie-Luce, M. (2009). Puerto Ricans in the United States and French West Indian immigrants in France. In M. Cervantes-Rodriguez, R. Grosfoguel, & E. Mielants (Eds.), *Caribbean migration to Western Europe and the United States: Essays on incorporation, identity, and citizenship* (pp. 94–108). Philadelphia, PA: Temple University Press.

Ministerie van Sociale Ontwikkeling, Arbeid en Welzijn (SOAW). (2014). *Regionale migratie en integratie op Curaçao.* Willemstad: Ministerie van Sociale ontwikkeling en Welzijn.

Ministerie van Sociale Ontwikkeling, Arbeid en Welzijn. (2014). *Regionale migratie en integratie op Curaçao.* Curacao: Willemstad.

Bibliography **153**

Miranda-Nieto, A., & Boccagni, P. (2020). At home in the restaurant: Familiarity, belonging and material culture in Ecuadorian restaurants in Madrid. *Sociology*, *54*(5), 1022–1040. doi:https://doi.org/10.1177/0038038520914829

Moya Pons, F. (2008). *Historia del Caribe: Azucar y plantaciones en el mudo Atlantico.* Santo Domingo: Editora Buho.

Narayan, K. (1993). How native is 'native' anthropologist. *American Anthropologist*, *95*(3), 671–686.

Nowicka, M. (2007). Mobile locations: Construction of home in a group of mobile transnational professionals. *Global Networks*, *7*, 69–86.

OECD. (2017). The Dominican Republic's migration landscape. In OECD/Centro de Investigaciones Económicas, Administrativas y Sociales (Eds.), *Interrelations between Public Policies, Migration and Development in the Dominican Republic* (pp. 37–55). Paris: OECD Publishing.

Oso Casas, L. (2009). Dominican women, heads of households in Spain. In M. Cervantes-Rodriguez, R. Grosfoguel, & E. Mielants (Eds.), *Caribbean migration to Western Europe and the United States: Essays on incorporation, identity, and citizenship* (pp. 208–231). Philadelphia, PA: Temple University Press.

Pacini Hernandez, D. (1995). *Bachta. A social history of Dominican popular music.* Philadelphia, PA: Temple University Press.

Parasecoli, F. (2014). Food, identity, and cultural reproduction in immigrant communities. *Social Research: An International Quarterly*, *81*(2), 415–439.

Paul, A., & Yeoh, B. (2021). Studying multinational migrations, speaking back to migration theory. *Global Networks*, *21*, 3–17.

Pécoud, A. (2004). Entrepreneurship and identity: Cosmopolitan and cultural constituencies among German-Turkish businesspeople in Berlin. *Journal of Ethnic and Migration Studies*, *45*(9), 3–18.

Perez Murcia, L. (2018). 'The sweet memories of home have gone': Displaced people searching for home in a liminal space. *Journal of Ethnic and Migration Studies*, *45*(9), 1515–1531.

Petree, J., & Vargas, T. (2005). *Dominicans in Switzerland: Patterns, practices and impacts of transnational migration and remittances linking the Dominican Republic and Switzerland.* Lausanne: Ecole Polytechnique Federale de Lausanne.

Petridou, E. (2001). The taste of home. In D. Miller (Ed.), *Home possesions: Material culture behind closed doors* (pp. 87–106). Oxford: Berg.

Philipp, A., & Ho, E. (2010). Migration, home and belonging: South African migrant women in Hamilton, New Zealand. *New Zealand Population Review*, *36*(1), 81–101.

Pizarro, J., & Villa, M. (2005). *International migration in Latin America and the Caribbean: A summary view of trends and patterns.* Santiago de Chile: CEPAL/CELADE.

Portes, A., & Rumbaut, R. (1990). *Immigrant America. A portrait.* Berkeley, CA: University of California Press.

Rabikowska, M. (2010). The ritualisation of food, home and national identity among Polish migrants in London. *Social Identities*, *16*(3), 377–398.

Reitz, J. (2002). Host societies and the reception of immigrants: Research themes, emerging theories and methodological issues. *International Migration Review*, *36*(4), 1005–1019.

Renne, E. (2007). Mass producing food traditions for West Africans Abroad. *American Antrhopologist*, *109*(4), 616–625.

Restler, L. (2006). *Intraregional Caribbean migrations: Exchanges of people culture, and ideas, the case of the Dominican Republic and Southern St. Martin.* Providence, RI: Brown University.

Román-Velázquez, P. (1999). The Making of Latin London. Salsa music, place and identity. London: Routledge.

Romero Valiente, J. (1997). *Las migraciones exteriores de Republica Dominicana.* Huelva: Universdad Huelva.

Ryan, L. (2015). Inside and outside of what and where. Researching migration through multi-positionalities. *Forum: Qualitative Sozialforschung/Forum: Qualitative Research*, *16*(2), art. 17.

154   Bibliography

Sandu, A. (2013). Transnational homemaking practices: Identity, belonging and informal learning. *Journal of Contemporary European Studies, 21*(4), 496–512.

Sansone, L. (2009). The making of Suriland: The binational development of a black community between the tropics and the north sea. In M. Cervantes-Rodriguez, R. Grosfoguel, & E. Mielants (Eds.), *Caribbean migration to Western Europe and the United States* (pp. 169–190). Philadelphia, PA: Temple University Press.

Saseănu, A., & Petrescu, R. (2011). Potential connections between migration and immigrant food consumption habits. The case of Romanian immigrants in Andalusia, Spain. *The Amfiteatru Economic Journal, 13*(5), 790–802.

Scandone, B. (2018). Re-claiming one's 'culture': How middle-class capital and participation in higher education can promote the assertion of ethnic identities. *Journal of Ethnic and Migration Studies, 46*(3), 1–18.

Slootman, M. (2014). Soulmates: Reinvention of ethnic identification among higher educated second generation Moroccan and Turkish Dutch. Ph.D dissertation University of Amsterdam.

Sørensen, N. (1994). Roots, routes and transnational attractions: Dominican migration, gender and cultural change. *The European Journal of Development Research, 6*(2), 104–118.

Srinivas, T. (2006). As mother made it: The cosmopolitan Indian family, 'authentic' food and the construction of cultural utopia. *International Journal of Sociology of the Family, 22*(3), 191–221.

Sullivan, A. (2006). *Local lives, global stage: Diasporic experiences and changing family practices on the Caribbean island of Saba.* Ph.D. thesis, University of North Carolina, Chapel Hill, NC.

Thomas-Hope, E. (1992). *Caribbean Migration.* Mona: University of the West Indies Press.

UN-INSTRAW. (2006). *Gender, migration, remittances and development.* Fifth coordinating meeting on international migration. UN Department on International migration, New York, NY.

United Nations Department of Economic and Social Affairs, Population Division. (2020). *International Migrant Stock 2020.* Retrieved from https://www.un.org/development/desa/pd/content/international-migrant-stock

Van den Berghe, P. (1984). Ethnic cuisine: Culture in nature .*Ethnic and Racial Studies, 7*(3), 387–397

Van Ginkel, R. (1994). Writing culture from within. Observations on endo-ethnography. *Etnofoor, 7*, 5–23.

Verbeke, W., & Lopez, G. (2005). Ethnic food attitudes and behaviour among Belgians and Hispanis living in Belgium. *British Food Journal, 107*(10–11), 823–840.

Vilar Rosales, M. (2010). The domestic work of consumption: materiality, migration and home-making. *Etnográfica, 14* (3), 507–525.

Vu, V., & Voeks, R. (2012). Fish sauce to French fries: Changing foodways of the Vietnamese diaspora in Orange County, California. *California Geographer, 52*, 35–55.

Wandel, M., Kjollesdal, M., Kumar, B., & Holmboe-Ottesen, G. (2008). Changes in food habits after migration among South Asians settled in Oslo: The effect of demographic, socio-economic and integration factors. *Appetite, 50*, 376–385.

Weller, D., & Turkon, D. (2015). Contextualizing the immigrant experience: The role of food and foodways in identity maintenance and formation for first- and second-generation Latinos in Ithaca, New York. *Medicine, Sociology; Ecology of Food and Nutrition, 254*(1), 57–73.

Werbner, P. (1999). Global pathways, working-class cosmopolitans and the creation of transnational worlds. *Social Anthropology, 71*, 17–36.

Wiles, J. (2008). Sense of home in a transnational space: New Zealenders in London. *Global Networks, 8*(1), 116–137.

Wood, J. (1997). Vietnamese American place making in Northern Virginia. *Geographical Review, 87*(1), 58–72.

Index

Acceptance, 120
Adaptation, 120
Algemeen Beschaafd Nederlands
    (ABN Nederlands), 56
Alternate food rituals, 73
Ambiente, 47–49
Ambivalent homes, 63
American dream, 100
Appelmoes, 121, 146
Arepa, 145
Arroz con coco/con fideo, 145
Arroz con leche, 127, 145
Aruba, 26
Aruban economy, 26
Asopao, 145
Assimilation, 3

Bachata, 3, 11, 13, 19, 43–46, 48, 74,
    96, 109–112, 143
Biefstuk, 121, 146
Bija, 145
Bitterballen, 121
Black telephone, 42
Bread, 122
Business opportunities, 103–107

Caribbean communities, 107, 139,
    143
    importance of, 125–129
Caribbean immigrants, 142
Caribbean migration, 18, 24, 71
Casa Migrante, 14
Chaca, 145
Chenchen con chivo, 145
Chicken madras, 146
Children, 30
Chimichurris, 145
Chinese, 135

Christmas, 69
Cilantro ancho, 145
Citizenship, 142
Co-ethnic community, 8, 95
Co-ethnics, 8, 10, 93, 95–96, 116–117,
    138
Commensality, 10, 106
Communal space, 17, 117
    contested homes in, 107–116
Community with expanding
    infrastructure, growing,
    45–46
Comparative approach, 139
Comparsa Sabor Dominicano, 46
Concón, 145
Contested homes in communal
    spaces, 107
    Dominican food initiatives in
    Netherlands, 107–109
    El Malecon, 109–114
    La Tienda, 114–116
Context, 7
Contextual embeddedness of
    immigrant homemaking,
    7–8
Cosmopolitanism, 84
Culinary essentialism 88
Culinary inventions, 120
Cultural adaptation strategies, 87
Cultural elements, 43
Cultural mosaic, 15
Cultural practices, 116–117
Culture of unity, 105
Curaçao, 24

Dance, 11, 13, 43–47, 65, 67, 77, 93,
    96–97, 106, 111, 115, 135
Data collection method, 10, 12

156 *Index*

Decision-making process, 30
Demasiado horrible, 55
Deprived economic migrants, 85
Diploma devaluation, 85
Discrimination, 58, 63, 85, 141
Distinctions, 94
Diversification in migration
    destinations and stepwise
    trajectories, 38
Domestic context, 139
Domestic space, 117
Dominican co-ethnics, 97
  co-ethnics, cultural practices and
    feelings of home, 116–117
  contested homes in communal
    spaces, 107–116
  feelings of home in Dutch-
    Dominican community,
    94–103
  food practices, business
    opportunities and
    dominican sociability, 103
  story of ingredients, 103–105
  story of sharing and celebrations,
    105–107
Dominican commodities, 43
Dominican community, 3, 14–15, 21,
    30, 46, 97, 114
  in Netherlands, 7, 17, 100
  in Saba, 27
Dominican condiments, 115
Dominican cuisine, 68
Dominican cultural practices, 1
Dominican culture, 14, 43
Dominican customers, 116
Dominican dishes, 109–110, 133, 136
Dominican dream, 100
Dominican events, 101
Dominican food, 7, 17, 43, 68–72, 76,
    79–80, 82, 86, 90, 111, 128,
    139
  broadening horizons, 77–79
  celebration food, 80–81
  cultural practices and feelings of
    home, 90–91

cultural pride, 75–76
Dominican food-serving
    restaurants, 109
Dominicans economic status and
    unfamiliar practices, 85–88
explaining Dominicans' attitude
    towards, 84
and feelings of home, 72
health and lifestyle, 79–80
human warmth, 73–75
importance, 73–77, 81–84
initiatives in Netherlands, 107–109
intermarriage, length of residence,
    identity and adaption,
    88–90
after migration, 77
practices, 69, 94
taste, 76
Dominican foodways, 69, 134
Dominican government, 97
Dominican immigrants, 11–12, 32,
    41, 46, 68, 85, 105, 125,
    137–138
  context, 13
  in Netherlands, 3, 33–34, 143
  in New York City, 133
Dominican infrastructure, 42
Dominican migration, 2, 141–144
  diversification in migration
    destinations and stepwise
    trajectories, 38
  emigration of Dominicans, 19–22
  migration to Kingdom of
    Netherlands, 22–30
  migration to Netherlands, 30–38
  to Netherlands, 137
  to Puerto, 28
  to United States, 20
Dominican Republic, 1–2, 10, 14–15,
    20, 24, 26–27, 31, 38–39,
    47, 49–52, 54, 56–61, 67,
    75, 82, 86, 93, 98, 102, 104,
    112, 115, 117, 127–130,
    132, 134, 142
  home in, 57–59

Index 157

Dominican Republic to the Dutch
Caribbean, 141
Dominican Republic Tourism Office, 56
Dominican sociability, 103–107
re–creation, 105–107
Dominicanness, 110
Dominicans, 25, 28, 32, 52, 56, 59, 63,
77, 80, 98–100, 102, 104,
107, 109, 113, 121, 123,
125–127, 130–131, 135–136,
138, 143
attachments, place of home and
feelings of home, 65–66
beginnings of Dominican social
and cultural infrastructure,
41–45
creation of Quisqueya in
Netherlands, 41–46
economic status and unfamiliar
practices, 85–88
encounters with Dutch contextual
characteristics, 46–57
ethnographic fieldwork, 10–12
home after migration, 57–65
homemaking through food
practices, 1–2
longstanding interest in dominican
migration and culture,
13–16
maintaining Dominican ways of
celebrating, 133–135
in Netherlands, 34, 141
population, 21
products, 114
prostitutes in Netherlands, 104
proximity to, 2
researching Dominicans'
homemaking in
Netherlands, 10
restaurant, 113
salami, 129
system, 59
women, 29
Dominicans to Dutch Caribbean
islands, 142

Dumpling, 70
Dutch army, 64
Dutch birthday parties, 119
Dutch *bruin café*, 110
Dutch Caribbean, 119
Dutch Caribbean Islands, 22, 24, 28,
104, 138, 142
migration to, 22–27
to Netherlands, 27–30
Dutch cheese, 74
Dutch climate, 55
Dutch context, 136
Dutch contextual characteristics
Ambiente, 47–49
coldness, 53–55
encounters with, 46
individualism, 50–52
language, 56
living inside, 49–50
overregulation, 55–56
Dutch custom, 131
Dutch dishes, 121–122, 124, 135–136
Dutch Food Practices, 79, 86, 89
dealing with encounters, 122–125
Dutch Food, 121–122
encounters with Dutch Food, 121
finding ingredients, 125–130
food customs in Netherlands,
130–135
receiving society characteristics,
practices and homemaking,
135–136
Dutch government, 29
Dutch man, 123
Dutch products, 121, 133
Dutch society, 7, 56, 59, 90, 104, 119
Dutch spekjes, 124
Dutch system, 107
Dutch-Dominican community, 103
feelings of home in, 94–97
Dutch-Dominican population,
characteristics of, 32
Dominican immigrants in
Netherlands, 33–34
region of origin, 32–33

158 Index

Eagle Petroleum Company, 26
Economic crisis, 29
El Vacilon Musical Amsterdam Latino,
    46
Elements of home, 6, 40–41, 66,
    68–69, 74, 137–138
Emigration of Dominicans, 19–22
English Caribbean islands, 70
Ensalada Rusa, 145
Entrepreneurship, 114
Erwtensoep, 121–122, 146
Ethnic communities, 94
Ethnographic approach, 10
Ethnographic fieldwork, 10–12

Familiarity, 4, 126, 128
Family-centred definition of home, 63
Flan, 145
Food customs in Netherlands, 130
    changed household composition
        and living alone, 131–133
    maintaining Dominican ways of
        celebrating, 133–135
    no warm meals at noon, 130–131
Food names, 145–147
Food practices, 8, 17, 90, 103–107
    Dominicans' homemaking
        through, 1–2
Frikandel, 146
*Fundacion de Emigrantes Unidos en
    Holanda*, 46

Gastronomic syncretism, 125, 136
Geographic dispersal, changing, 34
Gravy, 122
Grocery stores, 10, 17
Groenten, 146
Guantanamera, 77

Habichuela con dulce (sweet bean
    dessert), 1, 127, 145
Hachee, 121
Hageslag, 121
Haring, 121
Hello Fresh Box, 146

HelloFresh box (meal subscription
    service), 83
Heterogeneity, 141
Hindustanis, 126
Home, 40, 64–65
    in countries, 62
    concept of, 4
    cultural practices and feelings of,
        90–91
    in Dominican Republic, 57–59
    Dominicans, 95–103
    in Dutch Caribbean, 63–64
    food ingredients, 125
    after migration, 57
    in Netherlands, 59–62
Home feeling, 64, 66, 116–117
    in Dutch-Dominican community,
        94
Homemaking, 5, 8, 86
    as alternative lens for exploring
        immigrants' settlement, 2
    attention to emotions and micro-
        level experiences, 3–4
    contextual embeddedness of
        immigrant homemaking,
        7–8
    immigrant homemaking and
        differentiation in post-
        migration practices, 4–7
    of immigrant process, 142
    literature, 90
    process, 6, 138
    receiving society characteristics,
        practices and, 135–136
    studies, 77
Hospitability, 74
Hutspot, 121
Hybridization, 120

Identity, 10, 40
Immigrant homemaking, 5, 84, 140
    contextual embeddedness of, 7–8
    and differentiation in post-
        migration practices, 4–7
    literature, 81

Index **159**

nature of, 137
studies, 94, 120
Immigrants, 138, 141
communities, 128, 135
cultural practices and post-
migration experiences,
140–141
food practices, 9
integration, 139, 143
settlement, 140
settlement experiences, 137
Individualism, 50–52
Indonesian dishes, 121
Ingredient finding process, 9
Integration, 3
Intermarriage, length of residence,
identity and adaption,
88–90
Internal diversity, 141
Internal migration, 71
International migration, 5
International tourism, 33
Intra-regional migration, 22

J&J Embutidos, 107

Karbonade, 121, 146
Kingdom of Netherlands
from Dutch Caribbean Islands to
Netherlands, 27–30
migration to, 22
migration to Dutch Caribbean
Islands, 22–27
Kipe, 145
Knowledge, 116
Korean immigrants food practices, 87
Kroket, 121, 147

La Bandera, 145
La Comparsa Sabor Dominicano
(Dominican initiative), 95
La Tienda's products, 114
Labour migrants, 27
Lago Oil and Transport Company,
26

Lago refinery, 27
Location of home, 40, 50, 137–138,
140
Locrio, 145

Majarete, 146
Mamajuana, 145
Mangù, 146
Marital status of Dominicans, 38
Material practices, 117
Melting pot model of cultural
assimilation, 15
Merengue, 13, 19, 43–46, 77
Migrants, 4
communities, 128
Migration, 26, 120
background, 32
destination, 19, 27
to Dutch Caribbean Islands, 22–27
home after, 57–65
migration-related characteristics,
68
motive, 38, 85–86, 91, 100
process, 53
scholars, 3
Mofongo, 146
Mondongo, 145
Morir soñando, 146
Moro de habichuelas/guandules, 146
Moroccan immigrant communities,
119
Mosques, 111
Motoconchos, 15
Music, 43, 111

Nagelkaas, 121
Netherlands, 102, 139
characteristics of Dutch-
Dominican population,
32–38
creation of Quisqueya in, 41
Dominican Food Initiatives in,
107–109
Dominican immigrants in,
33–34

160 Index

from Dutch Caribbean Islands to, 27–30
food customs in, 130–135
home in, 59–62
migration motives, 30–32
sex industry, 29
New migrants, 24
Non-Dominicans, 111
Non-elite immigrants, 85

Oliebollen, 121
Opportunities, 6, 8
Orthodox food ritual, 73

Pannekoeken, 121, 147
Pastel en hoja, 146
Pastelón, 146
Patat met mayonaise, 121, 147
Pescado con coco, 146
Pica pollo, 146
Pimiento, 146
Pleasure circuit, 143
Plus (supermarket), 126
Poffertjes, 121
Population movements, 38
Porous food ritual, 73
Post-migration practices, immigrant homemaking and differentiation in, 4–7
Potatoes, 122, 133
Pre-migration
circumstances, 2
food traditions, 86
Principal European destinations, 20

Quisqueya in Netherlands
beginnings of Dominican social and cultural infrastructure, 41–45
creation of, 41
growing community with expanding infrastructure, 45–46

Racism, 58, 141
Re-inhabiting process, 41

Receiving society characteristics, 9, 120–121, 135–136
Resistance, 120
Restaurants, 17
Rookworst, 121, 147
Roti, 147
Royal Dutch Oil Company, 24
Rural agricultural model, 20

'Salad bowl' model of cultural pluralism, 15
Salsa Ranchera, 146
Sancocho, 133
Sancocho de siete carne, 146
Saté ku batata, 147
Scholars, 4–5
Segregation, 120
Semana Santa, 1
Sense of community, 4, 67, 77, 91, 106, 113, 117, 124, 138
Social mobility, 40, 100, 143
Sociale Ontwikkeling en Welzijn (SZOAW), 33
Somali immigrants in Australia, 86
Sopita, 146
Spaces-multifunctional, 117
Spaces–communal, 6, 8, 10, 17, 94, 103, 111
Spaces–domestic, 8, 17, 21, 27, 50, 111
Spaces–transnational, 75, 105
Spanish statistical office, 21
Stamppot, 121, 147
Stamppot met rookworst, 121
Stepwise migration, 14, 138
Stroopwafels, 121
Successful migration, 3, 100, 143
Surinamese, 135
community, 114, 125
dishes, 121
immigrants, 125
market, 75
supermarkets, 12
Sweet bean dessert (*Habichuela con dulce*), 134

Index   161

Tostones/frito verde, 146
Tourism, 31
Traditional Dutch food, 17
Transnational communities, 43
Transnational practices, 128
Tres leches, 146
Trujillo, Rafael Léonidas, 19–20, 44
Tu eres mas dominicana que un
    plátano, 10
Turkish immigrant communities,
    119

US Army, 29

Vegetables, 133
Vietnamese food products, 128
Vietnamese immigrants in California,
    128
Visa para un sueño, 19

Yaniqueque, 146
Yolas (small wooden boats), 20
Yucca, 125

Printed in the USA
CPSIA information can be obtained
at www.ICGtesting.com
JSHW050113250524
63705JS00003B/17